LIVING AND RELATING

In memory of my mothers

Violet Beatice Plankey Becker
1914—1989
&
Elsie Elizabeth Schmidt Luepnitz Kent
1912—1988

LIVING AND RELATING

An Introduction to Phenomenology

Carol S. Becker

SAGE PUBLICATIONS
The International Professional Publishers
Newbury Park   London   New Delhi

For information address:

 SAGE Publications, Inc.
2455 Teller Road
Newbury Park, California 91320

SAGE Publications Ltd.
6 Bonhill Street
London EC2A 4PU
United Kingdom

SAGE Publications India Pvt. Ltd.
M-32 Market
Greater Kailash I
New Delhi 110 048 India

Printed in the United States of America

Library of Congress Cataloging-in-Publication Data

Becker, Carol S., 1942-
   Living and relating: an introduction to phenomenology / Carol S. Becker
         p.   cm.
   Includes bibliographical references and index.
   ISBN 0-8039-3902-7. — ISBN 0-8039-3903-5 (pbk.)
   1. Phenomenological psychology.   2. Developmental psychology.
3. Interpersonal relations.   I. Title.
BF204.5.B43   1992
155—dc20   91-37435
                                                                CIP

92   93   94   95   96   10   9   8   7   6   5   4   3   2   1

Sage Production Editor: Diane S. Foster

Contents

PART I

❖

Introduction

This book is for people who want to understand their own and other people's experiences. It presents a phenomenological view of human living and relating, a view that begins and ends in human experience. *Living and Relating* is built around everyday events; these incidents are used to unfold a phenomenological outlook on life, development, and relationships.

I first saw the need for such a book as a university teacher. Each year while I prepared my syllabus for an undergraduate course, A Phenomenological Approach to Human Development, I wished for a text that would spark the interest of beginning students in phenomenology. I imagined these students enrolled in social science academic programs and preparing for a variety of human service careers. A phenomenological understanding of human nature, human development, intimate relationships, and helping relationships would empower them in their work with people.

As I wrote *Living and Relating,* I drew upon my expertise in phenomenological theory and research, as well as my work as a psychotherapist and a professor. In addition to a readership of social science students, I pictured the book being read by people outside of academic settings, people who thought about the meaning of life and wanted to learn about themselves and other people. I hoped, too, to make my insights available to social science colleagues who had not been trained in a phenomenological perspective but who wished to incorporate it into their professional work.

In its final form, *Living and Relating* is written to a wide-ranging audience and not only to a select group of phenomenological scholars. Because of this, I draw the classical thinkers in existential philosophy, as well as phenomenological philosophy and psychology, into the everyday world and show how their insights can provide a rich and useful orientation to human existence. Further, I blend these pure existential and phenomenological viewpoints with humanistic, descriptive accounts of living and relating that have been developed by fiction and nonfiction writers, as well as grief counselors and psychotherapists. In these ways, I share with readers the most interesting and vibrant parts of my psychological view of phenomenology.

Chapter 1 begins with an incident from my childhood, an event that I remembered on a recent Sunday afternoon. This experience launches us into the world of phenomenology which, at its best, explores and deepens our understandings of everyday life. The chapters in Part I explain the assumptions of phenomenology, discuss how phenomenologists view human nature, introduce the reader to prominent phenomenological thinkers, and show how phenomenologists think about and carry out research.

I outline a phenomenological approach to human development in Part II. Research and theory are used to illuminate important events in childhood, adolescence, adulthood, and old age and to bring the reader into the lifeworlds of different aged people. Part III extends developmental insights into the realm of intimate relationships. We deepen our understandings of essential life themes by exploring the nature of relationships between parents and children, friends, and sexual partners. The ending of sexual love relationships offers us further opportunities to learn about emotional life as well as the task of developing a family support system that surrounds and nurtures our individual lives and adds to life's meaning and richness. Finally, in Part IV, we study the experiential and relational aspects of several kinds of helping: that between client and psychotherapist, physically ill people and medical helpers, and students and teachers.

Upon finishing *Living and Relating*, the reader will have traveled a multifaceted, experiential path through many important aspects of human existence. She or he will have at hand a valuable map to the world of phenomenology and to its views of human nature, human development, and human relationships. My heartfelt hope is that each reader of *Living and Relating* will be stirred to step into the everyday world with new interest and wonder.

1

What Is Phenomenology?

For the phenomenologist, there are no layers, there is just one layer of life as such. There, in that life is the depth of life. There is the explanation of life, insofar as life can be explained at all. For there is much that cannot be explained in life and that never has been explained. Life is definitely not a nebula, but it is certainly a mystery.

J. H. VAN DEN BERG

A Moment In My Daily Life

It is a summer afternoon in Oakland, California. I am alone in my home after workers have finished remodeling it. As I walk through the kitchen and living room, my fingers trail over the round, smooth wall corners. The sunlight's dance on the maple floors catches my eye, and the gentle breeze that rolls through the open windows caresses my skin. I sigh with relief and settle into a comfortable chair near the couch to soak up the sensuous beauty of my home. I sit watching the eucalyptus tree leaves caper in the wind outside my living room window.

As I relax, I remember an incident from my childhood. I am 8 years old, and it is another summer afternoon in my parents' home in upper Michigan. My mother and older sister are in the kitchen; they are preparing dinner. I hear the clatter of pans and the pressure in my mother's voice as she instructs my sister. I feel my father's presence somewhere outside—he is helping a neighbor repair a broken down truck engine. I am playing in the living room.

Between the couch and the armchair I build a house. The card table is upright, and the gray army blankets are over it. I slide from the afternoon sunlight into my cave-house. My back rests against the wall and my legs are straight out in front of me. I balance myself with my hands at my sides. The dark air, scented with mothballs, is mysterious and delicious. Surrounded by the smells of myself and my house, I feel snug and safe. I sit listening to the muffled voices of my sister and mother. I am hidden from them, but they are still within my reach.

Suddenly, my young brother is there, in a doorway he has made in the blanket. He, too, likes my house and wants to join me. I bar his way and close the door. After several openings and closings of my door, his screams bring Mother to his side. The quiet is shattered by discussions of sharing and responsibility. I stand my ground. Mother stands hers, taller and firmer.

My brother enters and sits uncomfortably in the disturbed darkness. We look at each other and see that we have both lost the home for which we longed.

Why does this memory occur to me on a peaceful Sunday afternoon? Is it because, at age 48, I have regained my home and have finally done what I was trying to do at age 8? Has my life been an attempt to recover from my childhood and to reclaim my desires? Or was my table-house the first glimpse of my personality and adult self? My childhood and adult experiences are similar but different. In my childhood memory, a pleasurable experience becomes a traumatic one. In my adult experience, a traumatic event ends in tranquility.

I begin with this incident from my life because situations like this one are the essence of phenomenology. The description of an everyday event demonstrates the phenomenological viewpoint in several ways. First, the moment is experiential: It reveals my experience of myself, others, and the world around me, both as an adult and as a child. Second, by describing my behavior, I clarify my desires and intentions. Third, the events that I describe are ordinary; they are common parts of my life and other people's lives as well. As we will see, these three elements—experience, intentions, and everyday events— are the basic premises of phenomenology.

Many meanings of my adulthood and childhood are contained in these descriptions. I am explicitly aware of some of them, but others are beyond my grasp. I seek a comfortable place in the world; I desire a room that is just for me, exactly as I wish it to be. The location of my house in the living room of my parents' home is similar to my adult house; it is set apart from but surrounded by other people and homes.

As I elaborate on my adult experience of solitary reverie, I discover interpersonal parallels with my childhood memory. I imagine loved ones celebrating the remodeling of my home and see them talking and relaxing around a crackling fire in the fireplace. Just as the location of my card table house separated me from and connected me to family members, my adult house joins me to family and friends on my own terms. In both my childhood and my adult experiences, I am alone within a network of interpersonal relationships.

Dwelling on these parts of my life reveals richer meanings and themes than I had realized. These small moments express many large matters of my life and can even teach me about such lofty matters as time, space, freedom, and love.

Social scientists with different theoretical orientations would treat the foregoing life events diversely. Each would focus on different aspects of me and my houses. Some would arrive at conclusions and insights that diverge sharply from those that I have developed.

We will discuss the phenomenological understandings of situations such as these—moments from day-to-day life—to understand their meanings and to learn about a phenomenological view of life.

What Is Phenomenology?

Phenomenology is the study of phenomena, of things or events, in the everyday world. Phenomenologists study situations in the everyday world from the viewpoint of the experiencing person. This experiential view helps phenomenologists understand people and human life so that they can work effectively with them. Let us look at each part of this basic definition.

To study something, we must pay attention to it, notice it, seek it out. Generally, we investigate things that catch our attention, that we are curious about, or that are troublesome. We probe events to better understand them so that we can live effectively; our satisfaction in life is heightened by our understandings. Phenomenologists investigate people's experiences of life events and the meanings these events have to them.

Experience is with us during every waking moment; it is what we think, feel, remember, imagine, see, hear, smell, taste, or touch. When we are awake, our experience is usually complex. We experience many things simultaneously. We can, for instance, be thinking about reading while listening to a friend talk as we jog up a hill. Besides being complicated, our experience shifts constantly and one experience prepares us for others. As our life experiences grow, so do our knowledge and skills. Even when asleep, we continue to experience sensations, thoughts, and feelings.

When we study phenomenology, we take up a serious interest in experience, our own and that of other people, in ordinary life. The topics of phenomenology are, therefore, almost limitless; we can study anything we can experience and describe. As we pay attention to our experiences, we can increase our awareness of ourselves and other people. Awareness makes us efficient and effective participants in life.

What kind of phenomena can phenomenologists study? The life events that phenomenologists explore happen constantly; an adult imagines the perfect relationship, a child discovers the magic of mathematics, an elder pushes off the high-dive, an adolescent turns the ignition key in her first car, a reader reinterprets a classic text. For the phenomenologist, each of these life events can become a serious area of scientific investigation. The phenomenologically oriented researcher asks the experts of these life events, the people doing and experiencing them, to describe experiences from daily life. Then the researcher discerns the experiential components and the important aspects of the phenomenon. We will look more closely at the product of empirical phenomenological investigations in Chapter 4.

Because each moment of our existence resides in the everyday world, it is easy for us to describe this world. Daily life is always part of our experiences as we live through joyful, interesting, boring, or sad situations. Our day-to-day living is satiated with interactions with people, plants, animals, and objects. These events of the lifeworld are the beginning and the ending of any scientific interest in life; all pursuits of knowledge ultimately aim at improving the quality of everyday life.

Phenomenologists study people's experience of everyday life within a definite philosophical context that generates specific assumptions about human nature and human living. These philosophical insights were developed by European thinkers at the end of the 19th and the beginning of the 20th centuries.

A phenomenology of everyday life can be traced back to existential and phenomenological philosophers who lived during past centuries. The Danish philosopher Soren Kierkegaard (1813—1855) is credited with the beginning of the existential school of philosophy. He sought to understand each person as a unique individual. Kierkegaard (1954) focused on each person's responsibility to develop an ethical life based upon turning inward and becoming fully who he or she was destined to be. His writings sparked others to explore human existence and the unique, as well as the common, problems in life. Eventually, this exploration resulted in a diverse body of existential understandings about human nature and existence. These heterogeneous ideas all illuminated human nature as active, dynamic, creative, and larger and richer than theories. In an anthology of existentialism, the American philosopher Maurice Friedman (1991) overviews the wide-ranging scope of contemporary existentialism by offering the following definition:

> "Existentialism" is not a philosophy but a mood embracing a number of disparate philosophies; the differences among them are more basic than the temper which unites them. This temper can best be described as a reaction against the static, the abstract, the purely rational, the merely irrational, in favor of the dynamic and the concrete, personal involvement and "engagement," action, choice, and commitment, the distinction between "authentic" and "inauthentic" existence, and the actual situation of the existential subject as the starting point of thought. Beyond this the so-called existentialists divide according to their views on such matters as phenomenological analysis, the existential subject, the intersubjective relation between selves, religion, and the implications of existentialism for psychotherapy. (pp. 3-4)

Beginning with Kierkegaard, the existentialists took human existence as their starting point, explored the nature and meaning of
human life, and delineated its fundamental themes.

Influenced by Kierkegaard's work, the German philosopher
Edmund Husserl (1859-1938) developed a systematic method of
studying human consciousness and experience (1962, 1977). This
systematic reflection on conscious experience was the birth of phenomenology. Husserl believed that experience of life events in the everyday world, with theoretical understandings suspended, was an
invaluable source of knowledge. His famous statement, "Back to
the things themselves," expresses a basic principle of phenomenology. This statement, "Back to the things themselves," directed
philosophers, social scientists, researchers, and psychotherapists to
suspend theoretical understandings of life and to renew their
observations of people's experiences in the everyday world.
Husserl's phenomenological contribution was a method of inquiry
and empirical exploration that deepened existential understandings
of life.

Another German philosopher, Martin Heidegger (1889-1976) continued Husserl's phenomenological method of exploring consciousness and knowledge by undertaking a broader explication of being
and time. Heidegger's work (1962) is cited as the first union of existentialism and phenomenology, resulting in the existential-phenomenology viewpoint. Existential-phenomenology combined existential
philosophical foundations with a phenomenological method. With
the birth of existential-phenomenology, a diverse and broad-ranging
investigation of and reflection upon human existence began. Other
philosophers and social scientists joined in and contributed complementary and contrasting insights about human nature and human
existence. In the next chapter, I review some of these thinkers as I develop a phenomenological understanding of human nature. Like
most contemporary existential-phenomenologists (Valle & Halling,
1989), I use the term *phenomenology* to characterize the entire existential-phenomenological tradition. It is important, however, for the
reader to remember that I am drawing upon both existentialists as
well as phenomenologists when I do so.

The phenomenological viewpoint is based upon two premises.
One premise is that experience is a valid and fruitful source of knowl-

edge. Any person's knowledge is based upon what that person experiences, whether it be firsthand experience or vicarious, secondhand experience. Experience is the source of all knowing and the basis of behavior. Experience, what we are aware of at any point in time, is the foundation of our knowledge of ourselves, other people, and the world in general. Without human experience, there would be no human world. Rather than distrust human experience, as many social scientists do, phenomenologists see experience as the cornerstone of knowledge. As we will see in Chapter 2, phenomenologists believe that experience is always situated in the world (van den Berg, 1972a). Contemporary social phenomenologist Rolf von Eckartsberg (1986) has coined the term *experiaction* to capture this integration of experience and behavior.

A second premise of the phenomenological viewpoint is that our everyday worlds are valuable sources of knowledge. We can gain important insights into the essential nature of an event by analyzing how it occurs in our daily lives. For example, if we wanted to understand the creative process, we would ask ourselves, When have I created something? Then, by describing that situation as completely as we could, we would start learning about creativity.

As scholars went "back to the things themselves," they developed new understandings of human nature and phenomena. These formulations spearheaded radical changes in social science theory, research, and praxis.

First, I will look at how phenomenologically oriented philosophers and psychologists conceptualized human nature.

2

Phenomenological Understandings of Human Nature

As they paid closer attention to experience, philosophers and psychologists developed new understandings of human nature. A phenomenological view of life includes the following concepts.

Being-in-the-World

The German philosopher Martin Heidegger (1962) reevaluated his beliefs about human nature. He coined a new term for a person, *Dasein*. This German term breaks down into *Da*—"there," and *sein*—"being." *Dasein*, then, means "being there," or "the there of being." By defining a person as "being there," Heidegger emphasized that a person is always in the world; to exist is to exist somewhere. Existing in the world is an essential part of being human; a person is a "being-in-the-world." To understand people, we must understand their contexts—the worlds or situations in which they live. To separate person and world is false; to be a person is to be in a world.

Being-in-the-World-With-Others

Heidegger also understood people as "being-in-the-world-with-others." He saw people as networks of interpersonal relationships.

13

Try, for example, to answer the question, Who am I? Anything you say depends, explicitly or implicitly, upon relationships. If you describe yourself by your name, that name is connected to many people. If you define yourself by a social role—as a spouse, a student, a wage earner, or a parent—that aspect of yourself ties you to various interpersonal situations. The same conclusion can be drawn from whatever you say; even saying that you are alone brings up other people in contrast to it. Any experience of yourself or another person occurs within an interpersonal framework. By their very nature, people are interpersonal beings.

Reflective

Reflection—thinking about self, other, and world—is another attribute of human nature (Husserl, 1977). Human nature is an openness that illuminates the world; each person is a clearing within which the world presents itself (Heidegger, 1962). Not only are people aware of themselves and the world, they are aware of their awareness; they are self-reflective. Being self-reflective, people can think about experience, about thinking, about themselves, about the object-world, and about the interpersonal world. People are naturally reflective and self-reflective.

Thinking about the assumptions of theories and practices is one way people are reflective and self-reflective. Phenomenologists assert that the quality of life improves when people clarify their values and act in accord with them.

Active Subject

Phenomenologists maintain that people are subjects, not objects, and cannot be reduced to mechanistic processes. An active, experiencing person is at the core of every human action. People create or, as we shall see, co-create their lives. To be human is to be an active agent who organizes and reacts to influencing forces. No matter how terrible the life events are that befall a person, phenomenologists contend that each person remains the only one who can live that particular life. People are not accumulations of internal and external influences. They are experiencing centers of meaningful action and reaction; they transcend the facts of their lives.

People not only react to life's events and forces, but they also shape events that shape their lives. Rolf von Eckartsberg (1971) introduced the phrases "shaped shapers" and "shapers being shaped" to describe this aspect of human nature. As active subjects, people seek meaning in life and strive to attain valued goals. Living with purpose, people are the responsible and irreplaceable agents in charge of their lives.

Intentional

Active subjects are intentional subjects. When we intend something, we strive to make it happen. Human intentions are quests for meaning and are essential parts of life. Being intentional beings, people live in ways that are meaningful to them. For phenomenologists, intentionality is a natural part of human nature; to live intentionally is to construct a meaningful life and world, for both self and others.

According to the French phenomenological philosopher and psychologist Maurice Merleau-Ponty (1962), we are intentional on both reflective and prereflective levels of existence. Reflective intentions are those of which we are explicitly aware. We speak of these purposes readily and experience them as important contents of our lives. Almost anything can be a reflective intention in life: we intend to complete our schooling; we strive to be kind persons; we want our lovers to love us madly. Our lives are complex, and we have many meaningful goals. We may try to accomplish all of the above-mentioned intentions at once. Sometimes multiple intentions complement one another. Sometimes they clash.

Intentions can also be prereflective. Prereflective intentions are lived out versus thought about; we express them in our actions and think about them later. For example, we sleep in because we forgot to set the alarm; we stop work to reminisce over old photographs we found in our desk drawer; we embarrass ourselves by consistently calling "Joe," "Steve." These intentions are lived out and make us stop and look more carefully at our desires. With little effort we realize that we wanted to sleep in, to avoid working, and to stop having superficial conversations with Joe like the ones we have with Steve.

Prereflective intentions are different from the Freudian notion of the unconscious. Unconscious urges are cut off from consciousness and are compelled by biologically based drives and urges. Prereflective urges are intentions of which we are only slightly aware. Unconscious motives imply a self buffeted about by forces more powerful than the self; prereflective intentions are the work of active subjects in the process of learning about meanings that are integral parts of themselves.

Body-Subject

In his classic text *Phenomenology of Perception,* Merleau-Ponty (1962) reassessed the embodied aspect of human nature. He used the term *body-subject* for the mind-body unity that is the essence of human nature. In describing people as body-subjects, Merleau-Ponty bridged a Cartesian split and challenged current dualistic thinking about mind and body. Merleau-Ponty argued that people's minds and bodies are always interrelated. At any given moment, people's lives are both mental and physical. To be human is to be simultaneously mind and body.

As a body-subject, a person and his or her body are one. Bodies are thoughtful bodies just as minds are embodied minds. Our bodies are subjects too; they are we. Although we can objectify our bodies, that is, treat them like things to be manipulated at will, they are also our intentional selves.

Psychologically, our bodies are thoughtful just as our minds are bodily minds. If we are tired or hungry, it is difficult for us to think clearly. In a similar way, our bodies think about and manage our lives prereflectively. By listening to and understanding the prereflective meanings of our lives, we can clarify our desires and prioritize our goals. Knowledge helps us make desires become realities.

In many areas of our lives, our bodies know and navigate the world in a smooth, thoughtful execution of our intentions. Think, for example, of telling someone how to walk, dance, play a guitar, or hit a tennis ball. To describe actions that we perform unthinkingly, we must consult our acting bodies. Only then can we describe these skills as accurately as we do them.

With the rise of the natural sciences in the 1500s (Romanyshyn, 1982), people lost touch with the body as subject and became fascinated with it as a physical object that could be objectified, dissected, and analyzed. Once the person was extracted from the meaning of the body, anatomical understandings of it flourished. This body, filled with physiological systems and anatomical detail, helped medical professionals identify and cure physical illnesses. It also, however, moved the body-subject, the most fundamental ground of our being-in-the-world-with-others, into the shadows.

Beginning primarily with Merleau-Ponty's work, phenomenologists returned to an investigation of the body as subject and reclaimed it as the rich, original ground of human existence. Dutch phenomenological psychiatrist and psychologist J. H. van den Berg (1961, 1971a) advanced this understanding of the body by situating it within a historical psychology. He showed how sociocultural trends mold our view of the human body in particular and human life in general. American phenomenological psychologist Robert Romanyshyn (1982, 1989) continued van den Berg's work and highlighted the metaphorical depths of the lived, historical, and sociocultural body. He demonstrated that different ways of speaking about the human heart, for example, the divided heart, the courageous heart, and the heart as a mechanical pump, reflect varied relationships to the self, the body, and the world. Each experience of the human body embodies a particular orientation to life and living. It opens a vista of selected meanings that reflects back the style of our psychological life. Each vision of the body re-visions psychological life (Romanyshyn, 1982, pp. 100-142).

David Michael Levin (1985), a contemporary American philosopher, captures the richness of the current phenomenological understandings of the lived body when he describes human movement and gesture. Levin shows us that all of personal and interpersonal life, past, present, and future, are held in the body. He explains:

> [A]s soon as we begin to move and gesture in response to the presence of the human Other, we are held by our culture in the corresponding beholdenness of our bodies. In every human voice, there are echoes of the mother's tongue, echoes of significant teachers, respected elders,

close friends; and there are accents, too, which bind the voice to the history of a region, a culture, and generations of ancestors. The athlete of today repeats the race of the Olympic torch-bearers, bearing the history of centuries in the very span of his body. The carpenter of today repeats the gestures of skill which have always constituted his handicraft; and it is only by the grace of that ancient gesture that he belongs to the tradition of the craft as it has been handed down from generation to generation across thousands of years. Analogously, the mother nurses her child, repeating thereby one of the oldest of human gestures. In these ways, and in countless others, Dasein is held open to its history and tradition, and is granted the chance to find in this beholdenness the deepest dimensionality of its fulfillment as an historical and tradition-bound being. (pp. 174-175)

Understood as this vastness, it is easy to see that people's bodies are integral parts of themselves and the foundation of interpersonal living.

Co-Constitution of Meaning

How is meaning constructed? Do we create meaning and, thus, fill the world with connection and relevancy? Or does it come to us complete, from outside of us?

The first position is that of idealism, a classical school of philosophical thought. The idealists believed that knowledge resided in the thinking person. Each person discovered meaning within the self by mulling over knowledge until she or he arrived at its purified form. In this sense, the essence of thought was pre-given and the person had to dwell within the self to uncover it through the use of logical principles. Enlightened understanding could then be brought into everyday life.

The opposite school of thought—empiricism—purported that meaning comes to us from the world, that we discover it in the concreteness of existence. The empiricists believed that each person found meaning ready-made in the world and that valid truths about life could be gained by putting oneself aside and articulating what was observable and independent of the self, out there in the world. These schools of philosophical thought were searching in opposite places for lasting truths about human nature and human existence.

The philosophical and psychological debate between idealism and empiricism has continued for centuries. Merleau-Ponty (1962) developed a phenomenological position between these two extremes, that of the co-constitution of meaning.

Merleau-Ponty stated that meaning is created between person and world. Both poles of the dialogue—the person and the object—bring certain limits and possibilities to the development of meaning. Meaning is formed in this exchange; it is co-created between the person and the object. A simple example will help us understand.

Suppose each of you has been reading with a pen in hand. Turn your attention to the pen. What personal meanings does it have for you? What cultural meanings? Now, get outrageously creative with the pen. What new things can you think of doing with it? Write down what you think of and talk with other people about the conventional and innovative uses of a pen. If you compare the meanings and functions that a pen has for you with those that it has for other people, you will find that, within limits, the meaning of a pen varies from person to person.

All agree that a pen is used for writing, but some experience it as a treasured instrument of free expression. Others see it as a harsh taskmaster. Someone thought of using two pens as chopsticks; someone else used a pen as a doorstop. No one, however, seriously considered eating a pen for lunch. In and of itself, the pen presented limits to us. The pen's properties held each of us in check. These properties brought limits and possibilities to each person's interactions with it. Every person also brought limits and possibilities to his or her experience of the pen. In the interaction between the person and the pen, the pen's meanings were co-created.

The co-creation of meaning occurs between the self and the object and also between one person and another. Meaning is created in the back-and-forth movement, the dialectic, between self and object or self and other. It does not reside in the object, in the person, or in the other. Meaning occurs in between, and both person and object are necessary participants in its co-creation.

On a daily basis, we hardly notice this co-creation of meaning that surrounds us and the objects of our life. We become aware of it, as in the foregoing exercise, when something disrupts the smooth flow of our everyday world and forces or invites us to attend to ourselves and our surroundings in a new way.

When I am invited to reflect on the pens in my life, for example, I discover several that I use in different ways on varied occasions. I have numerous inexpensive pens that I often lose. Two others are treasured and are kept in special places: One fits into a snug pocket of my appointment book, and the other rests in a cubical of my grandmother's old desk. Each of my pens reflects a different me. The easily replaced pens belong to the hurried and functional me; the treasured pens are possessed by an intimate, contemplative me. The heavy black fountain pen that resides in my grandmother's desk can even return me to another pen and desk. This even older pen, one that I used in my fourth-grade schoolroom, must be dipped into the inkwell in the upper right-hand corner of that old, marred, wooden desk. The smell of my modern ink brings that older pen back to me now, and each pen adds definition and richness to the other. All of these pens, those that I still have and those that I have lost, are with me now and each reflects me. Each shows a particular way that I am in the world.

My experience of my pens happens between each pen and myself. As such, my experience is a psychological reality that occurs between fact and idea and between physical and mental realities. This experience, between myself and the pen and between the physical pen and the psychological one, opens up new visions of myself and the world. Robert Romanyshyn (1982) characterizes the psychological reality that is found in human experiences like these as metaphorical. He explains:

> Fidelity to psychological experience on its own terms leads us beyond these alternatives of fact and idea, thing and thought, empirical and mental reality toward a metaphorical reality. (p. 148)

> A metaphor, then, is not essentially a way of seeing how one reality is *like* another. It is a way of seeing one reality *through* another. Its resemblance, if we should call it that, is the resemblance that a reflection bears to the reality of which it is a reflection. It is not a real (factual) resemblance but a resemblance where likeness is a difference. (p. 153)

The richness of human experience lies in its metaphorical nature in which identity and difference appear simultaneously, when something both is and is not itself in its meaningful connections. My new pen brings my childhood pen back into my grasp, but there is never any confusion as to which pen I hold. Each pen is similar to and different from the other. Both are enriched by their reflective and prereflective meeting within my experience. New and old meanings come alive in my experience as thing and person, fact and image interact. This dynamic interplay is at the heart of the co-creation of meaning.

Thrownness

Thrownness (*Geworfenheit*) complements the understanding of people as active subjects (Heidegger, 1962). It means that people are "thrown into" a given world. People are born with many decisions already made: They are female or male; they are born into racial or ethnic groups; their parents are specific people; they are born in a particular part of the world at a particular point in time. People's cultures are well established when they enter life. As people grow up, they become active members in a life formed by factors outside their control.

Situated Freedom

If people are active subjects thrown into a world, how free are they? The phenomenological position, situated freedom, lies between complete freedom and complete determinism. Situated freedom means that in any given situation people can make choices. In each life situation, some intentional act is possible. People are influenced by interpersonal, social, and biological factors, but they also appropriate these conditions. They make choices that are meaningful to them and that fit into their life goals.

The French philosopher Jean-Paul Sartre's (1956) famous statement "People are condemned to freedom" exemplifies the phenomenological position. People must choose; even not choosing is an influential choice. Some choose "have to" lives and are simultaneously

comforted and frustrated by lack of freedom. Others are aware of
their ability to make choices in any situation.

What are examples of situated freedom? Some people are single-
minded in their life choices. You can, for example, decide to do well
in a college class. Then you go to class, read assignments, clarify
misunderstandings, and review class notes. Others may not be so
single-minded. They may want to do well in a class but also want to
see friends and have fun. Then study time gets absorbed by other
activities. If we say we want to do one thing and find ourselves
doing others instead, we should look more carefully at the confluence of our life choices. Clarifying our desires will help us accomplish the most multifaceted plans for life.

Perspectivity

Perspectivity means that any knowledge is from a particular, limited standpoint. Phenomenology is one perspective in the social sciences; it is a specific way of understanding people. Within this
viewpoint, some things are important that are inconsequential in
others. Phenomenologists believe that experience is the touchstone of life. Behaviorists, however, believe that behavior is the
only reality, and psychoanalysts proclaim that the unconscious is
the ultimate source of valid knowledge. Each viewpoint contrib-
utes valuable knowledge about people, but each is also limited.
Any discipline is an approach to the world as much as it is a body
of knowledge.

Along with their interest in human experience as the basis of
human knowledge, phenomenologists believe that knowledge is co-
constituted. What is known, perceived, or believed is influenced by the
standpoint of the knower, perceiver, or believer. The way in which one
approaches the world both opens up and limits what one finds there.

Knowledge is deepened by standing within a specific perspective.
A phenomenological psychologist studies, for example, a person's
experience of living with a chronic disease such as diabetes. A med-
ical researcher concentrates on micromolecular levels of the disease.
A medical practitioner focuses on medication, diet, and exercise.
Each of these areas of knowledge is necessary to the diabetic person's

living. Each offers a rich but limited view of the diabetic. The patient profits from each specialist's knowledge.

All knowledge is perspectival. We can deepen our insights into life by dwelling within a particular perspective. We can also enrich our understanding of life by accessing many vantage points.

Unique Experiences and Essential Themes

For phenomenologists, each person is unique. Everyone is different from everyone else; no two people are exactly alike. Phenomenologists see people as irreplaceable; no one can live people's lives for them or experience exactly what they experience. It is possible to empathize with someone and, in a sense, feel his or her pain or joy, but we can never experience all of the nuances and meanings that the person experiences. Thus we must listen to people rather than assume that we know what they are telling us.

Phenomenologists extract the common components from unique events and illuminate the essential themes of unique experiences. Knowing the common aspects of human experience helps us understand and work effectively with particular people.

A Phenomenological View of Human Nature

A well-thought-out philosophy of human nature provides a solid foundation for applying phenomenology to life. For the phenomenologist, people are active, intentional subjects who are aware of their worlds. Each person is inherently tied to a context and to other people, and these factors help define the person. A person is a unity of mind and body, a perspectival scholar, and a co-creator of meaning who embraces and transcends thrownness by exercising situated freedom. Unique experiences generate common themes that enable phenomenologists to illuminate the essential structures of life.

Having addressed the question, What is human nature? I will look at two fundamental dimensions of the world: time and space.

3

Now and Then; Here and There

For phenomenologists, time and space are basic dimensions of the human world (van den Berg, 1972a). We can gain useful insights by understanding how people perceive these dimensions of life and live in relation to them. Phenomenologists are concerned with experiential time and space, time and space as people experience them.

Time

Experiential time is more fundamental than measured time. Because we experience the passage of time, we can divide it into units and measure its progression with clocks and calendars. Clock and calendar time enables large groups of people to coordinate activities and to accomplish amazing feats. Phenomenologists believe, however, that if people become preoccupied with measured time and dismiss experiential time, they lose touch with an important quality of the lifeworld.

Experiential time, time as we experience it, may or may not correspond with clock time. When experiential time differs from clock time, we usually correct our experience rather than reset our watches. Unlike clock time, experiential time is measured in unequal minutes and hours. Some hours, those spent in enjoyable conversations, flash by. Some minutes, those spent in a silent, angry stand-off with someone, stretch longer than hours. Experiential time is a rich source of information about life. In noticing how different people live time, phenomenologists have gained helpful insights into the worlds of different-aged people. Children and adolescents run toward the future, adults struggle to relax in the present, and elders turn toward the distant past. Phenomenologically oriented clinicians (Binswanger, 1963; Boss, 1963; May, Angel, & Ellenberger, 1958) have understood depressed people, schizophrenics, and those experiencing anxiety by analyzing these people's experiences of time and space. Realizing how people live in relation to time can enhance our interventions with them.

Most of us believe that time is linear: the past comes before the present, the present precedes the future. In this linear progression of time, we take for granted that the past influences and even causes the present and future. Those of us sophisticated in psychology, for example, are apt to think that the events of our childhood have determined our current life and that the present, in turn, will determine our future. Likewise, we assume that our past is real, fixed somewhere behind us, and contains the important facts of our lives. Unless we have exchanged dissimilar memories of the same event with someone in our nuclear family, we may even believe that there is an interpersonally valid past, equally true for everyone.

These beliefs are our "natural attitudes" concerning time. Phenomenologists call them "natural" because we, unthinkingly, assume that this is how time really is. In fact, however, these common beliefs about time are ideas that we have reified and substituted for our actual experience of time.

If we suspend these natural attitudes about time and observe experiential time anew, we discover only one time, present time. Each moment that we experience is now. An unending sequence of "nows" feeds the flow of time. Indeed, we do remember the past and fantasize about the future, but we only do so here and now. The past that I remembered yesterday may be completely different from today's past; each past appears within the present moment and is influenced by it. The past, then, is always the present-past. Let us look at the moment from my past life that I described in Chapter 1.

I had not remembered the card table house from my childhood in Michigan for decades. Why did it reappear in my California home? And where had it been all those years that I did not think of it? I know, beyond doubt, that the card table house is part of my past today, but yesterday it was nowhere to be found. Now that it is with me again, I realize that my summer afternoon in Oakland allowed me to remember it. The present, then, brought back and orchestrated the past. Today, the card table house is present as the past; it is the present-past. The present called it forth, to take its place in a new constellation of meanings.

Someone might argue that the card table house was sitting in the wings all along, waiting to be brought on stage. The past was present, but I was unaware of it. Some could assert that the past (the card table house) was a prototype of the present (my remodeled home) and even caused it to occur; the present was reducible to the past. A psychoanalyst, for example, might say that the past was more real than the present and, then, I would be in danger of losing my eucalyptus panorama to the army blanket one.

For the phenomenologist, people cannot be reduced to the past. The past is influential, but it does not determine the present. Rather, the past changes in present time. The experiential past is dynamic, it shifts and changes as I pay attention to it. Something is there, in the past, that I remember, but its meanings are fluid.

When I first remembered the card table house, my brother and I were frozen in confrontation at the door. As I described it, I was pulled through this scene to the later events, and my brother and I were facing each other in uncomfortable silence. Just as I typed the final sentence, I experienced an empathic shift and saw my brother and me as tragic partners in a family drama. Which is the real past? Experientially, they are all real. One flows into and evokes the next as my present-past shifts before my eyes.

As I sit and ponder these memories, the telephone rings; it is my brother calling from his home in Pennsylvania. I tell him about the card table house. As soon as I mention it, he laughs and tells me his memory; he played with his trucks for many wonderful hours in that house. I am stunned. It is my card table house, and he does not even remember me being in it.

Now I am faced with two card table houses, mine and my brother's. Later that week a conversation with my mother helps me relate the two houses. She describes my brother playing in it while I was in school and exiting, without leaving a trace, when I stepped off the school bus. The past changes again, and I correct my earlier interpretation. Both I and my brother managed to regain our card table houses while we were still children, and my mother helped each of us do so. Not only has my past changed, but my brother and mother are different as well.

If these memories do not reveal a factual past and factual people, of what use are they? Their use lies in revealing intentional people in the act of being and becoming themselves. By tracking the changing directions of this memory, I have learned much about myself, my childhood, my brother, and my mother. During the years of training to be a psychotherapist, I have had many pasts: angry, sad, lonely, solitary, dreamy, happy, mischievous, thankful, loved. I regained a piece of my emotional self through each of them. For all of us, in the long run, knowing about ourselves is more useful than pinning down an objective past.

The same points apply to the future. The future is a present-future that stays constant or changes as the present unfolds. Most of us have been taught that the present causes the future. Indeed, many social scientists believe that the highest knowledge is that which we can use to predict the future with certainty. The most successful scientist knows life before it is lived.

We express this relation to the future in many parts of our everyday lives. We work hard today so that we can enjoy the benefits of our efforts tomorrow. We know that the future is being made now through diligence and persistence.

A closer look at our experiences show us that the future, as a present-future, influences the present. The future influences our actions because it is believed and desired, because it is real now. For example, I get up to attend my 8:00 a.m. class because I know that this class is required for my bachelor's degree. I follow a monthly investment plan because I envision a stress-free retirement. Without a real present-future, the present would be different; I would sleep late or spend my money more freely than I already do.

Without a viable future, my life is directionless and meaningless; even my past loses its meaning. When my present-future looks grim, my past becomes a series of futile and aborted gestures that led me to this listless state.

I call this expanded time—the present-past, the present, and the present-future—circular time. Time is circular in that all the moments of time influence one another. The past influences the present and the future, but the present and the future also orchestrate the past. The past sets the future, but the future narrows or expands the past. Each part of time influences the others in a dialectical dance. And, an active, experiencing person is the main character in experiential time.

Now is all there is. Now, however, is filled with the present-past and the present-future.

Space

Similar to time, experiential space is more fundamental than measured space. Because we first experience space, we can measure it in equal units of inches, feet, or yards. Measured space enables business to be conducted: we buy a house that has 2500 square feet of living space, we rent office space at $2.00 per square foot, we decide to walk to the market because it is only 1 mile away.

Measured space and experiential space can be the same, but they can also differ. The bucket seats in my car may be too far from each other when my lover and I are driving alongside the ocean. They may not be far enough away from each other, however, when my wet dog is sitting in the other one. In each case, the seats remain only 1 foot apart. But, in each situation, it is a very different foot.

When experiential and measured space differ, we assume that our experience needs correcting. Most of us would worry about our reality-testing ability if we assumed that the tape measure was wrong. But the fact is, the tape measure can be incorrect. Let us look at an example.

A woman in her early twenties, Kara, stops by my office between classes. She has heard that I teach a class on women and their bodies and wants to speak with me about something that is troubling her.

Kara explains that she has always enjoyed her body: she likes the way she looks, the way her body feels when she moves, and its shape. Yesterday, however, she read an article in a woman's magazine that cited measurements for women's bodies. To her amazement she discovered that her waist, which she has been perfectly happy with, is 2 inches larger than the average for her age and height. Even though she knows it is silly, she cannot stop thinking that her waist is too big.

Kara is in danger of losing her enjoyable, experiential waist and replacing it with an inadequate, measured waist. If she substitutes her measured body for her experiential one, she ruins spontaneous pleasure in her body and makes herself vulnerable to a cultural plague of negative prescriptions. It would be healthy for Kara to bolster her experience of her body and to realize that its measurements are incorrect.

Experiential space, the place in which we experience ourselves, can also be different from physical space. Many of us have had the experience of driving a familiar route, one we take everyday, and not really seeing the road or the landscape. Even so, we drive, pre-reflectively, in a responsible and alert manner. If the car in front of us stops suddenly, we stop before we hit it. Reflectively, however, we are somewhere else. We are at our destination, giving the business report that we stayed up so late to finish, or back home, making sure we did not forget something.

Where were you in the last scary movie you saw? Stiff and screaming, you were probably in the movie. Only after the scene ended did you return to your seat in the theater. Experientially, you were in the movie; even your body was there. If movies and books are successful, they transport us into different lives and worlds.

Here, then, can consist of many places. We are not always where an observer thinks we are. We may, instead, be over there, in an experiential reality invisible to their eyes.

4

Phenomenological Research

Research is part of every person's day-to-day life. Broken into its parts, the word *research* means "to search again or in a new way." This is something all of us do on a regular basis, either to solve problems or to explore life. When we ask and answer questions, wonder if information is reliable, or question whether what we know is really true, we are being everyday researchers. Although most of us think of research taking place in university laboratories, the lifeworld is the laboratory of phenomenological research. In this chapter, we will see how phenomenologists do research.

In a number of ways, formal phenomenological research differs from everyday questioning, noticing, and reexamining. For one thing, it is more systematic and rigorous. When doing research, phenomenologists set aside large blocks of time to think about the project, to word their research questions, to collect data, and to understand data. Also, the researcher has a goal larger than the solution of an immediate, individual problem. She or he wants to articulate essential insights into the phenomenon, ones that can be understood, recognized, and used by others. The researcher's purpose is to provide a tangible and penetrating overview of the phenomenon that evokes the reader's life experiences of it.

The topics of phenomenological research are countless: they can include all of human experience. Anything that is experienced and can be put into words can be investigated by phenomenologists. Phenomenological researchers have studied learning, decision making, chess playing, criminal victimization, presentence incarceration, swearing, anger, the creative process, humor, the natural athlete, friendship, sexual desire, the premenstruum, childbirth, cancer, anticipatory grief, and psychotherapy.

Currently, most phenomenological research approaches can be classified as either empirical or hermeneutical. Many phenomenological researchers collect data; they are empirical phenomenological researchers. Of these, some ask people to describe life events and then use these descriptions to understand the general structure or nature of a phenomenon. Most of the above-mentioned subject matters of phenomenological research are of this type. Other empirical researchers use descriptive data to show the essential features of a process: reconciliation, forgiving someone, recovering from the ending of a relationship, recovering from criminal victimization. Still others use data to validate phenomenological concepts.

Another research tradition, hermeneutical-phenomenological research, is even broader than these empirical approaches. Hermeneutical studies use such things as literary texts and works of art to understand human life. In these studies, researchers read texts, for example, interpretatively. Scholarly and creative works, as well as life events, can be the subject of this kind of systematic, interpretative study. In this research tradition, the reader-interpreter of life texts enters a "hermeneutical circle" of witnessing, responding to, reframing, and relanguaging the object of exploration. This process can be dynamic, creative, and open-ended. Von Eckartsberg (1986) explains:

> There does not seem to be a set starting point or a clearly outlined procedure to follow in hermeneutical-phenomenological investigations. One embeds oneself in the process of getting involved in the text, one begins to discern configurations of meaning, of parts and wholes and their interrelatedness, one receives certain messages and glimpses of an unfolding development that beckons to be articulated and related to the total fabric of meaning. The hermeneutic approach seems to palpate its object and it makes room for it to reveal itself to our gaze and ears, to speak its own story into our understanding.

> In hermeneutic work we grope for the single expression that will do justice to the integrity and complexity and essential being of the phenomenon. We become spokespersons and messengers for the meanings that demand to be articulated. We become intrigued and entangled in the webs and the voices of language and its expressive demands. In hermeneutic work we become engaged in an expanding network of meaning-enrichment contributing new meanings to the ongoing dialogue. It is a process of contextualization and amplification rather than of structural essentialization. Hermeneutic work is open-ended and suggestive, concerned with relational fertility. (p. 134)

The reader will find a thorough and lively discussion of these empirical and hermeneutical approaches to and methods of conducting phenomenological research in van Eckartsberg's (1986) book *Life-World Experiences*. Within this diversity of research approaches, I will concentrate on empirical phenomenological research that illuminates the essential components of phenomena.

A research project usually begins in the lifeworld. The topic is salient, either in a positive or a negative way, for the researcher. Personal interest sparks a desire to discover how other people experience the phenomenon. In general, phenomenological researchers want to know more about what a phenomenon is rather than what causes it to exist. Starting from his or her everyday experiences of a phenomenon and traveling through other people's experiences of it, the researcher eventually arrives at a general understanding of a phenomenon in its unique and essential manifestations. The goal of phenomenological research is to illuminate the phenomenon's essential, structural qualities. This is another way of saying that phenomenologists want to understand the common aspects of a phenomenon that permeate and also transcend diverse individual experiences.

Phenomenologically oriented researchers design empirical studies that highlight phenomena as they are experienced by people. They study everyday events from the inside, from within the world of the person experiencing them. In doing so, they strive to understand what phenomena *are* for the experiencing person. Phenomenological researchers ask large, structural questions such as What is learning? and What are the essential attributes of a friendship relationship? Unlike traditional researchers, they want to understand the nature of a phenomenon rather than to predict and control it.

Phenomenological research departs from traditional social science research in radical ways. As we have seen, phenomenologists assume that experience is a valid source of knowledge and that people's everyday experiences contain rich insights into phenomena. Therefore, without forcing it into predetermined categories, they ask research questions that allow this lived understanding of phenomena to emerge. Because phenomenologists see scientific truths arising from and returning to the everyday world, they stay close to the lifeworld when doing research. Their mandate—"back to the things themselves"—departs sharply from the natural science model of research to which social scientists have wittingly and unwittingly subscribed.

A contemporary phenomenological theorist and researcher, Amadeo Giorgi, has outlined and then questioned the traditional research model that modern social scientists hold in esteem. Giorgi (1970) delineates three parts to any empirical model of research: a subject matter, an approach to the subject matter, and methods of collecting and analyzing data. Giorgi's critique of social science researchers is that, in an effort to be accepted as legitimate scientists, they have unquestioningly adopted a natural science model of research. This model, developed to study inanimate objects, places a priority on realities that can be observed, broken down into smaller parts, systematically manipulated, and measured. Giorgi argues that this model's usefulness to the social sciences is limited because people are inherently different from inanimate objects.

The subject matters of the natural sciences—organisms and inanimate objects—are ones that people have access to only from the outside. As humans, we can only understand these beings through observations of actions and reactions. Experimental procedures for studying living and nonliving matter have evolved and have proved useful in such disciplines as biology, botany, chemistry, and physics. The experimental method has been transplanted to the social sciences, has been equated with science, and has supplanted different methods and approaches. One tragedy of this prioritization of the experimental method is that the human world has been reduced to what is observable and measurable; human experience has been relegated to the realm of nonscience.

Further, the natural science model of research, exemplified by the laboratory experiment, rests on philosophical assumptions with which phenomenologists disagree. For phenomenologists, behavior is not more real and reliable than experience, smaller units of behavior are not preferred to larger units, prediction and control are not the best ways to show that you understand something, and people are not merely collections of observable reactions to stimuli. Basic premises of the natural sciences, that methods of measuring behavior can ensure objectivity and that researchers do not influence their findings, are clearly in conflict with the phenomenological view that meaning is co-created. By translating people into behavior that can be repeatedly measured, phenomenologists believe that traditional social scientists have eliminated the heart of human existence.

Adoption of a natural science model of research has resulted in the prioritization of method in the social sciences. Subsequently, the other two aspects of any research paradigm—the subject matter and the approach—have been narrowed to what can be observed, measured, repeated, controlled, and predicted. Large questions of life have been reduced to phenomena that are defined by the operations used to measure them (i. e., friendship is defined as one person's ability to predict another's responses on an adjective checklist), and researchers have focused on what causes something rather than on understanding its nature. The meaning of life events, as well as the relevancy of research findings to complex people and events, has been replaced by concerns for repetition and control.

Giorgi believes that social scientists must adopt a different model of research. He calls this model a human science one. As developed by Giorgi (1970), human science research suspends belief in the approaches and methods that natural scientists have developed and returns to an open-minded investigation of the different approaches and methods appropriate to various research topics. In human science research, an ongoing dialogue must occur among subject matter, approach, and method. Rather than preferred methods eliminating areas of study, new ways are sought to access data within these areas. Depending upon the topic, different approaches and methods become favored. It is appropriate, for example, to collect data on friendship in a friendly manner. Because the phenomenon is an intimate one, the researcher needs to collect data in ways that enable people to describe its intimate, relational nature.

Because the subjects of human science research are experiencing, reflective, intentional, and verbal people, human scientists proceed differently from natural scientists. The research situation is an interpersonal one for phenomenologists, one in which both researchers and research participants are experiencing and co-creating meaning together. Rather than translating experiences and meanings into numbers and then statistically testing the significance of the numbers, phenomenologists try to capture the meaning of a phenomenon for each research participant. These experiences, filled with meanings, are summarized into essential themes of the phenomena that permeate individual lifeworlds. Because they do not believe in the predictability of people or the repeatability of human experience, phenomenologists strive to understand the variations of these essential themes across human lives. In doing so, they know that any person's life experiences of a phenomenon are fuller, richer, and slightly different from the product of their research.

Phenomenologists try to see, understand, and articulate the important aspects of a phenomenon as it is experienced by particular people. They try not to impose their categories of understanding onto data. If, for example, they wish to understand friendship, they ask research participants to describe their particular friendships. They believe that people who form and maintain friendship relationships know a great deal about them on both reflective and prereflective levels of awareness. By attending to moments remembered and events described, the researcher can piece together the essential aspects of particular friendships.

In studying something like friendship, phenomenological researchers assume that people's experiences of friendship are valid and reliable sources of information. They also assume that people know more about friendship than they usually talk about, that lived-through situations and moments hold the structural essence of this phenomenon. Rather than predicting friendship choices, as many traditional social scientists have done, phenomenologists, like myself, define the nature of friendship. For phenomenologists, understanding what something is prefaces knowing what causes and

influences it. Because phenomenologists believe that an experiencing, intentional, active person is always part of the subject studied,
they articulate phenomena from the perspective of this dynamic center.

Both research informants and the researcher are active participants in human science research. Phenomenological research strives
for valid and reliable knowledge about phenomena by including,
rather than eliminating, people and their experiences. Objectivity,
then, is redefined in terms of awareness of preconceptions. Rather
than trying to eliminate preunderstandings, the phenomenologist
becomes aware of them so that they can be set aside and new faces
of the phenomenon can emerge. Once data have been collected, preunderstandings can be used to delineate the essential nature of a
phenomenon.

The process that phenomenological researchers use to become
aware of their preconceptions about a phenomenon is a simple one.
It involves the researcher writing down and reflecting upon all of
his or her lived experiences of the phenomenon. For example, I kept
a research journal when I was doing my dissertation on friendship.
Over a period of many months, I described my experiences of
friendship. These descriptions consisted of detailed memories of
moments spent with friends. I described, elaborated, and clarified
each moment I remembered. I jotted down any ideas I had about
friendship relationships and continued until I felt that I had said as
much as I could. Then I summarized what I knew about friendship
from these entries. Here is a summary of the things I knew about
friendship relationships before I collected data (Becker, 1973):

> For me, friendship is a mutual, dynamic, and emotionally close rela-
> tionship between two people. It contains ever deepening and expand-
> ing sharing through talking and doing things together. As the friends
> know each other better and better, their love for and appreciation of
> each other grows. The friends are sensitive to and attuned to each other
> without losing their centeredness in themselves. Moments of not talk-
> ing, of simply being together in comfortable relaxedness, capture a
> taken for granted feeling and understanding between friends. There is
> give and take between the friends, as well as mutual dependence and
> independence. Each friend is comfortable being herself with her friend.
> She trusts and respects her friend and can be herself without fear of
> rejection or judgements. (pp. 42-47)

Explicitly knowing what I knew about friendship, I then set this knowledge aside. Phenomenologists call this process "bracketing," or suspending preunderstandings of the phenomenon. Bracketing is how phenomenological researchers control for biasing data. Pre-understandings that are acknowledged and validated are less apt to be imposed upon research participants.

At this point, I developed a general question that asked people to tell me about everyday experiences of their most important friendship relationship. I asked them to describe a particular friendship; I did not tell them what to say or how to say it. My main question was, Tell me as much as you can about your most important friendship. This is another way researchers control for biasing the data. By beginning with a general question that directs people to talk, in their own words and in their own way, about day-to-day experiences of the phenomenon, the researcher can discover salient aspects of the phenomenon. What the research informant says becomes the guiding structure for additional questions.

Descriptive data are collected in a variety of ways: questionnaires, videotaped interactions, interviews after something has happened, interviews while something is happening. Von Eckartsberg (1986) gives examples of these different data collection methods and their products. I will discuss one of these methods—the retrospective research interview. In doing so, I will outline the principles that phenomenological researchers follow and illustrate how we ask questions during an interview.

The Research Interview

Phenomenological researchers use an unstructured format when collecting data. We ask one open-ended question at the beginning of the interview and then develop other questions from the person's response. Interviews are audiotaped and then transcribed verbatim. A good research question evokes memories of events that have been lived through rather than thoughts about the phenomenon.

The researcher wants informants to begin in the events of their lifeworlds. These events are filled with the order that the phenomenon has in each person's everyday life. They may be typical moments, unusual highlights, nuggets of meaningfulness, or unresolved issues. The researcher wants to discover the phenomenon exactly as it appears in the person's experience, in all its descriptive detail and variation. By noticing what is mentioned first, what memories are linked together, what situations are returned to again and again, the researcher can illuminate the central aspects of the phenomenon for each person. For example, if someone begins an interview on friendship by talking about a painful disagreement that was later resolved, this can alert the researcher to the importance of living through conflict and healing wounds in friendship relationships.

Preferred participants in phenomenological research are those who have many life experiences of the phenomenon. They do not have to think about it; its manifestations in their everyday lives are simply there for them when they hear the research question. The phenomenon is clearly present in their lives, and they can talk about it without analyzing their experiences. They merely must spend time with their situated experiences of a phenomenon and describe them to the researcher. And, they may have to struggle with putting words to complex, prereflective experiences.

To facilitate this task, the interview situation should be private, free from interruptions, and one in which the interviewee feels comfortable. This format will maximize attention to the descriptive task. After asking the opening question, the researcher suspends further structuring. If asked for direction, the researcher directs the person back to his or her everyday experiences of the phenomenon. Often, the interviewee must be reassured that whatever comes to mind will be helpful. The researcher's main task is to help the person sink more deeply into these experiences.

The research interview is a task-focused, interpersonal meeting between people who are virtual strangers or, if acquainted, are meeting in a new way. The researcher's goal—to get thorough descriptions of the interviewee's everyday experiences of the phenomenon—is accomplished by sensitively and skillfully attending to the researcher-researchee relationship. The researcher must put the informant at ease and help him or her attend to and describe experiences without being evaluative. Examples are especially helpful. It is useful for the researcher to cultivate genuine interest in other people, willingness to learn from lived experience, and respectful empathy for others. Paradoxically, if the researcher is genuinely present and interested in individual life experiences, he or she will maximize rich descriptions of life experiences.

The research situation involves a unique meeting of individuals that cannot be fully orchestrated by predetermined techniques. Rather, general principles guide the researcher in each research relationship. The researcher does similar things in each interview, yet each successful interview is a unique, creative event.

Structurally, the researcher follows an initial open-ended question with requests to elaborate on the events, feelings, memories, meanings, and thoughts that have already been mentioned. This inquiry follows the order of the phenomenon that was initially given in the subject's first descriptions. The researcher asks for specific examples, encourages the person to say more about things mentioned, and eventually asks if other moments or events come to mind about the phenomenon. This process continues until what the interviewee says sounds familiar, until examples and meanings repeat themselves, and until the person runs out of things to add.

The way the researcher proceeds may vary with each interview. The desired goal, of obtaining rich, detailed description from a person's lifeworld, may be attained by listening to one person, questioning another, agreeing with someone else, or challenging another. All of these interactions accomplish the same purpose in different ways. A successful research interview is one in which the interviewee can take the research relationship for granted, can sink into the descriptive details of his or her experiences of the phenomenon, and can give details and nuances that bring the researcher into the lifeworld.

The skilled phenomenological researcher is involved simultaneously in multiple tasks. Throughout the interview, the researcher monitors the evolving relationship between self and other so that it remains the unproblematic ground that facilitates rich description. The researcher must evenhandedly probe the descriptions for elaboration and depth of detail while simultaneously noticing what aspects seem salient. While requesting examples, elaborations, and clarifications, the researcher is assessing whether essential features of the phenomenon are being described adequately. The following are some questions researchers silently ask while interviewing: Do I feel that I can summarize the essential aspects of this phenomenon for this person? Have I gotten enough examples and details? Can the person say anything else about this aspect of the phenomenon? Do experiences of the phenomenon exist that she or he has not mentioned yet? In this way, the researcher scrutinizes the depth and breadth of the data during the interview. The researcher pushes description to its limits, knowing that lived experience eventually will become ineffable. If aspects of the phenomenon are noticeable in their absence, they are raised before interviewing ends.

The research interview is paradoxical in a number of ways. It is a task-focused situation whose outcome depends upon the quality of the researcher-researchee's relationship. Also, it is structured, yet unstructured. The researcher is prepared and knowledgeable yet open-minded and naive, immersed in the data but standing back to get an overview of it, and receptively responsive but task oriented. The researcher must be resourcefully responsive without leading, join the other person's lifeworld without intruding, be personably goal oriented, and be flexibly focused.

Depending upon many factors—the researcher's purposes and time constraints, the topic, the quality of the data, and the informants' emotional and physical availability—research subjects may be interviewed one or more times, for an hour or hours. The researcher must make a qualitative decision about the adequacy of the data. This decision depends upon what the researcher is trying to do with the data. Generally, interviewing ends when both researcher and researchee feel that descriptions have been thorough and inclusive. This becomes evident when themes are repeated and the person has nothing new to add.

The researcher must decide also how many people to interview. Again, this is a judgment based upon realistic and research constraints. Because more data make it easier to see the phenomenon's general structure, as well as its individual variations, it is to the researcher's advantage to collect as much data from as many people as possible. When data are rich enough to reveal the phenomenon's essential features and constellation, interviewing stops and data analysis begins.

Contemporary Danish phenomenological psychologist Steiner Kvale (1983) summarizes the mode of understanding typical of phenomenological interviews as follows:

> The mode of understanding in the qualitative research interview may be briefly outlined in 12 main aspects. It is:
>
> 1. centered on the interviewee's life-world;
> 2. seeks to understand the meaning of phenomena in his life-world; it is
> 3. qualitative,
> 4. descriptive, and
> 5. specific; it is
> 6. presuppositionless; it is
> 7. focused on certain themes; it is open for
> 8. ambiguities and
> 9. changes; it depends upon the
> 10. sensitivity of the interviewer; it takes place in
> 11. an interpersonal interaction, and it may be
> 12. a positive experience. (p. 174)

During the interviews, the researcher can best accomplish his or her task by focusing on the descriptive process and the interpersonal context. At this stage, the primary commitment is to the subject's lived experiences of the phenomenon. When data analysis begins, the researcher's commitment and focus shift to the general, structural qualities of the phenomenon.

Data Analysis

Analysis of the data begins once the interviews are completed and the data have been transcribed. This process is a tedious and time consuming one that proceeds through clearly outlined stages. The goal of phenomenological research—to provide a holistic view of the phenomenon that is useful to people in their everyday lives—is, ideally, a blend of the general and the specific. By dwelling on many manifestations of the phenomenon, the researcher is able to identify common themes. By articulating the interrelationship of these themes, the essential structure of the phenomenon is revealed.

Phenomenological researchers who follow the procedures developed by Giorgi (1971, 1975) carry out data analysis in a similar manner. These steps are useful, especially to new students, because they help researchers bracket their preconceptions and rigorously focus on the phenomenon-for-the-other. By staying with, dwelling on, and reflecting upon the exact words and meanings of each person, the researcher uncovers the salient features of the phenomenon. What follows is my adaptation of Giorgi's approach and procedures.

When I work with new data, I read through the transcripts one by one. I study each interviewee's descriptions and note themes or units of meaning. I find that color-coded highlighting or jotting down key words in the margins is a good way of thematizing. When I was studying women's friendships, for example, Ann began by talking about the little everyday things she shares with her friend. Then she mentioned never being bored. Later she talked about the mutual affection, enjoyment, and knowledge between her and Beth. Each of these was a theme or meaning unit.

When I note themes and meanings, I see the phenomenon from within a particular person's life experiences and identify its salient features and meanings. As I read through the data, I ask myself, What stands out about the phenomenon? What is the most important aspect, what is next in importance? How do these different themes fit together? Taking each highlighted theme, I go through the data and put everything that the person has said about it in one place. Cutting and pasting a copy of the data, electronically or mechanically, is a good way to do this. Next, I summarize and edit the meanings and manifestations of each theme, still using the person's own words. Finally, I look for how all these parts of the phenomenon are interrelated, how these pieces go together to make one phenomenon. Then I write an overall portrait of the phenomenon for each research subject.

In this descriptive portrayal, I stay as close as I can to the person's words, while also trying to articulate the situated meanings of the phenomenon. This is another way of saying that I highlight the typical situations, events, and meanings that the phenomenon has in the person's life. From my study of friendship, here is an example of this level of data analysis, for a woman I named Ann, about her friendship with Beth (Becker, 1987):

Beth is the person I feel closest to on my level in an equal relationship. I can be myself with her and she is an important part of me and my life. When I think of Beth I picture her soft, warm smile, a mischievous look in her eyes and the sophisticated way she walks into a room. All of these bring back experiences we have shared together.

The most important moments of our friendship are the most mundane. They include having lunch together, calling her on the phone and saying nothing in particular, working on a paper together, or catching up on details after we have not seen each other for awhile. A familiar background of gestures, phrases, interchanges and activities fills these daily events. There are also elements of surprise and excitement. For example, we always eat lunch together in the cafeteria. Each of us does certain things the same every time. But an unexpected remark or a change of routine can make it a new experience, filled with surprise. While the daily routines are there, we never know for certain what is going to happen in them.

Times such as these are filled with all of our past moments together. They hold our caring for one another and the personal meanings and nuances that are present for each of us in our friendship. When Beth says something, I understand all of it: what she actually said, what it means to her, what she said especially to me. Things that are said and done are part of the creation of our relationship.

Beth and I have had the time to share many experiences, and to reveal diverse aspects of ourselves to one another. She has been with me when I have been sad and worried, consumed by ugly fears about myself. Beth has also seen me happy and carefree. She accepts my problems and my strengths, but encourages me to overcome my fears and helps me see them in a realistic manner.

Similarly, I know sides of Beth that few people realize exist. Most people know the poised and sophisticated Beth. I also know Beth's shyness, her fears and sorrows, and her need for other people to accept her. I look forward to knowing all aspects of Beth and care about her experiences in life. (pp. 62-63)

This level of data presentation is powerful because it brings the reader into the content and form of particular friendships and evokes the reader's experiences of friendships.

After I have completed this stage of data analysis for all research participants, I use the summary portraits to do the same thing at a higher level of generalization. I read through each summary, identify common themes, and reorder themes into a structural description of the phenomenon. Here, I leave individual lifeworlds behind and focus on the phenomenon itself; I strive for the most inclusive statement of the phenomenon's essential qualities. This structural description uses the language of my discipline (e. g., psychology or phenomenological psychology) and is oriented toward the audience I wish to reach (e. g., other psychologists, students in the social sciences). I will present my structural description of friendship in Chapter 10.

Contemporary phenomenological psychologist Frederick Wertz (1984) summarizes the researcher's presence to the data as involving five movements:

1. Empathic presence to the described situation
2. Slowing down and patiently dwelling
3. Magnification, and amplification of details
4. Turning from objects to immanent meanings
5. Suspending belief and employing intense interest (p. 42)

Within this stance, Wertz cites eight procedures that the researcher uses to arrive at the phenomenon's essential structure:

1. Recognition and utilization of an "existential baseline"
2. Distinguishing constituents
3. Reflection on judgment of relevance
4. Grasping implicit meanings
5. Relating constituents
6. Imaginative variation
7. Conceptually guided interrogation
8. Psychological languaging (pp. 42-43)

Now that you understand how empirical phenomenological researchers work with data, I will use the topic of criminal victimization to look at various ways phenomenologists present research results.

Two phenomenological researchers, Constance Fischer and Frederick Wertz (1979) show numerous ways to present research results. Depending upon the researcher's purpose, different levels of data analysis are preferred. Fischer and Wertz exemplify five forms that research findings can take. The ones I will review are individual case synopses, the illustrated narrative, and a general condensation. Respectively, these presentations become progressively structural

and abstracted from particular lifeworlds. Often, researchers concentrate on one level of presentation, while giving samples of the
other levels of analysis. The following excerpt from a case synopsis
vividly brings us into the experience of being criminally victimized
(Fischer & Wertz, 1979):

> Upon returning home from a family outing shortly after Christmas, the R.
> family noticed that the bottom panel of the front door was broken, the glass
> shattered. Mr. R. thought that children must have been playing.
>
> When he went inside, he saw the candy dish on the floor rather than
> on the stereo as usual. He looked around and saw a pair of pants lying
> on the steps and thought the house might be ransacked. He walked into
> the living room and when he saw the stereo gone, he was in disbelief.
> He knew robbing existed but felt "it would never happen to me." He
> screamed out to his wife, "Don't come in," thinking someone might still
> be there, but Mrs. R. had already gone inside. She was shocked to see
> the bare wall where their Oriental rug wedding present had hung. Their
> cedar chest was smashed and broken into. Her shock turned to fear.
>
> Mr. and Mrs. R. went next door to call the police and then went back
> home to figure out just what had happened. By this time, Mr. R. was
> angry, feeling "I'm gonna get somebody for this!" Taking stock, they
> found the children's Christmas toys gone, including a six-foot teddy
> bear. The back door was wide open, but the house was not cold, indicat-
> ing that maybe they scared the thieves away when they got home. The
> jewelry was gone. It was strange to the Rs, however, that candy was
> taken although some expensive gifts were left under the Christmas tree.
> There seemed to be no reason why the thieves took some things that
> were sentimental but of no monetary value. What hurt most was a
> bronze Infant of Prague bank which Mr. R's mother had all her life and
> gave him when she died. It was irreplaceable. (p. 140)

Next, Fischer and Wertz use the illustrated narrative to present an
overview of the sequential themes of being criminally victimized:
living routinely, being disrupted, being violated, reintegration,
going on. They develop each theme, accompanied by specific examples from the transcripts. For my purposes, I will summarize briefly
these five stages of being criminally victimized.

Before being criminally victimized, people live routinely, believing that crime occurs but that it will never happen to them. Once
their lives are disrupted by the crime, they imaginatively and per-
ceptually scan the immediate environment for an even worse outcome than the one that happened. A sense of being violated, with
accompanying feelings of outrage, despair, hopelessness, and resig-

nation, follows. Eventually, victims recover from the violation by doing something to ensure their future safety. They resume their lives with less trust and more caution (Fischer & Wertz, 1979, pp. 145-148).

Next, Fischer and Wertz give a general condensation of the phenomenon that highlights the essential structure:

> Being criminally victimized is a disruption of daily routine. It is a disruption that compels one, despite personal resistance, to face one's fellow as predator and oneself as prey, even though all the while anticipating consequences, planning, acting, and looking to others for assistance. These efforts to little avail, one experiences vulnerability, separateness, and helplessness in the face of the callous, insensitive, often anonymous enemy. Shock and disbelief give way to puzzlement, strangeness, and then to a sense of the crime as perverse, unfair, undeserved. Whether or not expressed immediately, the victim experiences a general inner protest, anger or rage, and a readiness for retaliation, for revenge against the violator.
>
> As life goes on, the victim finds him- or herself pervasively attuned to the possibility of victimization—through a continued sense of reduced agency, of the other as predatory, and of community as inadequately supportive. More particularly, one continues to live the victimization through recollections of the crime, imagination of even worse outcomes, vigilant suspiciousness of others, sensitivity to news of disorder and crime, criticalness of justice system agents, and desires to make sense of it all. (p. 149)

By presenting multiple levels of data analysis, researchers can provide results that have multiple uses. For example, case synopses might be most useful in working with victims of criminal acts. A general condensation might be most useful in training psychotherapists who counsel crime victims or law enforcers who intervene at the scene.

Why Do Phenomenological Research?

Phenomenological research's usefulness lies in providing an understanding of phenomena as they are lived by people in the everyday world. Because any experience that can be described can be studied by empirical phenomenology, this approach and method has expanded the subject matters that can be investigated systematically. The products of phenomenological research, descriptive portraits of phenomena's essential structure and experiential components, give views of topics situated within the real lives of whole people. This structural understanding of what something is for the people experiencing it, can provide crucial information in theoretical, empirical, and intervention realms. Because empirical phenomenological investigations result in descriptive summaries of what something is, they evoke the reader's similar and different experiences of the phenomenon and, through this resonation, convey a validness of the findings.

Certainly, this descriptive, experiential approach is controversial. But for those who are willing to rethink the reification of operational definitions, control of variables, and prediction of isolated responses, phenomenological research breathes new life into increasingly dehumanized social science research. By going "back to the things themselves," phenomenological researchers uncover rich storehouses of insight into human life. I will be discussing some of these treasures in Parts II, III, and IV, which explore human development and human relationships.

PART II

❖

Human Development

The next four chapters will show how phenomenologists understand people of different ages. Developmental phenomenology is a young discipline and, as yet, no inclusive text has been written on life span development from a phenomenological viewpoint. Further, considerable diversity exists in phenomenological approaches to human development. Some phenomenologists (Bachelard, 1964; Moustakas, 1961; Yalom, 1980) describe such universal, existential issues of life as dwelling, loneliness, freedom, responsibility, and meaningfulness, which must be dealt with from birth through death. Others, explicitly or implicitly, follow a stage theory orientation to human development. Richard Knowles (1986), for example, adds a Heideggerian explication to Erik Erikson's (1963) eight developmental stages. Many others, such as Maurice Merleau-Ponty (1964), Rod Michalko (1984), and Daniel Offer (Offer, Ostrov, & Howard, 1981), describe essential dimensions of particular stages of life. Still others (Alapack, 1984; Barritt, Beekman, Bleeker, & Mulderij, 1983; Hornstein & Wapner, 1985; Miller, 1978) illuminate central life events that provide deep insights into human life.

I will draw upon these diverse orientations to help us enter into the lifeworlds of different-aged people who encounter various life events. Chapter headings of "Infants and Children," "Adolescents," "Adults," and "Elders," reflect my belief that chronological age is an experientially salient organizer of human life. Knowledge of life stages, however, cannot replace knowledge of experiencing people. An emotionally healthy self is a continuous self, one who experiences both continuity and change through time and space. Certainly, life events, as well as time, shape the experiencing, co-constituting, evolving, continuous self. People realize and actualize themselves—develop—in an ongoing, dialectical process of being-in- the-world-with-others.

A growing literature presents phenomenological views of children, adolescents, adults, and elders. Some of these show how people of different ages live in relation to the existential a prioris of time, space, self, body, others, and world. Some illuminate the essential themes of important life events: perceiving, speaking, playing, falling in love, leaving home, making commitments, being creative, growing old, and dying. All strive to know people from within their dynamic lifeworlds and to communicate a contagious interest in understanding unique, intentional subjects who share common life experiences. Rather than helping us comprehend people through prepackaged knowledge, phenomenologists prime our interest in diverse lifeworlds and invite us into dialogue with developing people. For the phenomenologist, research findings and theories about human development are useful bridges into co-participation in the everyday worlds of people with whom we live. The phenomenologist seeks to understand others, over there, in and of themselves. They remember, however, that any understanding of the other is a co-constitution of meaning, an understanding of the other-for-me. The dialectic, then, of self and other is inherent in the study of development.

All of us begin a study of human development from inside our own lives. We are a presence, living in present time, that includes a present-past, as well as a present-future. This temporal dimension of existence enables us to experience our being. We are, in the context of who we have been and who we will be. We also experience our own becoming. We stay ourselves but we change. Our sense of becoming is our sense of development.

From a phenomenological perspective, it is important to begin here, in the everyday world of our own development.

When I think about myself developing, I think of changing in ways that I value and desire. Development implies growth, becoming more of what I am, of who I want to be, of stretching beyond the confines of my history and expectations. In becoming more of my desired self, I add skills and insights, I reclaim wounded parts of my emotional self, I gain a deeper and broader view of the small and large parts of my life. For children and young adolescents, development means growing taller and older, becoming sexually mature, and attaining autonomy and independence. For adults and elders, development means attaining goals, solidifying values by which to live and die, and gaining wisdom about the meaning of life. Most of us think of development as adding more, qualitatively or quantitatively, to ourselves and becoming better at what we do and are. But some of us know that we have developed through experiencing loss. Loss returns us to ourselves. It clarifies what matters to us, and it awakens us to our vulnerabilities and strengths.

Within Western European cultures, once we become adults many of us question our assumption that life is a continuous, upward progression of growth and change. We notice that we thread back through ourselves, that we learn and relearn, that we remain the same even though we change. Some of us experience our lives as circles, returning us again and again to the same issues. Some experience life as a linear, uphill climb to a summit. Others catch glimpses of a self spiraling through time, and life looping back on itself. Still others see sharp turns, juxtaposed shifts, and discontinuous breaks. From an experiential viewpoint, each of these different structures of development is a valid one. Although modern stage theories regard development as hierarchical and progressive, J. H. van den Berg (1961) reminds us that, historically, discontinuity and free occurrences of events have been regarded as equally valid. It behooves phenomenologists, then, to bracket their natural attitudes and reenter development through the door of life experiences.

Phenomenologists study development from within their assumptions about human nature. They see people as experiencing, diverse, intentional subjects who co-create meaning and
exercise situated freedom. In studying people of all ages and
in different life conditions, they seek to understand people on
the people's own terms. Developmental phenomenologists
ask questions about essential themes of human experience and
the nature of infancy, childhood, adolescence, adulthood, and
old age. They use knowledge gleaned to further their understanding of human existence.

Phenomenologists believe that a dynamic, intentional being
who is never totally within our grasp, is at the center of a systematic study of human development. Human development,
then, is not entirely predictable or knowable. People's actions
and reactions are manifestations of their reflective and prereflective intentions. In addition, although each life is similar
to the lives of other people, it is different from them as well.
Each person is, radically or subtly, different from all others
and deserves fresh investigation and understanding. A moment of life cannot be repeated. Life is a dynamic now that
builds on the previous moment and invisibly blends into the
next. To be a developmental phenomenologist is, above all, to
honor the unique, situated freedom of each person. To be a
developmental phenomenologist is to witness the co-creation
of life and the dialectic of thrownness and freedom from
which life span development is crafted. General knowledge,
then, can never replace knowledge of the active person who
remains at the center of life. In dialogue with particular lives,
however, general developmental understandings can alert us
to important issues and sensitize us to meanings and projects
that we could otherwise not consider.

Developmental phenomenology is at its best when it evokes
the living presence of unique people and ignites understanding of our own, as well as other people's, lives. It is as much an
approach and a presence as it is a method of examining and
articulating. By listening to people and sitting with and walking around in their lives with them, phenomenologists articulate the meaningfulness of human life at different points in

time and in various life situations. Much of the phenomenological orientation is about witnessing human life, appreciat-
ing its mysteries and complexities, and striving to articulate
its wholeness.

The importance of the meaning-making, intentional, relational person is being acknowledged in nonphenomenological
developmental perspectives as well. Current proponents of
the classical psychological systems of development, psychoanalysis and behaviorism, have added an experiential twist to
their formulations. One modern version of psychoanalysis,
self psychology, places a cohesive, experientially based self at
the core of healthy development. The founder of self psychology, Heinz Kohut (1977, 1984), defines the self as coming into
being and being maintained within a matrix of essential relationships. This sounds very similar to the phenomenological
understanding of people as being-in-the-world-with-others.
Because self psychology blends experiential and depth psychology perspectives, I will use the insights of Heinz Kohut
and Alice Miller (1981, 1983) to discuss relationships between
parents and children.

Self psychology is a radical transformation of Sigmund
Freud's early formulations of drive theory and the unconscious.
For Freud (1949), biologically based forces orchestrated life as
people oscillated between life and death, love and hate, sex
and aggression. Erik Erikson (1963) moved psychoanalysis toward the interpersonal with his emphasis on developmental
issues and conflicts: trust versus mistrust, autonomy versus
shame and doubt, initiative versus guilt, industry versus in-
feriority, identity versus role confusion, intimacy versus
isolation, generativity versus self-absorption, integrity versus
despair and disgust. Harry Stack Sullivan (1953) formulated
an explicitly interpersonal theory of development, one that
presented people's lives as chronologically linked, dynamic
organizations of meanings. Sullivan's emphasis on "dyna-
misms"—organizations of meanings expressed in actions—
prefaced the experientially cohesive self of self psychology.

Modern behaviorism has traveled a similar path from its
beginnings in Ivan Pavlov's model of classical conditioning.

According to Pavlov, the core of human behavior is stimuli and response patterns of the autonomic nervous system. B. F. Skinner's model of operant conditioning (1938) moved control of human behavior out of the nervous system and into the environment. Although he believed that people act to produce rewarding results, Skinner professed that environmental factors controlled behavior. Social learning theory, however, added cognitive factors to the understanding of behavior. Albert Bandura (1986) developed an interactional model of behavior, personal and cognitive factors, and environmental influences to explain human life (Santrock, 1989, pp. 53-56). For the phenomenologist, these historical shifts in traditional developmental paradigms are heartening indications that the experiencing person is increasingly being considered as essential to the study of human life.

Phenomenologists provide glimpses into the lifeworlds of people of different ages. Many people and areas of life have yet to be explored phenomenologically, but enough are available to enrich our appreciation of essential structures and themes of life and to whet our appetites for an experiential viewpoint.

The next chapter will begin the phenomenology of development in infancy and childhood. Psychologist Marc Briod (1989) exemplifies a phenomenological approach by describing the child's development as an "open, creative venture of living toward the future" (p. 119). He explains:

> Opening, of course, suggests the expanding, widening, enlarging, or emerging of children's lives, as well as Martin Heidegger's (1962) fecund notions of dis-closing, dis-covering, making manifest, letting be, and so on. So child development is perhaps most adequately conveyed by a language of disclosure. But it would be accorded its special metaphorical flavor of growing, flowering, emerging, making, and so forth in light of the narrator's sense of the texture of each developing life. Moreover, it would be described as a life of creative openness, not self-made, but creative in the exact degree to which it is open to the newness and freshness of experience, and to its own life as a continual return to the sedimented layers of existing, intentionalities, meanings, and projects.
>
> Every metaphor for development has its opposite term: decaying, declining, regressing, destroying, shrinking, collapsing, closing, covering

over, and so forth. A phenomenological approach to child development does not rule out the employment of any and all metaphors, including their opposites. But at the most fundamental level of narrative and hermeneutical work the child's experience is best regarded as opening, revealing, or disclosing a world, in keeping with the phenomenological approach to any lived experience, first mapped out by Husserl (1962) and later given existential underpinnings by Heidegger (1962), Merleau-Ponty (1962), and others. (p. 119)

Having gone through this general orientation to developmental phenomenology, I now step out into the everyday worlds of different aged people and discuss essential structures and themes of life.

5

Infants and Children

Many adult developmental psychologists have told us about infants and children. Some, like Freud (1935), have reconstructed the emotional maps of our early years from adults' retrospective accounts. Others, like Jean Piaget (1952), have used the actual words and actions of children to understand cognitive development.

A phenomenology of infancy and childhood is a difficult task for adults because they are not infants or children anymore. In addition, van den Berg (1961) thinks that we experience ourselves, our bodies, other people, the physical world, and time and space in fundamentally different ways at different chronological ages. He believes, for example, that the infant's relation to its body is quite different from the adolescent's. This is so for each of these fundamental dimensions of life; diverse lives have distinct meanings and structures.

Some phenomenological investigators run into more problems than others. When people cannot articulate and clarify their experiences, phenomenologists cannot be certain that they have bracketed their own preconceptions and are understanding the others' lived meanings. Because infants, and sometimes children, cannot put their experiences into conventional language, phenomenologists who study them must rely on observation. By listening to the language of gestures, tones, phrases, and actions, they gain access to the experiences and life structures of infants and children. We will see that phenomenologists formulate these developmental observations according to their philosophical understandings of human nature. They are apt to ask, How must the child be experiencing self, others, and world to do and say that? By bracketing their stereotypes and reflecting on the spontaneous expressions of children, they hope to awaken to the lived delights and difficulties of childhood. They hope to portray the intentionality of children in motion, in being and becoming themselves. Phenomenological writers also wish to invoke adult readers' reflective and prereflective memories of childhood. At their best, children can teach phenomenologists about unself-conscious lived experience prior to its being superseded by theoretical models of human life. To witness the child's fresh discoveries of self, others, and world is to behold central aspects of life.

Some phenomenologists have described different developmental meanings and structures at various ages. They try to characterize each age group in positive terms, without making one group a lesser form of another. The following are some insights about infancy and childhood that can be used throughout life.

Consciousness, Perception, and Language

Like many other philosophers and psychologists, Merleau-Ponty (1962, 1964, 1973a, 1973b) has studied consciousness, perception, and language. Unlike many scholars, Merleau-Ponty believes that these phenomena are first interrelated and later become separated. In normal infancy, consciousness, perception, and language are all a unified whole. The initial unity of consciousness, perception, and language enables later differentiation and reintegration. For the healthy, normal infant, to be conscious is to perceive the world and to respond to it. Structurally, consciousness, perception, and language are, at first, unified. For the infant, consciousness appears to be primarily a prereflective or bodily awareness. This prereflective infant is very much an active, intentional being-in-the-world-with-others.

Merleau-Ponty adds the body to our study of consciousness. The infant's first awarenesses are bodily ones; the infant is a body-subject who thinks by moving eyes, lips, tongue, hands, and legs. Initial thinking is prereflective: it happens as the infant acts in the world. As the infant matures, he or she forms a sense of self, as well as a knowledge of other people, by crawling, walking, and running around, over, under, and through the world. Through this sensory process, the identities of self, others, and world are constructed. For example, crawling all over Dad and tasting, smelling, touching, seeing, and hearing him enables the infant to know Dad and to know herself in relation to him. More obviously than at any other life phase, the infant is its body. The self is a behaving, bodily self.

When the infant, child, or any person engages the world, she or he attends to some things and not to others. The infant's attention is focused upon things that are meaningful, human faces as well as things to be sucked, eaten, and grasped. The sensory world is structured; it is organized into meaningful units when it first appears to the infant. Out of the array of possible things to attend to, the infant selects some and ignores others. Merleau-Ponty asserts that the infant's first blinking awareness of the world is an active, intentional one. Even traditional researchers tell us that, at birth, infants attend to figures and ignore backgrounds or horizons. Attention is active and selective from the very beginning of life. If an infant does not show preferences and does not selectively engage the world, we worry that something is wrong. This is so throughout life.

Through their perceptual, bodily involvement in the world, infants co-create and bring into being themselves, others, and their worlds. In the dialectic of self and world, human life is created and evolves. In understanding attention and perception, Merleau-Ponty (1962) suggests that attention is consciousness in the act of learning. He says:

> [I]t has long been known that during the first nine months of life, infants distinguish only globally the coloured from the colourless; thereafter coloured areas form into "warm" and "cold" shades, and finally the detailed colours are arrived at. . . . The first perception of colours properly speaking, then, is a change of the structure of consciousness, the establishment of a new dimension of experience, the setting forth of an a priori.
>
> Now attention has to be conceived on the model of these originating acts, since secondary attention, which would be limited to recalling knowledge already gained, would once more identify it with

acquisition. To pay attention is not merely further to elucidate pre-exist-
ing data, it is to bring about a new articulation of them by taking them
as figures. They are preformed only as horizons, they constitute in reality new regions in the total world. It is precisely the original structure
which they introduce that brings out the identity of the object before
and after the act of attention. Once the colour-quality is acquired, and
only by means of it, do the previous data appear as preparations of this
quality. . . . The miracle of consciousness consists in its bringing to
light, through attention, phenomena which re-establish the unity of the
object in a new dimension at the very moment when they destroy it.
Thus attention is neither an association of images, nor the return to itself
of thought already in control of its objects, but the active constitution of
a new object which makes explicit and articulate what was until then
presented as no more than an indeterminate horizon. (pp. 29-30)

Like experience, perception is filled with meaning. It is possible to
break it down into its sensory parts only because it is first a coherent, meaningful whole. Without this immediate, meaningful coher-
ence, the sensory details of perception would be random events. A
linear, sequential analysis of perception presupposes its wholeness.

We can understand children's perceptions through their actions
and words. A child psychologist, who wishes to understand the experience of a child, asks him or her to draw a picture of something:
a person, a house, a family. The psychologist enters children's experiential worlds by studying their drawings. Merleau-Ponty has used
children's drawings to form a structural description of children's
perceptions from inside of their perceptual worlds.

For Merleau-Ponty (1973b), the child's perceptions are a co-creation
of meaning that occurs between the child and the environment.
As seen in the child's drawing, a child's perceptions have their own
truth and logic, which are simultaneously global and fragmentary.
The first recognizable picture of a person that a child draws shows
these perceptual principles. It is a lumpy circle, a head with empty
holes for eyes. Later, another hole is added for the mouth. Still later,
stick arms grow out of the head and fragile legs reach toward the
still invisible ground. At each point in the child's development, his
or her drawings show the essence of a person for the child. A person
is a head and eyes that talks and then moves limbs. But, from the
very first, the child captures the essence of the person. Actually, we
confirm the truth of this essence each time we look at someone

approaching us on the street; we look at his or her face and eyes if we wish to discover who is there.

A delightful example of the simultaneously global and fragmentary logic and truth of the child's perceptions is found in the beginning of *The Little Prince*. Antoine de Saint-Exupery (1943) tells of his experience, at age 6, of seeing a magnificent picture of a boa constrictor swallowing an animal. Under the picture was written: "Boa constrictors swallow their prey whole, without chewing it" (p. 7). After much pondering, de Saint-Exupery made his first drawing, a picture of a boa constrictor digesting an elephant. Upon showing his frightening drawing to grown-ups and finding that they mistook it for a hat, the boy made a second drawing, this time an inside view of the boa constrictor. His second drawing depicted an elephant standing inside the enlarged mid body of a boa constrictor. The grown-ups' response to his second drawing was even more disheartening than the first. De Saint-Exupery says:

> The grown-ups' response, this time, was to advise me to lay aside my drawings of boa constrictors, whether from the inside or the outside, and devote myself instead to geography, history, arithmetic and grammar. That is why, at the age of six, I gave up what might have been a magnificent career as a painter. I had been disheartened by the failure of my Drawing Number One and my Drawing Number Two. Grown-ups never understand anything by themselves, and it is tiresome for children to be always and forever explaining things to them. (p. 8)

Grown-ups should heed these lessons from a childhood vividly remembered. The essential elements of the boa's feeding habits were present in de Saint-Exupery's drawings, only the details needed refining.

Similar to consciousness and perception, human language begins in bodily action in the world. The infant's first words are gestures and sounds. Coos and babbles soon follow and repeat the rhythms and accents of the culture. The infant is bathed in the language of the culture and thus learns to swim in it (Merleau-Ponty, 1962, pp. 179-191). Experientially, the infant's world is flooded with verbal language, and objects and actions are saturated with names.

When the child utters its first word, Merleau-Ponty believes that this word is experienced by the child as a quality of the thing itself; it is the thing speaking. The child experiences the word *ball* and the ball itself as one thing. A child says "ball" because the word is over there in the ball, it is the ball speaking itself. When he or she speaks, the child is expressing the unity of a languaged world, a living connection between the word and the object (Merleau-Ponty, 1973b, pp. 84-97).

Adult speech is similar. We do not associate a person's name with her or him as traditional psychology teaches us. Experientially, the person is his or her name. An example illustrates this characteristic of language.

It is a Saturday morning, and I am facing the vegetable section in a large produce market. I test the yellow zucchini for firmness and picture the antipasto recipe lying on my kitchen counter. How many pounds do I need? Someone calls my name and I turn, still preoccupied with the zucchini. I exclaim, "Tom," as I see the man behind me. How did I recognize him after nine years, with hundreds of students passing through my life since he graduated?

When I spoke Tom's name, I did not associate the person standing there with Tom. Tom was full of "Tom-ness," and I caught up to myself after I spoke his name, thinking quickly—this is Tom of the class of 1980 who had radical ideas, spoke vigorously, and handed in a 96-page paper for seminar. But these thoughts came after his name, pulled along by it. Even on other occasions when I turn and do not find the person's name on my lips, it is not a matter of associating the name with the person. Rather, it is a process of shifting through my worlds until I find the world they have been in—the world of students, clients, colleagues, or friends of casual acquaintances. If I know people well, once I find the world in which they belong, their names are essential parts of my experiences of them.

It is the same when we speak in any way; our thoughts and words are integrally connected. If speaking is not a spontaneous event, we stumble over words that have lost their living connection to our thoughts and actions. Normal speaking is extemporaneous. We can think through what we want to say, but the actual saying is a creation somewhat different from what we planned. As an experienced speaker, I know that a good speech is a unique occurrence that I create from my notes, from my goals for the speech, and from my feeling for the audience. Speaking takes place between the speaker and the audience and between the intentional person and his or her cultural language.

When one person speaks to another, many complex events occur. Both persons assume a common language with comprehensive grammar and syntax and conventional vocabulary. This shared language forms the basis for conversation between individual members of a culture. As each person speaks, all of the rules and words are taken for granted; each person assumes them as she or he jumps into the information and meanings at hand.

In speaking, each of us performs what Merleau-Ponty calls a coherent deformation of language (1964, pp. 84-97). Each time we speak, we deform the language we use, but we do so in a way that enables someone else to understand us still. Each use of language is an intermingling of meanings that are simultaneously shared and unique; as we speak, personal and social meanings commingle. Often we take this complex interpersonal process for granted and assume that our meanings are true for everyone. Occasionally, we catch a glimpse of the deeper nuances we skim over in our day-to-day conversations.

An example: On a Monday morning I meet a friend I have not seen for a year. We order breakfast, lean across the table, and begin catching up on our lives. I ask her how she has been, simultaneously remembering that the last time we talked she was happily involved with a new man, enjoying her work, and had just returned from a vacation at the beach. She says that she has been very well. If we stopped the conversation at this point, my assumptions about her statement would be obvious. To me, her "very well" means that she is still involved in a satisfying relationship with the same man, that her work is stimulating, and that she is still rested from that last vacation. As she continues, I realize that we almost missed each other in our initial sentences.

Her account is quite different from my assumptions. She has ended her relationship with Hal, cut back on her work hours, and begun a doctoral program. Yet, her initial words remain true; she is "very well." Even though we exchange more and more details, this initial process continues as we talk. We understand and misunderstand what the other is saying each time we speak. Each exchange contains coherent deformations of language and meanings. Misunderstandings remain minimal, however, and we leave the conversation feeling that we understand and have been understood.

Language is co-created in speaking. Periodically we must update our dictionaries with current meanings, uses, and constructions that we create in our everyday usage of language.

The progressive development of children can be gauged by their ability to put ideas, feelings, and experiences into words. This development helps them manage the relation of past, present, and future and to understand life. In a comparison of incidents in the day-to-day lives of three children, aged 3, 6, and 9, respectively, Briod (1989) concludes that development involves an increasing ability to use language to make sense of one's experience. Through naming and telling their experiences, children know the power of their own voices in appropriating life events and in discovering and recovering themselves.

Existential Themes
of Children's Play

Phenomenologists study childhood by paying attention to the events that preoccupy children. Many of these incidents are in the realm of play, which Erikson (1963) believes is the child's work. In play, children live out the reflective and prereflective themes of their lives. By taking children's play seriously, phenomenologists discover essential themes of human existence. Such is the case with many games.

When I think back to my card table house that I first described in Chapter 1, I sense the seriousness of my play. Even now, when I am in my late 40s, I do not make fun of myself. Intuitively, I see existential themes of my small life, and I bend toward myself and my house with respectful attention. These issues may have been even more important then than they are now, because now I am a bigger and more powerful person in the world. Reading Gaston Bachelard (1964, 1969), I am filled with deep understanding of myself, my card table house, and life itself.

Bachelard discusses the spaces in which we dwell, small places that surround our beings, that offer us a womblike comfort. These enclosed spaces cradle our bodies and enable our souls to soar to the far reaches of what might be possible. When we are snuggled into our safe spots in the world, we can, in imagining or in dreaming, face the cosmos.

Bachelard fills my card table house with cosmic light when be brings me into the inner worlds of nests, shells, and corners. He shows me that my house was a corner of the world where I could take root. This small space that enclosed my body and confined my movements was a place of solitude, a haven for dreaming. Being immobile in an enclosed space, I could soar into life's possibilities and dream the immensity of my being. According to Bachelard, small things attract us because, through imagination, large things can materialize within them. As an 8-year-old child, I expanded into life from beneath the roof of my card table house. By sitting inside my small house and arranging it just as I wished it to be, I built it, and life itself, from the inside. To my busy mother, I was sitting alone in musty darkness when I could have been out playing in the afternoon sun. To me now, looking back at my childhood from within my reading of Bachelard, I was sowing a vital, inner life.

When adults treasure the seriousness of their own childhood play, they are more apt to be delightful play companions of children. This is the case with games of peekaboo and hide-and-seek.

Loren Barritt, Ton Beekman, Hans Bleeker, and Karel Mulderij (1983) have observed, described, and reflected upon the universal and age-old games of peekaboo and hide-and-seek. They ask, Why is it so pleasurable for children to see and be seen, to hide and be sought? None of us can refuse a game of peekaboo offered by a child in a store checkout line. When we remember twilight games of hide-and-seek in our childhood neighborhoods, we are catapulted into rich sensory images. Here are two descriptions of games of hide-and-seek that Barritt and his colleagues recorded. The first situation is an interaction between Nancy and her mother:

Nancy (2 1/2 years old) calls to her mother, "Find me. I'm hiding."
Mother tells her, "All right" and walks over to the closet where Nancy is standing in full view. Mother calls out in mock distress, "Oh, dear, I can't find my Nancy. I wonder where she's gone? Perhaps she's only

gone out to buy some bread and milk, but I didn't hear the door. Oh dear, she's disappeared." Nancy is chortling with delight. Mother pulls back the clothing and looks in at Nancy. She shakes her head and says: "I guess she isn't here. There is a little girl here but her name is Mary. I still don't know where my Nancy has gone." Nancy laughs and hides her eyes. Nancy continues as mother enacts variations of the theme of "Where has Nancy gone?" (p. 143)

The second example takes place in an Amsterdam train station:

> Amsterdam, Central station; a narrow grey platform with steel masts in the form of I beams and countless bizarre little constructions, the remains of earlier efforts and new additions, modern benches. Grandpa, grandma and grandson, 3 or 4 years old, grandpa moves a few yards away toward the train schedule board. Grandma and grandson see a beautiful chance and hide themselves behind a pillar. Grandpa comes back, misses them and looks around. The moment that he sees them (grandma and grandson are dancing about, talking softly but frequently) he acts as though he didn't see them, goes farther looking on the wrong side swinging his cane as he goes forth. Grandma and grandson venture out, bent over, from the shadow of their hiding place in order not to miss the role that grandpa is playing. And grandpa plays for his audience. Others waiting, see what is going on but they act as though they don't see it. As grandpa pretends to be ready to give up grandma and grandson appear at exactly the right moment to laugh at how dumb grandpa was at not being able to find them. They saw him very well. And the little boy is now dancing and jumping about in enjoyment over grandpa's act. Grandma also beams. (p. 143)

It is easy to see that children and adults delight in hide-and-seek games because the loveable, special child is reaffirmed in them. Children are privileged to watch a loved adult search for them, and adults have the opportunity to play to an appreciative, absent audience. Children safely disappear because they are right there and can observe how the adults act in their absence. They are delighted that their absence leaves a hole in the world and that adults become playfully worried, even distraught.

Nancy's mother responds to Nancy's invitation to play by dropping her world of work to search unproductively for Nancy. Nancy's skill in disappearing defeats her mother, and she watches her mother be baffled by a problem Nancy can easily solve. She is surrounded by her mother's concern, care, and worry while being there, but absent. Nancy elatedly discovers that she is important enough to be missed and searched for by her mother. A consequence of this game is that Nancy is assured that her Mother will miss and remember her. She realizes that it is safe to leave because she will not be forgotten.

In the second example, the grandson has the delicious company of his grandma in the prank on Grandpa. He is safe because she is hiding with him, and this embellishes the pleasure of their mischief. Together, they befuddle Grandpa. Grandpa draws the drama to a crescendo with his exaggerated foolery; he makes a public display of being flustered by the loss of his loved ones. The grandson and Grandma hold his happiness in their hands when they jump into existence again. They have celebrated their treasured relationships as they wait for the train.

Essential themes of human existence are enacted in these playful moments. Children and adults long to be seen, sought, and brought back into existence by a loving gaze. Hide-and-seek games, which happen in full view of absent children, reassure them of their stable place in the family world before they run out to join peers. These games solidify trust in a stable self, one that is remembered and remains continuous as the child steps off the edge of his or her familiar world into independence.

As the child becomes older, games of hide-and-seek are played with peers. The child hides farther out in the world, away from home in the yard and neighborhood. Here, surrounded by other hidden children, the child waits in dread and excitement to be found by the person who is "it." Isolated hiders are joined by their shared plight; they are stalked by the person "it." With each step, the stalker builds the tension of his or her absent presence. Children can celebrate newfound independence and cunning as they are together in their aloneness and are certain of being sought (Barritt et al., 1983, pp. 155-156).

The human desire to be seen, to be missed, and to be separate from and together with other people unites all these games. By taking such games as these seriously, phenomenologists gain important understandings of children and, indeed, all of life.

Learning to Read

Along with play, school and learning are important parts of
children's lives. The skill of reading is first achieved in first grade.
Long before school envelops their lives, children enter the world of
storytelling. Stories are engaging when they are as interesting as life
itself. The child who is read to, as well as the one who reads, lives
stories with the people and animals who reside between the covers
of books. They are invited into stories by adults who are physically
and emotionally available, who create a special, quiet, and cozy relationship with the child in which the story unfolds. Here, within
the circle of a protective arm or in the hollow of a soft lap, the child
can become absorbed in the sounds, actions, and feelings of the ad-
venture. In shared solitude, he or she can be led into new dilemmas,
dreams, and dramas.

Once stories are meaningful parts of a child's life, reading naturally follows. The fun in stories pulls children into them, and children
become caught up in stories' actions, sounds, pictures, and, eventually,
letters and words. According to phenomenological educator Valerie
Polakow (1986), reading, like speaking, is a transformative act. In
reading, meaning is made as the child becomes part of a story and
the story seeps into his or her life. The active, intentional child
engages with letters and skillfully weaves them into a world alive
with meaning and possibilities. Polakow observes this in 4-year-old
Sasha:

> I observed Sasha experimenting with letters and numbers, frequently
> blending the two systems together. The multiple possibilities that he
> saw in letters extended across many dimensions of his perceptual
> world. When writing K for Kimberley (the name of a friend at day care),
> Sasha turned K into X and said, "Now I have a railroad track cross-
> ing"—and followed that with a drawing of a train. (p. 44)

Through these creative acts, Sasha was making letters into living
words. In the process, he was becoming a creator of words. As he
approached being able to read, Sasha made his own words, spelled
the way they sounded to him, and self-published homemade books.
He explains how this was part of learning to read:

SASHA: Well, see, when I was writing like this I was learning to read and I was spelling my own way and I would only read the words in the way I made them—not the way *books* did.

VAL: How did you change from spelling your way to the book way?

SASHA: Oh, when I started getting used to *Ant and Bee* and reading *Frog and Toad*. . . then later, see, when I saw book words I *would just break through and spell through the words*—like you know a few days [ago] I found out difficult (smiles delightedly) which is a very difficult word! Right? (p. 39)

At 5 years of age, Sasha became a reader. He tells how it happened:

"Well, see, . . . it just happened one day and suddenly it felt like Yippee, I CAN READ," and he threw up his arms and laughed, "and it made me feel different inside my tummy. I felt kind of powerful." (p. 37)

When the world of words is an active, alive one, it invites the child into it and makes him or her the delighted master of words.

Clearly, enjoyment pulls children into becoming readers. Polakow found that 5-year-olds who acted as her reading specialists were drawn to complex stories that were humorous, had scary plots, or spoke to the meaningful themes of their lives. These children's favorite stories contained interesting and difficult sounds, as well as challenging, complex plots. Such stories as these invite children to live stories. Alive stories are thresholds to "word-worlds" (p. 46).

With a solid history of living, hearing, telling, and reading stories, children can use reading skills to further expand their worlds. To such children, the world of words is an inviting and magical one. As an adult, Bachelard (1964) captures this magic when he describes a word as the germ of a dream. He explains:

When we read the works of a great word dreamer,. . . we find ourselves experiencing in words, on the inside of words, secret movements of our own. Like friendship, words sometimes swell, at the dreamer's will, in the loop of a syllable. While in other words, everything is calm, tight. . . . Words—I often imagine this—are little houses, each with its cellar and garret. Common-sense lives on the ground floor, always ready to engage in "foreign commerce," on the same level as the others, as the passers-by, who are never dreamers. To go upstairs in the word house, is to withdraw, step by step; while to go down to the cellar is to dream, it is losing oneself in the distant corridors of an obscure etymology, looking for treasures that cannot be found in words. (p. 147)

Reading, play, and dreaming are treasures of childhood that need to be nurtured throughout life. For many adults, contact with children helps them nourish the child they once were and still are.

Recapturing the Adult's Childhood

As an adult, childhood returns to me at unexpected moments. Sometimes it is my own childhood. At other times, it is a childhood I never knew. I am catapulted back in time when I come upon a puppy wiggling after an absorbing scent on a forest path, am enveloped by the smell of fresh-cut grass, or feel a rush of wind through my hair. These experiences return me to the moments and places of my life, those that have been lived and those of which I have dreamed. Memories of childhood reverberate through adults' souls. When memories are painful ones, our task is to transform these difficult ghosts into kinder spirits (Bentz, 1989, p. 4). When they are happy ones, we have only to let them ripple through our hearts and let them transport our lives. As we age, we gain appreciation of the grooves that childhood experiences wore into us. From the vantage point of her 70s, Eudora Welty (1984) tells how the chiming clocks of her childhood have continued to mark her life time:

> In our house on North Congress Street in Jackson, Mississippi, where I was born, the oldest of three children, in 1909, we grew up to the striking of clocks. There was a mission-style oak grandfather clock standing in the hall, which sent its gong-like strokes through the living-room, dining-room, kitchen, and pantry, and up the sounding board of the stairwell. Through the night, it could find its way into our ears; sometimes, even on the sleeping porch, midnight could wake us up. My parents' bedroom had a smaller striking clock that answered it. Though the kitchen clock did nothing but show the time, the dining room clock was a cuckoo clock with weights on long chains, on one of which my baby brother, after climbing on a chair to the top of the china closet, once succeeded in suspending the cat for a moment. I don't know whether or not my father's Ohio family, in having been Swiss back in the 1700s before the first three Welty brothers came to America, had anything to do with this; but we all of us have been time-minded all our lives. This was good at least for a future fiction writer, being able to learn so penetratingly, and almost first of all, about chronology. It was

one of a good many things I learned almost without knowing it; it would be there when I needed it. (p. 3)

Welty's words are even more powerful for those of us who know that she wrote them at a desk in her childhood home.

When we travel back in time, either in memory or in geographical reality, to the places and events of our childhoods, we seek the invisible past, the one imbued with personal meanings. Those of us who are lucky enough to walk through the rooms in which we once lived are searching for the private home contained in the public one. The factual house is useful only if it enables us to reenter our childhood home, where our lives took form in intimate spaces filled with family members, as well as our secret intentions and desires. Bachelard (1964) believes that this childhood home, the one we remember and dream, is the one that we must rediscover and reclaim. He says:

> [T]he real houses of memory, the houses to which we return in dreams, the houses that are rich in unalterable oneirism, do not readily lend themselves to description. To describe them would be like showing them to visitors. We can perhaps tell everything about the present, but about the past! The first, the oneirically definitive house must retain its shadows. . . . All we communicate to others is an *orientation* towards what is secret without ever being able to tell the secret objectively. What is secret never has total objectivity.
>
> What would be the use, for instance, in giving the plan of the room that was really *my* room, in describing the little room at the *end* of the garret, in saying that from the window, across the indentations of the roofs, one could see the hill. I alone, in my memories of another century, can open the deep cupboard that still retains for me alone that unique odor, the odor of raisins drying on a wicker tray. The odor of raisins! It is an odor that is beyond description, one that it takes a lot of imagination to smell. But I've already said too much. If I said more, the reader, back in his own room, would not open that unique wardrobe, with its unique smell, which is the signature of intimacy.
>
> Thus, very quickly, . . . the reader who is "reading a room" leaves off reading and starts to think of some place in his own past. . . . The values of intimacy are so absorbing that the reader has ceased to read your room; he sees his own again. He is already far off, listening to the recollections of a father or a grandmother, of a mother or a servant, . . . in short, of the human being who dominates the corner of his most cherished memories. (pp. 13-14)

These experiences are the rich treasures of our past. Harvesting the meanings and integrating them into our adult selves are more important than possessing the actual objects of our childhood. Reclaiming the memories, hopes, and dreams of our pasts is important because it enlivens adulthood and makes the future pulse with possibilities. Bachelard (1969) describes this aspect of childhood for adults:

> Childhood is a human water, a water which comes out of the shadows. This childhood in the mists and glimmers, this life in the slowness of limbo gives us a certain layer of births. What a lot of beings we have begun! What a lot of lost springs which have, nevertheless, flowed! Reverie toward our past then, reverie looking for childhood seems to bring back to life lives which have never taken place, lives which have been imagined. Reverie is a mnemonics of the imagination. In reverie we re-enter into contact with possibilities which destiny has not been able to make use of. A great paradox is connected with our reveries toward childhood: in us, this dead past has a future, the future of its living images, the *reverie future* which opens before any rediscovered image. (p. 112)

Recapturing one's inner childhood is the strengthening work of adulthood. These descriptions and reflections illuminate some of children's core involvements. Each topic is a segment in the child's process of becoming an emotionally vital and viable interpersonal self. When we are able to stand in their shoes, we can almost see life through their eyes. Our own childhoods are evoked as well, and we can re-experience memories, feelings, and meanings that are the foundations of our adult problems and joys. This is also true of the adolescent years.

6

Adolescents

In Western European cultures, adolescence is a taken for granted developmental stage. This is so despite its recent emergence in the early 1900s as a time of special human needs and characteristics (Santrock, 1990, pp. 12-15). Since the early 1900s, many researchers and theorists have identified and discussed important themes of the adolescent years, those from 12 through 20. Erikson's (1963) idea, that a main task of adolescence is to form an identity, a viable sense of self for self and others, is one that is commonly held. For Erikson, identity consists of a psychosocial sense of well-being. This includes feeling at home in your body, knowing who you are and where you are going, being able to share yourself with people who are important to you, and being able to rely on a congruence between your private and social selves. In adolescence we become reflexively aware of ourselves as interpersonal agents in the world.

Phenomenologists see adolescents as continuing their dynamic evolutions as beings-in-the-world-with-others. As they mature cognitively, emotionally, and physically, adolescents gain reflective and self-reflexive skills. While they remain who they have been, they also change and become different. Their experiential worlds shift away from nuclear families, and they establish primary relationships with peers. They decide on career paths and set out on personally crafted life paths. Phenomenologists seek to know the experiential

73

world of adolescents, to follow the unique and common themes that thread through their lives, and to understand their intentions and desires.

Adolescence is generally understood as a transition period between childhood and adulthood. The transition is achieved by a self that becomes increasingly autonomous, resourceful, and resilient. In this chapter, I will explore descriptive accounts of adolescents' phenomenal selves and experiential worlds. I will look at several experiences of adolescent life: experiences of self, shifting boundaries between self and others, first experiences of falling in love, and experiences of leaving home.

The Adolescent's Room

Often, the move into adolescence is first noticeable in the adolescent's physical presence in the world. A new self-consciousness becomes evident in attire and grooming. Doors that were once left open are now closed. The adolescent's room, always a haven, now becomes a closed chamber, off-limits to other family members. Like a cocoon that holds a transforming larva, the adolescent's room becomes a sanctuary from which a changing self is birthed.

The adolescent's room is a nest that helps him or her enter the larger world. Here, surrounded by music, posters, memorabilia, and artifacts of ongoing projects, teenagers discover, recover, and renew themselves. Alone in their rooms, adolescents digest life. They turn back onto themselves, to wish, to remember, to plan happy moments, or to recover from disappointing ones. Adolescents withdraw into their rooms for hours, lost in a thought, a song, a dance movement, a video, a computer game, or a book.

The adolescent's room is a second skin that holds a becoming self, a self in transition. This is a self between selves, one that cannot be grasped because, as yet, it has no visible substance. It is first obvious in what it is not, in what it is leaving behind. Author Annie Dillard (1987) looks back at that time in her life:

> I saw already that I could not in good faith renew the increasingly desperate series of vows by which I had always tried to direct my life. I had

vowed to love Walter Milligan forever; now I could recall neither his face nor my feeling, but only this quondam urgent vow. I had vowed to keep exploring Pittsburgh by bicycle no matter how old I got, and planned an especially sweeping tour for my hundredth birthday in 2045. I had vowed to keep hating Amy in order to defy Mother, who kept prophesying I would someday not hate Amy. In short, I always vowed, one way or another, not to change. Not me. I needed the fierceness of vowing because I could scarcely help but notice, visiting the hatchling robins at school every day, that it was mighty unlikely. (pp. 172-173)

As Bachelard (1964) has already told us, privacy is vital for daydreaming, and daydreaming is essential to an inner life. For Bachelard, an adolescent holed up in his or her room is constructing a self from the inside. In exploring the metaphor of a shell, he says:

A creature that hides and "withdraws into its shell" is preparing a "way out." This is true of the entire scale of metaphors, from the resurrection of a man in his grave, to the sudden outburst of one who has long been silent. If we remain at the heart of the image under consideration, we have the impression that by staying in the motionlessness of its shell, the creature is preparing temporal explosions, not to say whirlwinds, of being. (p. 111)

Adolescents form a vital and viable self from a mixture of solitude and social interaction. They craft an experientially cohesive self that enables them to live with and relate to others.

Diaries and Secrets

Most adults intuitively know enough to respect adolescents' closed doors and hidden lives. For many young women, this is a time of secret conversations, intimate feelings, and diaries. For many young men, it is a time of unspeakable feelings, passionate projects, and secret vulnerabilities. In different ways, adolescent men and women set boundaries between themselves and others. They exaggerate the space that separates inside from outside, private spheres from public ones. This exaggeration enables them to dwell in personal and social worlds and, eventually, to move easily between them. At points during the adolescent years, however, these boundaries are sacred ones and dare not be crossed. A recent experience with another adult impressed this upon me.

A friend has just returned from her childhood home in Boston. At age 43, she has only now brought her childhood diaries with her, to be stored in her California home. Some, from grade school, are ordinary notebooks. Others, from junior and senior high school, are official diaries with locking tongues. She has been buried in them since before I stopped by to meet her for lunch, and now reads excerpts of her young self to me. She draws out one of the official diaries, pushes the lock, and finds it closed. Both of us pause, as all respectful people do, at this boundary of her younger self. Even she has no thoughts of forcing the lock open but sets it aside and continues, using other diaries that were left unlocked.

The self locked inside a diary is a secret and fragile one. It is a self that we know is easily violated. Like our movements in the presence of an infant, our gestures soften and our voices lower as we approach a diary. We want to enter its world in the proper manner, with the turning of the small key and the loosening of the leather tongue. A violent entrance, which would cut the strap or break the lock, is unthinkable. Then we would know ourselves as plunderers of secrets that were not meant for our eyes. Rather, we must be invited in, enter with receptivity, and be willing to wait for secrets to reveal themselves to us. The little key, the button, and the latch all instruct us in waiting and silence.

A diary is a safe place to pour out one's soul, a soul that grabs onto pieces of life in search of itself. My friend, returning to her words after 30 years, finds fragments of experience that are clues to an inner world. Why had she written that? Where had that thought come from? What was the desire of that passion? Her young musings reveal what later became bold strokes of her life. These artifacts from long ago invite her to ponder past and current selves. Secrets well up. Some are discarded shells of a being that has transformed and disappeared. Others become labyrinths that lead to deep, underground areas still rich with treasures.

Like one's own room, a diary provides a place to come back to oneself, to contemplate life and to see its future horizons. Here, we encase the pieces of life we wish to preserve, the ones that we want to last forever. Here, too, we search for something to hold onto, something that gives direction and meaning to our lives. Our efforts to write life, to contain it in a paragraph or a page, give us a hold on it. Small handfuls of life, sifted through and pondered between the covers of a diary, help us grasp the mysteries of life and touch its expanses.

Secrets, like those contained in diaries, give the self a place to dwell, a base upon which to stand, and a sense of specialness. Shared secrets bond friend to friend and separate one person from another. They demarcate intimate areas within the social world and tie one to a place where one belongs.

Adolescent Subgroups

Adolescents also find private worlds in public realms. Immersed in music, videos, clothes, hairstyles, and food, adolescents carve out areas of life that are their signatures. These socially shared symbols and interests give form to the self and situate it in a shared, interpersonal world. In this world, boundaries are clearly visible and people are easily distinguishable from one another.

The adolescent who listens to heavy metal, has two-toned hair, hangs out at a particular cafe, and dresses in a distinct style can be identified immediately with others who subscribe to these practices. These external signs show the person's preferences and choices; they reveal the person's nature. These public manifestations reveal a particular self that belongs to a group, one that is beyond the reach of outsiders. Others who are different and, therefore, do not belong cannot enter. Adolescent subgroups give social reality to the individual self. They simultaneously tie the adolescent to kindred spirits and distinguish her or him from people with different tastes and values. Subgroups ensure the adolescent a protected place where he or she belongs. Subgroups also provide an overview map that simplifies the complexities of the social world and orients the adolescent to social diversity.

Dress, hairstyle, and music are central modes of expression for adolescents. With these tools, the adolescent constructs a valued and viable social self, a self joined to others and distinguished from them. This self is pointed toward the future, where dreams will be actualized and longings fulfilled. In describing a young woman's preparations for an evening walk into the city, van den Berg (1972a) shows her actions to be preparing a different self, one who is sexually mature. He says:

> A young girl has an evening off. She decides to go into the city and hopes to attract the attention of the boys she will see. She puts on her best dress and applies some makeup. When she is ready, she examines the result in the mirror, or, rather she has other people, seeing through her eyes, look at the girl in the mirror. If these other people say, "Does she not look pretty," she gets up, and for a moment or two, trips about in her room. *She is in the city already, then;* otherwise, she could not walk like that, nor could she look so sexy. Then she leaves her room and says goodbye to her parents. She behaves differently, saying goodbye. She walks in another way, and she does not even think of a daring look. . . . Then she leaves. As soon as she is in the city, . . . the streets are glittering with a light she never saw when she was a child. This is evidence of her maturity to her. The way people look at her tells that she is dressed like a young woman and that she has a mature body. Again her body responds: it trips about and looks sexy. (pp. 56-57)

With a certain style, gesture, and manner, adolescents create desired adult selves.

An adolescent buried in earphones is also one who is developing a future self. Enfolded in the sensuous pulsations and lyrics of contemporary music, adolescents simultaneously define and differentiate themselves from adults. Especially with music, generation after generation of adolescents have established boundaries between themselves and adults. With sheer loudness, words not understandable to adult ears, or rhythms that jar adult sensitivities, adolescents create walls of sound that repel adults. These rhythms and lyrics put expression to longings, dreams, feelings, and values that are, as yet, unspoken in their hearts and minds. Music that grabs the soul and feeds it, nourishes the developing self. The adolescent who changes classes surrounded by his or her favorite musical group on a Walkman is going far beyond the next class. He or she is moving into the ideals and hopes of a future that pulses and reverberates with unrealized dreams.

The Paradox of Adolescence

Rod Michalko (1984) notes a paradox of the adolescent period of life: it is a preparation for full participation in society by people who have been immersed in their culture since infancy. Adolescents, then, are preparing for something they have already achieved. Given this paradox, Michalko asks what adolescents are trying to achieve and what is unique about this period of life. He suggests that adolescence is best understood as a metaphor for a particular orientation to life, irrespective of chronological age. This orientation is different from an adult's and is based upon new, specialized developmental events.

Adolescents' experiential worlds expand as they mature physically and cognitively. They gain the ability to distinguish between a self-centered world and one that is separate from them. Cognitively, adolescents can distinguish between an experiential self and a self that is visible to others; adolescents' worlds expand to include an awareness of other people's experience of them. Michalko believes that this new perspective makes adolescents insecure. A previous, unquestioned security about self and world now seems fragile, arbitrary, and relative. In light of these developmental changes, adolescents must reconstruct a secure place in the world. This regaining of security involves developing a relation between self and appearance. It also involves figuring out how one's particular, individual life is connected to the life of society and where one fits in a multilayered, interconnected world. Managing one's appearance, developing a world view, and finding one's place in the larger social world are all necessary if adolescents are to reachieve a secure sense of self in a stable world.

Faced with these complex tasks, adolescents feel insecure and want to be secure. They long to feel complete, to experience their legitimate place in the social world, to be assured of a future full of meaning and promise. In an effort to attain these signs of a life that is complete and whole, a mature life, adolescents can act as if they are complete when they really are not. This orientation to the insecurity and incompleteness of life, to act as though one's life is whole, secure, and complete when it really is not, is the unique quality of adolescence. Moreover, sometimes adolescents strike an appearance of being whole and complete and of having overcome their vulnerability because they feel pressured by society to show that they are grown-up.

On the other hand, adulthood is oriented differently toward life's lack of wholeness and security. Adults replace a longing for wholeness with a way of living with its lack. The transition into adulthood is marked by a realization that the lack of wholeness in life is a limit of life that is part of life. A goal of mature adulthood, then, is to live an incomplete life with completeness; to live an unwhole life with wholeness. Understood as a metaphor, adolescence can extend throughout life, until we come to terms with our incompleteness and vulnerability.

The Adolescent's Phenomenal Self

Another phenomenologist, Daniel Offer, has done extensive research on adolescents' experiences of self and others. Offer (Offer et al., 1981) raises questions about whether an experiential perspective or an observational one is the more useful for understanding adolescents. He asks:

> Is the teenager just one more observer of his "me," whose judgement should be overridden by a consensus among seemingly objective adults, or is the observed teenager in a unique position to declare the truth about himself? Can adults infer, for example, that the truth about an adolescent's self-experiences and perceptions are his alone to reveal or not to reveal as he chooses? It is in the answers to these questions that many insights into the nature of the self can be found. (p. 13)

Offer opts for studying the phenomenal self, the self-experienced me. If we understand the self-experiences of adolescents, we can empathize and work with them and help them conceptualize and shape their lives. Offer believes that adults working with adolescents should stop trying to manipulate, predict, and control them, and start facilitating the choice-making power of adolescents. To further our understanding of the "phenomenal me," Offer delineates five experiential selves of the adolescent: the psychological self, the social self, the sexual self, the familial self, and the coping self.

During the 1960s and 1970s, 15,000 adolescents living in the United States, Australia, Israel, and Ireland filled out a questionnaire designed by Offer and his associates. The questionnaire consisted of statements constructed by the researchers about psychological, social, sexual, and family areas of adolescent life. It was distributed in high schools and contained 130 questions. Teenagers responded by saying whether each statement "describes me very well, describes me well, describes me fairly well, does not quite describe me, does not really describe me, does not describe me at all" (p. 137). Statistical procedures were used to group results into portraits of adolescents' various selves. Overall, Offer presents a more positive view of the adolescent's world from this experiential perspective than is available through other methods of inquiry. His analysis of data compares younger and older adolescents, males and females, ordinary with differently abled, and cultures and generations with each other. There are few subgroup exceptions to the positive self-reports summarized below. Based upon these anonymous self-reports, adolescents proved to feel positive about themselves, comfortable with peers and family members, responsible and in control of their lives, and optimistic about the future. What follows is a brief elaboration of each of these areas.

The psychological self includes the adolescent's experience of impulses, feelings, moods, and emotional evaluations of body and self. Most adolescents endorsed the following statements about themselves:

> I enjoy life.
> Most of the time I am happy.
> I feel strong and healthy.
> I feel relaxed under normal circumstances.
> The picture I have of myself in the future satisfies me.
> Usually I control myself. (p. 46)

Another aspect of self, the social self, also proved to be a positive one. It consists of the adolescent's experiences of his or her place and level of comfort with peers, moral codes of conduct, and vocational-educational goals. These are the statements that adolescents said described their social selves:

A job well done gives me pleasure.
Being together with other people gives me a good feeling.
I feel that there is plenty that I can learn from others.
I enjoy most parties I go to.
I like to help a friend whenever I can.
I would not hurt someone just for the "heck of it."
At times, I think about what kind of work I will do in the future.
I am sure that I will be proud about my future profession. (pp. 53-54)

Teenagers also reported feeling positive about their sexual selves. The sexual self comprises adolescents' orientations to their sexual bodies, their level of comfort regarding sexual information, and how optimistic they feel about being sexually attractive. Here are some statements adolescents said described their sexual selves:

Sexual experiences give me pleasure.
I think that girls (boys) find me attractive.
Having a girl/boy friend is important to me. (p. 151)

Adolescents' views of their families, of their happiness with family life, of their place in their families, and of their desire to emulate parents' life-styles constitute the familial self. Offer's respondents stood behind the following statements about family life:

I think that I will be a source of pride to my parents in the future.
My parents are usually patient with me.
Most of the time my parents are satisfied with me.
I can count on my parents most of the time.
I feel that I have a part in making family decisions.
Most of the time, my parents get along with each other.
When I grow up and have a family, it will be in at least a few ways similar
    to my own. (p. 152)

Offer's coping self consists of adolescents' experiences of their ability to persist in the face of life's problems, to trust their ability to master future challenges, and to remain emotionally optimistic and secure through it all. This, too, was a positively toned self, evident in agreement with sentences like:

If I put my mind to it I can learn almost anything.

When I decide to do something, I do it.

I feel that I am able to make decisions.

I believe I can tell the real from the fantastic.

If I know that I will have to face a new situation, I will try in advance to find out as much as possible about it.

Whenever I fail in something I try to find out what I can do in order to avoid another failure. (p. 153-155)

Offer's findings sensitize us to the adolescent's self-experiences and provide us with an optimistic, responsible, self-confident, and emotionally balanced adolescent self-portrait. Taking this self-view into account can increase our effectiveness in understanding, relating to, and influencing adolescents.

Best Friends

To understand adolescents on their own terms, one must understand their important peer relationships. Close friendships are bridges out of the nuclear family that lead into equal, primary relationships. Especially in same-gender friendships, adolescents find soul mates who share their deepest and most important developing selves. Without the complications added by sexual attraction, friendships provide a behind-the-scenes view of another person and give teenagers information on how they are similar to and different from other people. This comparative process helps them build a realistic self-picture, as well as an inside understanding of other people.

Having a best friend is an important developmental task (Sullivan, 1953). A best friend is someone we dare tell everything to, to share special secrets with, and to open up our most private pain. In doing so, we bring these self-experiences into the interpersonal realm and open them to corrective responses. Pain shared is pain on its way to healing. Revealing essential aspects of ourselves to someone else and, in turn, seeing his or her similar depths can make lasting heart bonds. When I open myself and my life to someone I care for, who I trust cares for me, I experience a reciprocal relationship. Reciprocity, the back-and-forth give-and-take of empathic understanding, is an essential attribute of intimacy. With a best friend, we come to know and care for someone else in special ways.

Adolescent friendships can be some of the most intense in life. As we push away from primary attachments to parents, many of us long to find a peer to whom we are special. Because women typically develop a sense of self in and through relationships with others (Gilligan, 1982), special friendships are focal among young women. Recently, an 18-year-old woman, Marge, told me about how her current best friendship began when she was 13 years old. Her most prominent memories are of how a group of nine girls struggled with wanting to be special to one another. She remembers:

> The first day of school in eighth grade was when I met Jessie's best friend. We liked each other right away. It took a few days to meet everyone else in the clique. By the time Jessie finally met me, she hated me, not for who I was, but for what I was—I was new and I had befriended her best friend. I felt hurt, so I hated her back. But, she was the person who was connected to everyone else, so pretty quickly we got to know each other and we really meshed well. Then, all kinds of petty jealousies started happening behind my back until one day I was surrounded by eight girls who were screaming at me for taking their friend away. Two of the girls were also angry because I wasn't their best friend. Jessie was standing behind the circle; she had focused everyone's frustration on me and wasn't taking any of the heat. I just lost it and started screaming and cursing. That cooled everyone out for a while. But, as Jessie and I remained best friends, other girls continued to feel threatened by it and to do things that would break us apart. All the way through high school, other girls kept trying to get in on our special relationship.

Being special was a longed for and vital emotional anchor in the unpredictable social world of these young women. Marge was one of the lucky people because her primary friendship lasted through the high school years. She and Jessie were inseparable; they became as close as any two people could. Marge describes the best times in their friendship:

> When we got along, we really got along. Both of us were nonconformists and liked to do crazy things. We skipped classes together and spent our money on senseless things. We both prided ourselves at being able to spend incredible amounts of money and have nothing to show for it. Jessie and I did what we wanted to, regardless of where it got us. We spent all of our time with each other; we could make anything fun by

doing it together. We stood up for each other when we got into fights with our parents. Jessie even ran away from home with me once after my Mom restricted me for getting a "D" in a class.

Since we were always together, we spent our money in the same places, on the same things. Neither of us had enough money, so we pooled it and opened a joint checking account. That way, my paycheck held us over until she got paid and vice versa. It all balanced out. Our parents thought we were crazy. No one thought it would work, but it has and we still pool all of our money.

After high school, we moved away from home to attend the same junior college. Now we're together even more than before. We share a room, wear each other's clothes, eat the same food, drive to school together, and work at the same business. We know each other so well, we don't even have to say something to know what each other's thinking.

Everything's not always great between us. We have some long-standing, irresolvable disagreements between us. We've gone over them so many times that we don't talk about them when they come up. It comes down to "You're this way and I'm this way, and I don't agree with you." It's useless to argue, she thinks her way and I think my way. I don't know how she works it out, but I go off and work it out in my head and then it's over. We can't fight for long because we're always in each other's faces. Eventually one of us acts normal again, and we're back. Both of us are relieved; when it's good between us, it's really good.

For both Marge and Jessie, this friendship has been a lifeline of stability. Throughout high school, they watched other women throw friendships away when they started dating. They vowed that they would never do that. But Jessie has become seriously involved with a man and the two friends are finding that they are separating. For Marge, much of the pain comes from Jessie not being clear and not letting go of her. Instead, Jessie wants Marge to spend as much time with Stan as she does. Marge is at the point where letting go of the old relationship seems less painful than being with Jessie. She explains:

I can see that Jessie's relationship with Stan is the best she's ever had. They work really well together. I want them to go off and do their thing, but Jessie keeps trying to get me to be part of it. I go over there with her, but they have their own thing going and, besides, I get tired of sleeping on Stan's living room floor. Plus, I can see that things are good between them and feel that Jessie is lying to me when she's acting like their relationship is about to fall apart any minute. So, I make excuses and make other plans. That really sets Jessie off, and we've been getting into terrible fights about really stupid things. I know there's no point in talking about it, because Jessie gets on auto-focus and won't agree with what I think is going on. Lately, I feel better being alone than I do when I'm with her. I can't wait for classes to end because we'll be living in different places this summer.

Both Jessie and Marge are changing. They are losing their old selves and their old relationship without being ready for the loss this involves. Jessie's inability to have separate intimate relationships is forcing Marge to set her own limits and to take care of her own emotional necessities. She and Jessie are being pulled into a painful life transition: they are growing beyond an intimacy that has, until now, been life sustaining. Like any change, it signals loss and an unknown future. But these changes can also enable each woman to clarify and affirm her preferences and values, to honor the fragility of even strong relationships, and to face the choices of individual, separate lives.

First Love

Phenomenological psychologist Richard Alapack's (1984; Fischer & Alapack, 1987) research gives us a glimpse of adolescents' first love relationships. Alapack asked undergraduate and graduate students: "Describe the relationship you experienced with the first person you truly loved." Heterosexual students gave retrospective descriptions of an adolescent experience of falling in love. Alapack (Fischer & Alapack, 1987) describes the general atmosphere of this first love relationship:

> Whenever the relationship happens, it is neither accidental nor caused. A ripeness is requisite if one is to notice the epiphany of the other's entrance into one's world; a readiness is necessary if one is to respond to the appeal in the other's eyes. But although the individual might be anticipating the other, or actively searching to find the other, she or he lacks both the power to make the other appear and the control to make that other come to one. The other must come of his or her own desire. If that person flows out to one in trust and with risk, and if one flows back meeting the other, then they might know the fulfillment that is first love. (p. 96)

The power of virginal love is that it transcends aloneness. First lovers go beyond themselves as they reach toward the other, as another and not simply as a self-extension. This first experience of opening up to an other consists of spiritual and sexual self-realization and the mutual coordination of two lives.

Experientially, a first love is absolute, unique, perfect, ideal, and innocent. It is an experience of togetherness in which "our" world is created through reciprocal involvement. It pulls each person beyond his or her previous, self-absorbed world. Verbal and nonverbal communication is heartfelt and never finished. Previously unexperienced painful and elating feelings open up emotional connections and understandings to oneself and one's beloved. Experiences of first love tie adolescents to their family history and values and open up a future world founded on interpersonal commitment.

A person who is in love for the first time feels awakened on multiple levels. The following are typical statements made by Alapack's (1984) first lovers:

I love everything about you.
We'll never part.
There's nothing I wouldn't do for you.
Nobody has ever loved like we love.
Our love is flawless.
We did everything together.
Our love will never end.
We listened to our song and gazed at our moon.
We couldn't take our eyes and hands off each other.
We talked long into the night.
Joy, jealously, pain, and tenderness exploded inside me.
From her and with her I learned how to share a life.
Now I knew why people got married.
I couldn't wait for Mom and Dad to meet him. (pp. 103-107)

With first lovers, we birth our sexuality and begin integrating it into our interpersonal selves and worlds. Our excitement about knowing and caring for the other person pulls us out of our self-centeredness and drops us into an other-centered love. First love invites us into our interpersonal potential and unearths the hopes, dreams, and illusions that we carry with us from our childhoods. The great joy of a first love is that we acknowledge and risk these longings. The great suffering is that we are disappointed and left alone once again. Whether first love ends in a breakup or a marriage, it is the blossoming of our sexual, loving selves and is, thus, a milestone of life.

Leaving Home

With a closed door, a secret, an ornament, a Walkman turned up loud, an intense relationship with a peer, adolescents transform their childhood selves into ones viable in the adult world. In doing so, they establish boundaries between themselves and their parents. Initially, these boundaries may need to be rigid and extreme ones so that separation can occur. Once they are securely in place, boundaries between parents and adolescents can become permeable in a back-and-forth sharing between separate, distinct individuals. Most adolescents separate from their parents in these ways while still living with them. If separate lives can be respected within the same home, differences can be acknowledged and disagreements negotiated. These skills help both adolescents and parents change and grow while still maintaining their relationship.

One of the last tasks of adolescence is leaving the parental home. In doing so, adolescents begin their individual life journeys in earnest. Separating from the physical support net of the family gives adolescents room to create their own homes and their own primary family ties. Rather than being satellites in their parents' lives, they launch into their own life trajectories. As they cross over the threshold of their parents' front doors, they step into the wider social world, one that is not defined and limited by their parents' choices. Within this world, they can begin to build their own homes, composed of places, people, and things they grow to love.

Richard and Melodie Alapack (1984) articulated leaving home as the hinge of the door to authentic adulthood (p. 45). By leaving home, adolescents can actualize their truly autonomous, adult selves and resolve old battles between themselves and their parents. Sometimes, physical separation from parents enables emotional separation. At other times, leaving home continues the struggles and negations that have always gone on between parents and children.

Using a blend of theoretical, clinical, and research sources, the Alapacks illuminated three movements of leaving home: the actual leaving, the experience of the absence, and the return visit. To leave the parental home is to step into an undetermined future. Often, the path leads through anxieties, fears, ambivalences, and insecurities to a self that is more knowledgeable about and confident in its abilities to live life in an independent and responsible manner. Leaving home forces us to work with existential themes of life: being dependent and independent, being with and being separate from, being the same as well as different from others. The physical act of leaving symbolizes our courage to grow up, to change our relationship with our parents to a more equal one, and to establish our own frame of reference for life. These gains also involve losses. They touch us with our vulnerabilities and, through loss, give us anticipations of death. In the process of leave-taking, adolescents realize their finitude along with their freedom.

Experiencing the loss of what was is an important part of establishing what can be. Homesickness and heartache are, therefore, essential aspects of truly leaving home. Losses that are grieved become touchstones for revitalizing changed, and changing, relationships. Acknowledging what is missed can clarify values and show us our needs and desires. Once we have left home physically, this internal leave taking becomes possible. It is through grief that we resolve old hurts and longings and separate our emotional self from parents. Losses that are acknowledged can strengthen our emotional self.

Paradoxically, homecoming is the final movement in leaving home (Alapack & Alapack, 1984). In returning to the parental home, the adolescent, now a young adult, can witness how far he or she has traveled. Stepping back into the original home, adolescents experience the degree to which they have become seasoned explorers of life. They long to be welcomed and celebrated, to be appreciated for the achievements they value. They wish, also, to see that there is still a place for them, that their favorite foods are served, and that family members re-enfold them into their lives. They search for signs that their parents can welcome them back as adults, on the adults' own terms. Young adults want parents to listen to them; they want to teach their parents about the younger generation. A universal human hope is to return home and to be welcomed and loved by our parents as a changed, maturing, and differentiated other. All of us wish to be supported for being the person we are and wish to become.

These are some of the existential challenges and circumstances we confront during our adolescent years. We carry these early experiences and meanings with us into adulthood where we spiral back through them, again and again, as we become ourselves.

7

Adults

The complexities and mysteries of life increase as we become adults. Many essential themes of adulthood have been discussed by traditional scholars: love and work (Freud, 1949); intimacy, generativity, and integrity (Erikson, 1963); actualizing an integrated self through differentiation and synthesis of opposite sides of the personality (Jung, 1960); and the progressive development of life structures through a series of crises and commitments (Levinson, 1979). Phenomenologists add topics to this array of fundamental dimensions of adulthood. They discuss basic issues of human existence, as well as contents of life that are focal in adulthood. First, I will look at some existential a prioris of life.

Existential A Prioris

As we have already seen, to be human is to face our responsible yet vulnerable place in life. We confront thrownness and freedom as we co-constitute our lives and negotiate interpersonal relationships. On the dark side of life, we confront fundamental issues of life as we grow older—loneliness, anxiety, death, meaninglessness, and unfinished actualization. The opposite of these—relatedness, security, vitalized living, meaningfulness, and actualization—are equally prominent dimensions.

LONELINESS

Loneliness is an ontological fact of life. To be human is to be lonely. Our loneliness arises from two sources: our separateness from others and our uniqueness. No one is exactly the same person I am. No one can experience my feelings and meanings, perceive exactly as I do, be me, or live my life. Each of us holds the responsibilities, joys, and burdens of his or her particular life. Being existentially alone, each of us is fundamentally separate from everyone else.

Clark Moustakas (1961) calls this basic aloneness, existential loneliness. In existential loneliness we experience the vulnerability of our interpersonal existence. Being with others is part of our nature and yet, fundamentally, we are alone. Coming to terms with our existential loneliness is an important task of adulthood. We can flee from this loneliness, or we can befriend it. Even if we flee loneliness through activities or other people, however, we cannot outdistance it. If we befriend it, we can learn to feel comfortable with our solitary existence and even treasure being alone. Being thrown back upon our aloneness can be painful but it can be self-renewing as well.

When I face my existential loneliness, I become acquainted with an important aspect of my being. I discover some of the implicit and explicit themes of my life and relationships; I notice my fears, insecurities, and dependencies. Stripped back to me, I greet myself as the foundation of my interactions with and perceptions of the world. As I come to know myself in existential loneliness, I often face things about myself that I dislike. But as I work with these qualities, I can become receptive to and forgiving of myself and renew my self-appreciation. I may even begin to treasure my time alone and look forward to knowing myself better. Working with my existential loneliness helps me be peacefully alone. Existential loneliness acts as a vehicle for personal and interpersonal regeneration. It enables me to treasure being alone, and it can teach me how much I want and require satisfying relationships with other people.

A second loneliness, loneliness anxiety (Moustakas, 1961), has a different emotional origin and tone. Loneliness anxiety occurs when I lose touch with myself whether I am alone or with other people. If I am uncomfortable with myself, I may rush into action—any action that distracts me from my fears of facing myself. I lose touch with myself by unthinkingly voicing other people's opinions, by associating with people who intimidate me, by cultivating relationships that deplete me, by being dishonest about myself and with myself. All of these ways of leaving myself result in loneliness anxiety, an anxiety of running away from myself without, paradoxically, being able to leave my body, myself, and my life. In loneliness anxiety, I am divided against myself, caught in an impossible quandary that leaves me empty and panicked.

Existential loneliness gives rise to existential anxiety—the anxiety that shakes the foundation of our existence and leaves us fearful and trembling (Kierkegaard, 1954). Through interpersonal relationships, we bridge this isolation. As other people meet our gaze, respond to our words, and reach toward us, they help us feel less alone; they understand us, share our dreams, sympathize with our pain. Isolation and relationships are fundamental dimensions of life with which all adults struggle (Yalom, 1980).

DEATH, MEANING, AND FREEDOM

Three other sources of existential anxiety—death, meaninglessness, and freedom—thread through life (Yalom, 1980). These, too, are universal, existential issues that are painful to face but ultimately strengthen our celebration of day-to-day living.

All of us are born with one certainty—that we will die. This realization becomes an increasingly personal one as we reach middle age and experience the death of our parents and close friends. We are mortal beings; our lives are finite rather than infinite. The certainty of our death makes all of us afraid and anxious. Some of us flee into exercise and energetic projects. Others become depressed and listless. We think, If everything ends in death, why not just give up now? The struggle to remain actively involved in a life that will end in death is one of the existential tasks of life. Facing and accepting the certainty of our death can enable us to treasure each moment of life and to treat life as a bountiful gift.

As we confront death, we question life's meaning. At some point, all of us ask, What is the meaning of life? We wonder why we struggle so hard, why we care, why we keep working. We ask ourselves, What am I searching for? Can I find it? Will it satisfy me? These questions all probe life's meaning. Each of us will experience a crisis of life's meaning, a time in which life will seem incoherent, senseless, and arbitrary. All of us need personal, social, or spiritual purposes in life, even if these purposes are to live a meaningless life as best as we can. Confrontation with meaninglessness is a normal theme of life; constructing a meaningful life in the face of its arbitrariness is our plight.

As we struggle to craft a meaningful course through life, we confront our freedom and responsibility. I shape my life by making choices and acting on my perceptions. As I select some of life's possibilities and leave others behind, I co-constitute my life. People who dare not risk living as they wish to, choose to live inauthentically (Heidegger, 1962). Living inauthentically involves refusing to actualize important parts of myself. Sartre (1956) calls this "bad faith." When I live in bad faith, I never notice my desires, wishes, and needs. I can deny my desires (live in bad faith), or I can try to actualize them (live in good faith). In either mode, I live out my human freedom and responsibility.

COMMITMENT

It follows, then, that commitment is a core issue of adulthood. As adults we make commitments to ourselves, to others, and to the structures of our lives. A person forms his or her existential self by making commitments to persons, projects, and groups. Our commitments call us out of ourselves, to someone or something. A person's adult identity is formed in this process of being called and responding.

Often, commitments are made without fully realizing their open-endedness and consequences. Doubts and personal struggles surface as the commitments we have made demand more and more of us. If their benefits carry us through periods of questioning and turmoil, we deepen commitments through actions. Reaffirming our commitments, in turn, increases our felt satisfaction and decreases our negative feelings. The process can clarify values, as well as identities.

At some point, however, habitual ways of being and definitions of ourselves are challenged by the commitments we have made. Just as we become ourselves through commitments, so also do these commitments change us. Paradoxically, we have to know ourselves to make and keep commitments, but we also can only know ourselves through the commitments we make. It is risky to make and keep commitments, but avoiding them is worse—it negates possibilities of finding and being one's self. Reaffirmed commitments enable us to go beyond our current identity and to develop in new and desired ways. Responding honestly and responsibly to our ever-changing lives keeps us on the edge of being true to ourselves and truly ourselves. From a Heideggerian perspective, phenomenologist Richard Knowles (1986) calls this a process of living authentically. He says:

> As with all the authentic experiences, one does not arrive at a static state of commitment but continues in the dynamic pattern of call and response, of doubt and reaffirmation, an ongoing process spiralling upward and/or becoming stagnant. Also, the process is never perfectly lived out or realized. People become more or less authentic and, if they do become more authentic, it is by modifying the inauthentic mode or habituality, not by some denial of inauthenticity. (p. 136)

We construct ourselves and our lives in and through commitments. Daring to be who we are, as well as who we wish to be, we can face ourselves honestly by clarifying commitments. This process enables us to grow increasingly self-reflective and to live in accord with our values and beliefs.

Along with these foundational life dimensions, everyday life contains numerous contents and events. There is not, as yet, an inclusive phenomenology of essential themes of adult development. Phenomenological studies of adult life events, however, are growing in number. In recent years, more and more phenomenologically oriented researchers have collected descriptive data on aspects of life that have been of special interest to them. The topics we will look at in this chapter range from such difficult experiences of adulthood as self-understanding, fathers' experiences of their sons leaving home, and anticipatory grief, to such less disturbing topics as exercise, creativity, and swearing. Although not inclusive of all of adult life, each of these topics is a window into adulthood and expands upon the above-mentioned existential themes.

Life Themes of Adulthood

SELF-UNDERSTANDING

Paying attention to experiences of ourselves and our lives is an important task of adulthood. To this end, Ien Dienske (1984) investigated women's experience of self-understanding by asking them to write down some of the important stories of their lives. To Dienske, these stories reveal the woman and her world, they tell what is important to her at a moment in life when something essential became clear. All adults experience this process of self-understanding. The descriptions summarized by Dienske show the particular problems women face when they try to understand their own experiences. Women's lives, like the lives of all people who are discriminated against, are in danger of being socially negated in ways that deprive them of meaning and make them invisible. This lack of social celebration of women's lives and attributes takes up residence inside their souls and gives them a sense of illegitimacy.

The following story was written by a 40-year-old Dutch woman in March 1981. She had finished reading Virginia Woolf's *A Room of One's Own* and realized how books gave people a tradition within which to fit. She also realized that such a tradition was lacking in her own life. She wrote (Dienske, 1984):

The Emptiness Behind Me

Then, very slowly, the feeling was there. It was behind my back, an emptiness I had never realized before. I knew it had been there ever since I was a little girl. An emptiness, unnamed and unrecognized. A long, long nothingness. It sucked at my back. It hurt me. There is no tradition to which I belong. I can't live a life like my mother's or my grandmother's. There is no line of women, generation after generation, where I fit in, from where I can go on. There is no greatness, no history of great women. I never learned any names. No triumph, no glory to my kind. Not a single beam of greatness has fallen on me because I am a woman. There is no continuity to support me. We are not part of the ever-growing history written down in standard works. I'm an outsider. I am not an heiress to this culture.

I looked at the emptiness behind me. There, somewhat aside, was my mother and, somewhat more aside, my grandmother. We are not in one line. The line is broken. I can't and won't live like my mother, my grandmother, and the generation before them. There is a perceptible emptiness behind me. (p. 368)

This powerful portrayal of one woman's understanding of a deep problem in her self-understanding is easily recognized by any minority person in a culture. It exemplifies how much of the personal meaningfulness of lives depends upon social validation. Without a sense of our similarity to and continuity with other people, it is difficult for us to experience our lives as full and fulfilling. When we do not have a sense of our place in human history, our present and future lives become fragile.

In a sweeping sociohistorical analysis of the last 2,000 years, psychologist Philip Cushman shows how the erosion of traditions, community, and family has made this experience of emptiness a common one. With the breakdown of socially shared meanings, people experience themselves as lacking conviction and worth and needing to be filled up. Cushman (1990) describes this empty self:

It is a self that seeks the experience of being continually filled up by consuming goods, calories, experiences, politicians, romantic partners, and empathic therapists in an attempt to combat the growing alienation and fragmentation of its era. (p. 600)

In Western European culture, the middle-class self has evolved from a Victorian, sexually repressed self to one that is empty and fragmented. Cushman believes that the results of this inner emptiness—low self-esteem, values confusion, eating disorders, drug addiction, and chronic consumerism—can only be corrected by revitalizing sociocultural structures that give context and shared meaning to individual lives. Psychotherapists such as Heinz Kohut (1977) and Alice Miller (1981) envision a dyadic solution to this systemic problem. They believe that these sociocultural changes have eroded the self by making it difficult for people in general, and parents in particular, to be responsive and empathic to other people. They see inadequate interpersonal validation of people's spontaneous, experiential selves as the core problem. For Kohut and Miller, healing results from recognizing how each of us has been loved out of our spontaneous self, feeling healthy anger at this injustice, and mourning the loss of our emotional grounding in our own experience. Both poles, a socially shared meaning context and personal work with experiences of invalidation and meaninglessness, seem important in reconstructing an emotionally satisfying and viable social self.

EXERCISE

As we saw in chapter 2, our bodily being-in-the-world is an existential dimension of our selves. During childhood and adolescence, many of us take our bodies for granted. Especially as we reach our 30s and 40s, we find that our muscles lose their tone and we gain weight. In societies in which work is increasingly technical and mental, people must make explicit commitments to exercising if they are to stay physically fit and healthy.

Physical exercise and the discipline of working out is the subject matter of psychologist Heather Devine's phenomenology of training (1984). She distinguishes among dilettantes, social athletes, and serious athletes in the world of exercise. Even those of us who do not wish to be seen as dilettantes can sheepishly recognize ourselves in the following description:

> The "dilettante" in the training environment is different from the serious athletes in terms of intent and commitment. The dilettante concerns herself with the externals—she *appears* to train—she *appears* to be athletic, but she does not have the commitment necessary to achieve the mind-body experience that athletes crave, an experience that is only accessible after the body has reached a certain level of mechanical efficiency and stamina. The dilettante is obsessed with the "trappings" of training. The clothes she wears are "appropriate" for the sport; by donning this costume she hopes to endow herself with a certain amount of integrity—or credibility, if you like. Unfortunately these clothes never acquire the reliability, the "equipmentality," of those belonging to the serious athlete, because they are primarily for show. They do not acquire a "character"

from the individual's athletic endeavors; they remain unintegrated, separate and apart from the individual. When the dilettante "trains" she resembles a person at a costume party; she is "all dressed up and no place to go." (p. 174)

According to Devine, the dilettante only *plays* at being an athlete. She is caught up in the external manifestations of the sport—the clothes, the equipment, the settings—and these become ends in themselves. For her, working out is not disciplined and, unlike the serious athlete, she is not trying to reach new depths of her self through it.

The serious athlete trains with intent and commitment. She forces her way through bodily and spiritual inertia with an eye on her immediate and distant goals. She nourishes her hope of a fit body, a beautiful physique, a disciplined spirit, or a calm soul by keeping her daily vow to run, to swim, to work out. She seeks more than mastery of the sport; she strives to develop her inner power and potential. Observable gains in skill and endurance are only way-stations on the road to a larger goal. Devine says:

> Our training-search is a quest for a new being-in-the-world, a new sense of self. Through training we have the opportunity to mold—to recreate—ourselves. This is the "power" that is the epitomy [*sic*] of "fitness." Only the fit person gains the stamina and skill required to bend and prune the body, and we gain this fitness through the rigor of training . . .
>
> One needs hope to initiate training. But to carry through the training process, one needs faith as well. . . . One must believe in oneself. . . . When the person commits herself to "work out" she is keeping faith, in the sense that she has made a promise or given her word of honor. (p. 170)

The serious athlete trains her body, mind, and spirit to overcome external and internal obstacles. She abandons her old self and strikes out for new horizons; she goes beyond old accomplishments and the limits of her being. These experiences, in turn, transcend her everyday life. Devine explains:

> The lasting residue of these transcendent training moments, . . . is a heightened awareness of the capability of the body—a sense of awe and wonder. Concomitant with this sense is a renewed faith in oneself apart from the training milieu. Problems diminish in size and obstacles seem

less forbidding. The integration of mind and body for a few moments each day, that "peace-making" with the warring physical and spiritual elements of one's nature, leaves an afterglow of tolerance and optimism. Through getting reacquainted with that spiritual center through physical exercise, one learns to trust and like oneself again.

Why do people train? They train to gain a sense of the universe, a sense of the limitlessness of their own potential, that sense of power and freedom and ecstasy one feels when there is the realization that there are no boundaries, that one can do anything, that one can lose oneself in experience, can surrender one's rational being-in-the-world and come back, renewed and stronger than before. (pp. 176-177)

To train is to explore one's existential depths. Although most of us do not reach the cutting edge of our beings through physical exercise, we recognize the general flavor of this descriptive reflection. It rings true to our experiences and illuminates shared dimensions of exercising.

SWEARING

Being a phenomenological psychologist who occasionally swears, Burke Mealy (1972) wanted to understand swearing. He asked, What does it mean to swear? When do we swear and why do we do it? Even though more and more people swear, it is still prohibited. When we swear, we break conversational convention but we do so according to implicit rules. There are appropriate and inappropriate ways of swearing. Often we swear when other words fail us. But swearing is also a culturally specific, universal language: within a specific culture, we can swear and everyone understands our meanings.

Mealy asked white, middle-class men and women in their 20s and 30s to describe a recent situation in which they swore. He used these descriptions to specify the ways people swear and the occasions of swearing. Mealy found that swearing was most commonly used to express anger. But people swear for many reasons: to make or emphasize a point, to rebel, to shock, to express intimacy, to gain attention, to be accepted, to relax, to be playful. The following is an essential structure of swearing that Mealy (1972) described:

Swearing is the conventional expression for what is unconventional, especially the forbidden. Swearing refers to matters to which one is not supposed to refer, which are too sacred or profane to be sanctioned by convention. It expresses the holy, the exceptional, the vulgar, the base, the intolerable, the alien or whatever is otherwise inexpressible in ordinary terms.

Swearing is a conventional means of disengaging the limits or boundaries of convention. Swearing is, or is an expression of, going against, being beyond, crossing or otherwise altering conventional expectations, such as those delineated by roles, standards of conduct, mores or other defined social relationships.

The language of swearing is easy to use and versatile. Although the words, themselves, may have a specific, literal meaning, in use they are neither specific in meaning, nor complex, nor technical. They are simple, concise and direct. Moreover, the action intended by swearing is not dependent upon the past or deferred until the future. The meaning of swearing is immediate.

Swearing is a highly prereflective activity. Understanding and using swears is an automatic, body experience, which is associated with strong and, often, primitive feelings. (pp. 97-99)

Swearing puts words to the forbidden or inexpressible. We swear when other words fail us and express ourselves more passionately by doing so. Swearing is a prereflective, spontaneous breaking through of a verbal impasse. By swearing, we express what defies expression. Swearing breaks through limits and taboos that defeat calm, usual words.

If we notice when and how we swear, we can learn about some of our deepest passions and intentions. Deep meanings of our lives can be found in this verbal means of bursting through social conventions to make room for our emotional selves.

CREATIVITY

A different phenomenological reflection on adulthood was done by psychologist Mary-Perry Miller. Miller wanted to understand the important components of the creative process. She asked women poets who lived in the San Francisco Bay Area to describe their creative process. Yi Ling, a 27-year-old Asian-American actor, writer, and artist, describes her creative process as one that is personally and spiritually transformative. It is a process that does not come totally from herself. Here are excerpts from Miller's (1981) summary of Yi Ling's descriptions:

I remember the first batik that I did. It was a red moon. When I took it out of its final dye bath and ironed all the wax out, I looked at the moon and it was really incredible because inside the moon was an iris of an eye and a tear. It's like the material, the wax, and the dye also had a hand in the creative. I feel like I'm just a tool and that the art comes through me from some place, perhaps it's inside of me, or perhaps it's just the great ocean of creativity that's here, there, and everywhere. It's like I can have a vision of what I want, but I can't totally control it because all these other elements that I work with also have a hand. What I set out to do is not necessarily what is going to come out.

I feel that every piece of art begins as an unknown in the artist's mind. And it grows. It's like going on a path, walking a mountain trail that you don't really know where it's going, you just know it's a path. And, for me, the creative process is putting a step in that path and walking the whole way until you get to the end of the path or until—if it's a circle— you get back to the beginning. . . .

My writing starts from ideas, and the ideas usually become characters. I don't write about issues or situations. I write more about characters who are in situations. It begins with a vision or idea or notion of the whole—a feeling that this is what I have to work on next. And then I procrastinate, sometimes for weeks, . . . I read other things, work in the garden, type up my resume, and sharpen pencils. . . .

Other times I begin more methodically. Like the recent poem that I wrote about my grandmother. It's a dialogue between a grandmother and granddaughter. . . . The poem about my grandmother started from some journal notes that I had been keeping when she was dying. I would sit with her in the hospital and write notes and sketch pictures of her in my journal. I drew her face and wrote down bits and pieces of what was happening to her; the kind of powerfulness of her situation because she was dying. It started when I was going through it. . . . I looked back at the journals that I had kept during that time and just got the details here and there and pulled them into the poem. I decided that it would be a dialogue. I wanted to start it at a point when she physically made the discovery of her illness. That was my intellectual process. When I thought of that, then I heard in my mind's eye, I heard and saw my grandmother bitching about something. That's how it started and it progressed like that, moving from a dialogue to a monologue. It was all just a very natural sequence of events. When I would hear the voices, my grandmother's voice, I would write down what was said. Going through my journal and recalling those events and being touched by some of them led me to hearing her voice. So it was kind of an interweaving of them. I feel like I was led on this journey through the creation of the poem. So I would interweave these bits and pieces and pull the threads together. Either it is something that I see right then or it's something else from another day that I take and put down. So I followed the dialogue and the voices until I reached the movement. At that point I wouldn't quite know what the next movement was, so I'd puzzle over it and try different things. But always the right one seemed to come to me. I knew when it was the right piece. It's the feeling of "Of course, there it is, this is it." The same kind of feeling I get as I'm writing something and the next piece falls into place. It's like a little bird talking in my ear saying, "This is it!" It's a feeling inside of me. I know when something is right, when the word works or the dialogue is good. It is a bodily feeling, a physical feeling.

The poem begins with the grandmother's discovery and moves into a dialogue between the grandmother and the granddaughter, and then moves to a monologue. The first monologue is when the grandmother thinks back. Then it becomes a dialogue and monologue blended together with narration. It tells of how they lived through the grandmother's dying. The turning point is when, during one of the visits to the hospital, the granddaughter sees her grandmother as herself when she was young. Then it comes back and ends, like the circle is complete. All of the obstacles have been worked through and the journey is complete. (pp. 115-119)

Miller gives us a general understanding of the creative process by reflecting on Yi Ling's, and other women's, particular experiences. Her insights seem to also apply to men who are involved in creative work.

As formulated by Miller, creativity is an intentional act that is open to the not yet known or formed. It involves being willing to take the next step in the process, being willing to be taken where this leads, and then, actively, taking another step. Once an idea or starting point is chosen, nontask time helps the creative project germinate. This time, that Yi Ling calls procrastination, is an essential part of the process. Ideas, moments, sounds, and feelings all are essential players in creating something.

Miller helps us understand the creative process for women poets as a dialectical movement between self and image, self and other, images and words, body and mind. It involves immersing oneself in the concrete details of life and finding the universal in the particular. It takes place between the self and the "not yet." One is found as much as one finds; one listens as much as one speaks. Miller's insights apply specifically to art and poetry but also illuminate many everyday experiences in which we co-create life and form something that, until then, had not existed.

FATHERS' EXPERIENCES
OF A SON LEAVING HOME

When young adults move out of their parents' homes, it is an important life transition for parents, as well as adult children. Some studies have shown it to be a time of loss and depression for mothers, while more recent research has portrayed it as a time of relief and renewal for women (Rubin, 1979). Almost no studies have been done on fathers' experiences of adult children leaving home.

Psychologist Mima Baird (1983) asked fathers about their first son leaving home. She queried men in their mid to late 40s about how this transition affected their lives. Here is what one man said:

> Friends . . .were looking forward to my problems before I even knew I had a problem. They would say, "Getting ready for him to go?" and I would say, "Yeah, he's going next weekend." "Does it bother you?" I'd say, "No, why should it bother me? I'm happy for him." It never occurred to me that . . . right before he went away, I made him teach his younger brother how to wash my car. . . . I was thinking to myself, "I'm going to miss him because now I'll have to wash the car myself or get my other boy to wash it, and he won't do as good a job." . . . I think my friends were really referring to emotional feelings which I didn't even suspect. Even in the weekend before he left, . . . that was the furthest thing from my mind that emotionally I would be feeling bad. Beforehand I wasn't the least bit suspicious how I would feel. I guess I was just too busy with my own thing, too busy at work, too busy to even think about it. (pp. 66-67)

This father experienced his son's leaving in his typical world of action and doing. As he noticed the change, he focused on getting another son prepared to take over his oldest son's jobs. Caught unprepared for the feelings and meanings that this change brought into his life, he only dealt with these aspects after the change had occurred.

The fathers to whom Baird spoke were surprised by their emotional reactions to their sons' leaving. Another man had a similar experience but was able to experience his reaction in his son's presence:

> We loaded up the car one day and moved on over to his school and helped him get settled in his room, and I want you to know that I don't do any cleaning at home, and here I was helping him clean out his drawers and cleaning windows and getting everything organized. Kind

of reminded me of when I went to school. Seems like my parents helped me move in and swept the room. I am sure the place is in a shambles now . . . but at least we got him started off on the right foot. He said, "Gee Mom, I can't believe Dad has the 409 in one hand and a rag in the other." And I did. It didn't seem very long ago when I had arrived at college, and I found it somewhat incredulous to realize that my first child is now a college student. In fact I still find it a little shocking. (pp. 67-68)

In general, fathers were surprised by atypical feelings when their sons left home and, like this father, found themselves acting and reacting in unusual ways.

From in-depth interviews with 10 fathers, Baird formulated the following understanding of this phenomenon:

The essential structure of a father's experience in launching his first child emerges as one of change, separation and loss, evoking a variety of responses, embracing paradoxical emotions. As a prism refracts light into myriad patterns, so each father's personal history and web of relationships refracts the essential structure into multilevel experiences that are unique for each individual.

Launching of the first child is a marker event, announcing and demanding change, challenging a father to integrate the changes in his environment with changes in himself, his primary relationships and his experience of time.

The launching consists of three phases: preparation, the actual departure, and the adjustment after departure. Every father progresses through the phases at his own pace, with an agenda influenced by the past relationship with his own father and the quality of the relationship with the child who is leaving. Careful preparation of the child and anticipatory grieving by the father eases the transition.

The departure of the child challenges a father to recognize and resolve the conflict between cognitive acknowledgement of the need to disengage from the child and a less conscious desire or need to remain attached. Making the conflict conscious facilitates disengagement.

Initial awareness of the multifaceted experience known as "missing the son" can expand to a recognition of paradoxical experiences of grief and gladness, rejoicing and resignation, alienation and acceptance, frustration and fulfillment. The intensity and duration of emotional reactions or distress are mediated by past attachment experiences and the quality of interpersonal relationships in the present.

Amorphous anxiety and feelings of grief accompany an experience perceived as separation from, and loss of, a beloved object. Separation from the child in daily life represents loss of a beloved person, loss of control, loss of an essential identity and/or loss of meaning. Launching a child constellates earlier losses in life, unresolved issues in relationships and anxiety about aging and death. The impact of the figurative or literal loss of a man's father by alienation or death is heightened during the launching experience.

The experience provides an opportunity for emotional growth, resolution of old conflicts, moving into a more adult relationship with the child or a new awareness of larger existential issues of loneliness, death and meaninglessness. Launching a child invites a father to move from casual awareness of change and missing, through successively deeper levels of self-awareness as he seeks to find meaning and understanding of an experience perceived to be one of separation and loss. Increased awareness of the dynamics involved in the launching not only facilitates disengagement from the child but also enhances the father's own process of ongoing differentiation and individuation. (pp. 50-52)

Despite the fact that fathers do not anticipate being changed by a son leaving home, the changes affect their day-to-day activities and their emotional lives. Not only can this event clarify important past, present, and future aspects of life, but it can revitalize relationships and renew and prioritize intentions as well.

LOSS AND GRIEF

As we grow older, our physical, emotional, and social selves change and we experience losses. Some phenomenologists have explored common points of loss and change that occur during our adult years. All of us have experienced or will experience the death of someone we love. Although much has been written about mourning and grief (Freud, 1957; Kubler-Ross, 1969; Shneidman, 1973), little has been written about anticipating someone's death. Mary-Perry Miller (1978) investigated how we deal with grief that we anticipate, grief that we know is coming but has not yet arrived. Here is what a 24-year-old man, Jim, says about the anticipated death of his father. His father has lived with a brain tumor for the past 8 years. He has had two operations to reduce its size. The year before Jim spoke with Miller, a major heart attack further complicated his father's terminal condition. Jim describes his complex experiences:

I am very aware of a balance which I keep within myself between taking care of myself in this situation and taking care of and protecting my father. I feel like I am walking on thin ice when I talk with my father about it. I am never clear or assertive enough to tell him what my feelings are and that I am afraid that this might be the last time I see him alive. I do not want to impose my pain on my father as he is already suffering enough with his own painful feelings about it. But it is not as selfless as it sounds. Part of it is that I do not want to face it or his pain. . . .

When I think about it as a real situation in which he is going to die, I often find a kind of superstitious belief that I can effect [*sic*] the situation by how I think of it. If I think of my father as dying, he will die. If I think of my father as dying, then I am not giving what energy I could to his process of living. It is a conflict which cannot be avoided. It is trying to strike a balance between being realistic about the fact that my father is going to die soon and not dwelling on it or being preoccupied with it to the extent that it gets in the way of what we have now. . . .

I know that as hard as I work to prepare myself for my father's death, there is no way that I can be prepared for it. As badly as I feel about it now, I know that it is going to be much worse when he does die. When the reality hits me, it is going to hit me in the head and eliminate all of my preparedness. It will be like the time my father came home after his first operation. Although I thought I had prepared myself for that, when I saw him so helpless and vulnerable, it knocked all of my preparedness out of me. That visual reality was devastating. . . .

There seem to be two levels of my awareness of my father's dying. I know that my father is dying from the medical records, from what I have been told and have read, and from my knowledge of the operations. But there is another level of awareness which is much more immediate and powerful. This is the way in which I see him dying everyday. There is a certain closing-in, inhibition and cynicism that I see creeping in. . . . He was such a vital person in the world. He has been robbed of the best years of his life. My father is not only going to die, but he is dying and being changed by the situation.

My feelings of closeness to my father and not wanting to let go have intensified. It makes it more difficult for me to separate my feelings about him and my feelings about myself. What do I want for my father, and what do I want for myself? What part of me is going to die with my father? What part of me am I going to have left? I feel a sense of urgency to define what is me and what is my father. When he dies, a part of me will not exist anymore. One of the immediate reactions when you know that someone is dying is "thank God it is not me." But, at the same time, if that person means something to you, somehow it is you who is dying. . . .

There are also feelings of deep pain, sorrow and grief which are very different from my feelings of rage and guilt. I feel this grief and sorrow very acutely, but find the feeling very difficult to communicate. Sometimes it feels like an emptiness which puts me in touch with my own death and my own vulnerability. I experience it as a physical sensation rather than a direct emotional sensation. I feel a lump in my chest and stomach and a tightness in my throat. It is a feeling of being about to cry.

It is something that is not intellectual at all, but a most elementary and primal emotion which I have great difficulty putting into words. The words that come to mind are that a part of me is dying, and a part of me is going to be dead when my father is dead. That is very frightening and upsetting. To a certain extent I am mourning my own death.

It also feels like something very lonely. My father is going to die and leave me. I am going to be the person stuck here with all of these feelings. It feels very lonely because it is something that I cannot get help with, and that I am stuck with. At the same time that I am feeling intruded on by others who ask about my father, I am screaming out to people to help me with it. But they cannot. I have to work through it on my own. (pp. 41-49)

In anticipating his father's death, Jim is caught between many paradoxical movements: facing his father's death and facing his own death, raging against death and welcoming it, reaching out to people and pushing them away, being overcome with ineffable feelings and searching for words to express his feelings.

Because it has not happened yet, the anticipated death of a loved one is simultaneously present and not present. Whether we focus on it or relegate it to the background of our lives, it is always present as a "not-yet" significant loss. We cannot fully deal with it because it has not happened yet, and we cannot forget it because it is coming. Miller (1978) labels this phenomenon anticipatory grief for the survivor-to-be, and portrays the essential structure of it as follows:

For the survivor, anticipatory grief is a highly stressful emotional experience lived alone within the context of a significant relationship. The phenomenon is experienced on alternating contextual and figural levels, and may be lived either more contextually or more figurally depending on individual stylistic differences. Persistent feelings of helplessness, frustration and loneliness are associated with the contextual living of the phenomenon, while more fluctuating intense feelings of fear, anger, guilt, resentment, pain and sorrow merge with the persistent emotions to characterize the figural living of anticipatory grief. These expressions of grief are oriented toward the other, the relationship with the other, and the self in response to both an anticipated loss in the future, and an actual loss of what was being experienced in the present. Grief in relation to the other involves a recognition of the other's losses, a genuine concern for his/her well-being, and sympathy for the other as an individual in-the-world. Grief for the relationship involves a painful giving-up of the meaningful relatedness which the survivor and the dying other shared. The survivor grieves for the loss of all of that which they had "between" them, and of that which they "were" *for* each other, and all of that which they "would" have continued to be *for* each other. Grief for the other and for the relationship bring [*sic*] the survivor to a transcending personal awareness of his/her own finitude and aloneness in the world and a grief for self. Grief in relation to self embodies a presently experienced loss of a part of self and an anticipated loss of self. The fundamental structure of time molds the experience of anticipatory grief resulting in a vascillating [*sic*] past-present-future and a sense of being suspended in time, held in limbo between an unreachable longed-for past and an unavoidable painful future. (pp. 69-70)

Grief is something all of us have or will anticipate. It is a painful process that forces us to clarify ourselves, our values, and our relationships. It forces us to confront the fragility of life, the tenuousness of life's meaning, and our helplessness and aloneness. Learning from the losses in our lives will help us come to terms with our own aging and eventual death.

8

Elders

Unless we die young, all of us will grow old before we die. Our aging and eventual death become intense concerns for us during middle age. This is the period of life when children leave home and parents become physically frail and die. When we become elders, around age 65, we face special developmental tasks and events. These include retiring, making sense of our lives as we near death, living with the results of physiological aging and chronic illnesses, and, eventually, experiencing the dying process.

Most people within Western European cultures fear aging and dying. We handle these fears by holding onto youth. When signs of physical and mental aging become obvious, we medicalize people and move "patients" to hospitals or nursing homes. In many ways, our understanding and treatment of elders reveal ageist beliefs. Ageism is an irrational belief in the superiority of one age group over another and, therefore, its right to dominate. Within Western European cultures, it is assumed that young middle age is the prime of life and that other age groups, especially the elderly, are inferior. Ageism results in both negative and positive stereotypes about old people. Negative stereotypes teach us that old people are no longer sexual, are mentally and physically incompetent, are alone and bitter, are close minded and rigid, are needy and helpless, are crotchety and self-centered. Positive stereotypes go to the opposite extreme.

They typify old people as unusually capable, as wisened by age, as atypically youthful. On one hand, we idolize atypical elders and applaud the signs of their triumph over aging: their independence, alertness, activity, emotional competency, and productivity. On the other hand, we infantilize other elders by making them into cute, endearing, and entertaining oddities.

Both negative and positive stereotypes objectify old people, blur their individuality, and make the realities of their lives invisible. Stereotypes encourage us to believe we know old people without meeting them. In this way, we bypass the realities of aging and think of optimal aging as a psychological matter of attitude and will. Reducing the realities of aging to an attitude toward it amounts to expecting elders to think young so that they do not become old. If old people do not act their age, they buffer us from our dread of becoming old. Our fears of death, along with fears of losing our mental and physical independence and, thus, becoming vulnerable and powerless, fuel these stereotypes and distance us from old people.

Phenomenology illuminates old age experientially, from within the elder's lifeworld. Interacting with particular elders helps us differentiate old people from our stereotypes about them. Writers and researchers who have bracketed their internalized stereotypes of aging and the aged can help us dwell in the day-to-day experiences of old people. In this chapter, I look at some essential themes of being old and facing death.

Within feminist literature, writer Barbara Macdonald (Macdonald & Rich, 1983) is a recognized advocate of the rights of old people. She believes that the only way to avoid ageist bias is for old people to speak their own lives and experiences. As she aged, Macdonald experienced herself becoming increasingly different from and devalued by Western European culture.

Given our ageist culture, Macdonald believes that growing old can provide a final opportunity for confronting our differentness from other people. Having less and less status to lose, the positive outcome of being an old man or woman is gaining more and more freedom to be who one wants to be, to follow one's desires, and to be authentically one's self. At age 65, Macdonald looks herself in the eye and describes discovering her aging self:

I am less than five feet high. . . . I weigh about a hundred and forty pounds and my body is what my mother used to call dumpy. . . . "Dumpy" was her word and just as I have had to keep the body, somehow I have had to keep the word—thirty-eight inch bust, no neck, no waistline, fat hips—that's dumpy.

My hair is grey, white at the temples, with only a little of the red cast of earlier years showing through. My face is wrinkled and deeply lined. Straight lines have formed on the upper lip as though I had spent many years with my mouth pursed. This has always puzzled me and I wonder what years those were and why I can't remember them. My face has deep lines that extend from each side of the nose down the face past the corners of my mouth. My forehead is wide, and the lines across my forehead and between my eyes are there to testify that I was often puzzled and bewildered for long periods of time about what was taking place in my life. My cheekbones are high. . . . My chin is small for such a large head and below the chin the skin hangs in a loose vertical fold from my chin all the way down my neck, where it meets a horizontal scar. The surgeon who made the scar said that the joints of my neck were worn out from looking up so many years. For all kinds of reasons, I seldom look up to anyone or anything anymore.

My eyes are blue and my gaze is usually steady and direct. But I look away when I am struggling with some nameless shame, trying to disclaim parts of myself. My voice is low and my speech sometimes clipped and rapid if I am uncomfortable; otherwise, I have a pleasant voice. I like the sound of it from in here where I am. When I was younger, some people, lovers mostly, enjoyed my singing, but I no longer have the same control of my voice and sing only occasionally now when I am alone.

My hands are large and the backs of my hands begin to show the brown spots of aging. Sometimes lately, holding my arms up reading in bed or lying with my arms clasped around my lover's neck, I see my arm with the skin hanging loosely from my forearm and cannot believe that it is really my own. It seems disconnected from me; it is someone else's, it is the arm of an old woman. It is the arm of such old women as I myself have seen, sitting on benches in the sun with their hands folded in their laps; old women I have turned away from. I wonder now, how and when these arms I see came to be my own—arms I cannot turn away from. (pp. 13-14)

This powerful description penetrates physiognomy to reveal an old woman struggling to see herself honestly and, in the process, to reclaim her soul from both external and internal negations. Macdonald helps us see that becoming old eventually brings us face to face with our finitude. As we age, we lose the power to outdistance our

vulnerabilities and to flee from ourselves by cultivating socially valued attributes. We are caught in our bodies and in our lives; we are
left facing ourselves, facing into our own death. This can be a pow-
erfully clarifying experience. Often, accepting the inevitability of
death can increase appreciation of life. It also can reveal the meanings of ourselves, our lives, and life itself. Letting go into death can
enable us to let go into life.

When we let go into life, we can discover an expanded view of
ourselves. Through a fictional description, the writer Herman
Hesse gives us a portrait of this larger view of ourselves, one that
can contradict many of the concerns and values that directed our
younger lives. The narration is by Goldmund in the novel *Narcissus
and Goldmund* (1968). Goldmund is the sensuous and sexual explorer
who has spent his life seeking gratification and fulfillment through
heterosexual relationships in his vagabond life. The excerpt occurs
after Goldmund returns from his final journey:

> After a while, since he could not fall asleep, he got up and walked heav-
> ily to the wall to look into a small mirror that hung there. Attentively he
> looked at the Goldmund who stared back at him out of the mirror, a
> weary Goldmund, a man who had grown tired and old and wilted, with
> much gray in his beard. It was an old, somewhat unkempt man who
> looked back at him from the little mirror's dull surface—but strangely
> unfamiliar. It did not seem to be properly present; it did not seem to be
> of much concern to him. . . .
> Carefully he read the mirror face, as though he were interested in
> finding out about this stranger. He nodded to him and knew him again:
> yes, it was he; it corresponded to the feeling he had about himself. An
> extremely tired old man, who had grown slightly numb, who had re-
> turned from a journey, an ordinary man in whom one could not take
> much pride. And yet he had nothing against him. He still liked him;
> there was something in his face that the earlier, pretty Goldmund had
> not had. In all the fatigue and disintegration there was a trace of con-
> tentment, or at least of detachment. He laughed softly to himself and
> saw the mirror join him: a fine fellow he had brought home from his
> trip! Pretty much torn and burned out, he was returning from his little
> excursion. He had not only sacrificed his horse, his satchel, and his gold
> pieces; other things, too, had gotten lost or deserted him: youth, health,
> self-confidence, the color in his cheeks and the force in his eyes. Yet he
> liked the image: this weak old fellow in the mirror was dearer to him
> than the Goldmund he had been for so long. He was older, weaker, more
> pitiable, but he was more harmless, he was more content, it was easier

to get along with him. He laughed and pulled down one of the eyelids
that had become wrinkled. Then he went back to bed and this time fell
asleep. (pp. 302-303)

This fictional account shares a common theme with Macdonald's
nonfictional description—confronting physical changes of aging
that show the marks of life. It also reveals a man facing himself in a
more vulnerable, exposed, and honest stance than in his younger
years. Cut down to its essence, life reveals as much weakness as
strength, as much to pity as to admire, as much to accept as to
challenge. Both Macdonald's and Hesse's accounts celebrate the
maturity of psychological and spiritual development that can be
contained in a long life.

Grounded in these experiential portraits, let us now look at some
phenomenologically oriented views of maturity.

Maturity

Both throughout life and near its end, many people contemplate
the meaning of human existence. As we look back through time,
some of us see the sense our lives have made and experience their
fullness. Others are befuddled by the events that have occurred and
hope these events make a meaningful pattern even if we cannot see
it. Erikson's (1963) classical theory of old age, integrity versus despair and disgust, stresses finding meaning in a review of one's life.
For Erikson, the accomplishment of integrity involves accepting and
treasuring your life as the creation of a unique combination of
events. A sense of integrity comes from looking back over life and
valuing each event, whether joyful or tragic, as something that
helped a person become a unique self. When a particular life is experienced as having integrity, it has emotional continuity. Every
event that is and has been part of it is treasured as necessary to its
outcome. The person accepts who he or she is and takes responsibility for the lessons learned and the contributions made. Integrity connects individual lives to human life as a whole. A life of integrity
becomes a symbol of human life and reaches in all directions into
time and space.

Developmental psychologist Robert Peck (cited in Kimmel, 1980) has further differentiated Erikson's stage of late adulthood. He suggests that mature elders value wisdom over physical powers and have retained emotional and mental flexibility. These shifts in values can help elders adjust to social and personal changes that are part of their aging process. Successful aging also consists of letting go of work role preoccupation and finding pleasure and meaning in nonwork areas of life. Peck believes that the ability to go beyond physical pain and self-concerns adds enjoyment and meaning to life. As people live with chronic illnesses and approach death, they let go of embodied life and find gratification in being and having been part of other people's lives, lives that will continue after they are gone (Kimmel, 1980, p. 17).

Wisdom results from viewing one's life with integrity rather than with despair and disgust (Erikson, 1963). It consists of a detached, yet active, concern with life in the face of death. When we are wise participants in life, we are actively present and engaged, while simultaneously letting go and giving up a desire to control life and other people. Knowing with certainty I will die, I live my life according to the values I most treasure. Being conscious that each moment may be a last one, I live it as fully as possible.

Sociologist Valerie Bentz (1989) draws upon the work of philosopher Bernard Boelen (1978) to develop a phenomenologically oriented definition of maturity. She formulates maturity as a process of becoming mature. Becoming mature is the project of a person striving to be his or her most authentic, loving, creative, responsible, and aware self. As an ongoing part of life, becoming mature does not outdistance human vulnerabilities and failings. Rather, it engages the person in dialogue with his or her immaturities and emotional wounds. Becoming mature involves confronting and coming to grips with oneself and other people who have significantly influenced one's life. For most of us, becoming mature involves confronting our ghosts—internalized, negating voices that haunt us and block us from being all we wish to be—and transforming them into spirits. Spirits inspire rather than haunt and weaken us; they help us become the best and most valued parts of ourselves (Bentz, 1989, pp. 4-16). For example, Macdonald's description contains the echo of her mother's negations of her body, which she is still in the process of reclaiming.

According to Bentz, a mature person forms interpersonal relationships that are emotionally alive and stimulating and last through time. A mature person is empathic, responsive, honest, and caring. She or he can defend the self against overwhelmingly difficult experiences, is aware of a wide array of feelings, is in control, finds meaning in life, and can be playful. A mature self is a competent, congruent communicator and bases interpersonal relationships on positive, clear attributions and expectations. At the core of becoming mature is an integrated sense of self over time, a self that is in emotional, moral, and intellectual tune with significant others (pp. 81-100).

Becoming mature is a process with which all of us are engaged. We expect to reap the benefits of working toward it when we are old. The above descriptive definition, however, makes it evident that many of the qualities of maturity are necessary throughout life. These qualities are, indeed, the work of a lifetime.

Retirement

Our natural attitude toward retirement, especially if it is not our personal and anticipated retirement, is of a straightforward event with commonly shared meanings. But when psychologists Gail Hornstein and Seymour Wapner (1985) asked 24 retirees about their experiences of retirement, they discovered that this life event had different meanings to diverse people. Hornstein and Wapner distinguish four meanings of retirement. Retirement can be:

1. A transition to the less active period of old age
2. The beginning of a new phase of life in which one can live as one pleases and enjoy life to the fullest
3. A continuation of one's previous life, with less pressure and more satisfaction than previously enjoyed
4. A time when one must stop working even though one desires to continue (pp. 299-306)

The meaning of retirement can be different for each person; it can even shift for the same person over time. Hornstein and Wapner urge people to understand retirement from an experiential viewpoint. Only when we stand in retirees' worlds can we understand their desires and expectations. This understanding facilitates relating to and helping elders.

In addition to these diverse meanings of retirement, retirees vary in how aware they are of expectations and desires. Their expectations can include attitudes toward change, the degree of interpersonal involvement they want, and their general orientation to differences. Some retirees want spouses and adult children to be involved actively in this transition. Others wish to handle the changes themselves. If the retiree wishes others to help with retirement plans and they do not do so, lack of involvement can be experienced negatively. If, however, people try to help when the retiree wants to handle things himself or herself, this can also be experienced as unsupportive. The crucial factor is the desires and expectations of the person going through the transition and how people in the retiree's social support network fulfill these desires.

Any particular retirement goes more smoothly if all people involved are aware of their desires and expectations. The most difficulties occur when all have expectations they are unaware of, expectations they live out and are unable to verbalize. And too, a satisfactory adjustment to retirement is more likely when the retiree's expectations are congruent with the realistic factors of life. Even if people differ in their expectations, differences that are acknowledged provide a place to disagree and to arbitrate. Being able to negotiate conflicts at this stage of life depends upon previously developed skills.

Expectations of changes in life due to retiring are also important. If changes are desired and they do not occur, people feel disappointed. Disappointment can arise also from undesirable changes. A successful retirement actualizes a person's life goals. When a person's intentions are frustrated by the events of retirement, she or he feels defeated.

Hornstein and Wapner alert us to the diverse meanings and themes of retirement. In doing so, they remind us to get to know the intentions and wishes of particular elders.

An Experiential Account
of Having a Heart Attack

For many of us, the aging process involves living with chronic physical problems. Adjusting to these changes is a necessary part of life. Especially with cardiovascular disease, changes in life-style and awareness of our physical selves can mean the difference between life and death.

Having a heart attack is a frightening experience of middle or late adulthood. According to psychologist Sandra Levy (1981), acute myocardial infarction is the leading cause of death for adults between the ages of 40 and 65 years. Levy asked men who were recovering from a heart attack to recount their experience of having a heart attack and recovering from it.

Based upon interviews with 28 blue-collar workers between the ages of 42 and 74 years, Levy traced the process by which these men realized they were having a heart attack. Here is what she found.

Looking back, men first noticed unusual physical pain or discomfort during their work day. They continued to focus upon work and tried to ignore or dismiss the symptoms by attributing them to something usual (e. g., indigestion or another chronic physical problem). As the symptoms worsened and the men were surprised by more intense pain, they realized that something extraordinary was happening. Even then, however, some self-medicated with alcohol. Many denied that anything was wrong. Finally, unbearable pain incapacitated them, and they called upon others to help them, verbally or behaviorally.

People who have had a heart attack often reconstruct their histories so as to identify what led up to it. Creating a past that ended in an unexpected present is an important way of incorporating a trauma into one's sense of self. It is an effective way of making a trauma meaningful and gaining control over it. If the men could see how their life-style had resulted in the attack, they knew what to do to avoid another one. Levy suggests that men who do not reconstruct their lives to make sense of having had a heart attack wait longer to get medical intervention when having a second one. Since quick intervention can mean the difference between living and dying, increasing experiential awareness is crucial. Levy's study is an example of how useful an experiential understanding can be to the survivor of a heart attack, as well as to medical personnel. Above all, it points to the necessity of engaging the patient in health maintenance.

Managing Physical and Emotional Pain

Much of life is spent resisting its dark side: life's pain, disappointments, and losses. Emotionally, we try to forget our hurts and to stay safe from further harm by outdistancing disappointments and not looking back. Those of us raised by the adage "Don't cry over spilled milk" have learned not to express sadness. We assume we should not bother people we care about with our difficulties.

Most of us work with emotional pain throughout our lives. Some of us do it alone. Others are fortunate to share pain with loved ones. A wonderful outcome of this work is that we heal our emotional wounds by the time we are old. When this happens, we are at peace with our selves and our lives as we approach death.

Although some people live with chronic physical illness and pain throughout their lives, most of us have our first experiences with chronic physical discomfort as our bodies age. Then too, some elders retain their physical agility and vitality. Many old people, however, experience their bodies becoming increasingly frail. In cultures where physical illnesses are understood and accepted as legitimate, physical illnesses can also be vehicles for the expression of psychological needs and desires. And too, when we are disabled, our independence is threatened and we must grapple with being more physically and emotionally dependent. Often, this physical state returns us to whatever unfinished emotional work we have left to do. As elders, our encounters with emotional and physical pain can open us to deep lessons of life. Indeed, chronic pain can open our hearts to loving ourselves and others.

When pain, either physical or emotional, is chronic, we must learn to live with it rather than try to extract it from our lives. According to grief counselor Stephen Levine (1982), our resistance to pain makes for much of the pain we feel. He suggests that we change our relationship to pain. Rather than avoiding or fighting it, Levine asks us to face pain and seek to know it. Welcoming the pain and inviting it to come forth and show itself loosens our resistances to it. When we receive pain and incorporate it into our selves, we change our selves. These changes involve the loss of a tighter, more fearful and in-control self, a self that thinks it must be in charge of life. This loss is filled by an other self, one that gives up control, places itself in the hands of forces larger that itself, and opens itself to the lessons and gifts that are contained in the pain. Letting go of pain brings us to the edge of our resistance to life and catapults us into a large, more open self. Often, opening ourselves to pain involves going beyond fear and opening our hearts to love (Levine, 1982, pp. 114-145).

Resting in pain and letting it be there, we rest in a larger self than our previous one. This self contains but goes beyond previous ways we closed against pain. This new perspective can help us see our orientation to life. Levine (1982) explains:

> As one person said after opening to and exploring their pain, "It isn't just the pain in my spine or my head or my bones, it's all the pains in my life that I have pulled back from that have imprisoned me. Watching this pain in my body makes me see how little of the pain in my life, in my mind, I've given any space to."
>
> Many who have worked with these exercises have said that it wasn't just the pain in their body that they hadn't understood, it was also the fear, the boredom, the restlessness, the self-doubt, the anger which they had always pulled back from, which they had never allowed themselves to enter into. That they had never fully met themselves in life or dealt with death because they had always been encouraged to withdraw from anything that was unpleasant. The unpleasant had always acted as their jailer. (p. 118)

Resisting pain can shrink our lives and selves. When we withdraw from pain, we withdraw from life. Once we move beyond fear and resistance to face the dark side of life, we can more readily embrace the wholeness of ourselves.

Pain can be a wise teacher that tears our hearts open and throws us into the complexity of life and its wounds and discomforts. As we work with pain, we learn to treasure life and the mysterious ways it enables us to transform our spirits and reach wholeness.

Senility

A phenomenology of later life can be as difficult to do as a phenomenology of life's beginnings. Experientially, where are we, for example, when organic brain changes cause us to leave consensual reality and inhabit inner landscapes that are invisible to others? It is clear that ordinary, everyday time and space are replaced by different times, places, meanings, and concerns.

Especially when very old, some elders lose their orientation in time and space; they disengage from the interpersonally shared world and live in a different experiential one. We can take many attitudes to the disorientation of elders who suffer organic brain changes. Writer Russell Baker (1982) describes his evolving understandings of his mother at this stage of her life. His descriptions show an exquisite ability to enter into the experiential world of his mother and to respect her meaningful reexperiencing of her life as it draws to an end. He says:

> At the age of eighty my mother had her last bad fall, and after that her mind wandered free through time. Some days she went to weddings and funerals that had taken place half a century earlier. On others she presided over family dinners cooked on Sunday afternoons for children who were now gray with age. Through all this she lay in bed but moved across time, traveling among the dead decades with a speed and ease beyond the gift of physical science.
> "Where's Russell?" she asked one day when I came to visit at the nursing home.
> "I'm Russell," I said.
> She gazed at this improbably overgrown figure out of an inconceivable future and promptly dismissed it.
> "Russell's only this big," she said, holding her hand, palm down, two feet from the floor. That day she was a young country wife with chickens in the backyard and a view of hazy blue Virginia mountains behind the apple orchard, and I was a stranger old enough to be her father. (p. 1)

As he sat with his dying mother, Baker faced his relationship with her, their struggles against one another and their inabilities to know and accept each other. Eventually, he stepped past the doctors' diagnosis of senility and stopped trying to reorient her to his world. Instead, he attempted to be present with her in her swoops through the past.

Descriptions like this can help us disengage from a medical and physiological explanation of the dying process. Baker is able to stay with his dying mother, experientially, as she leaves his world. To stay with his mother, Baker must let go of his self, the one that formed in complement to his mother's old self, and simply bear witness to her changes. The loss of old selves, both Baker's and his mother's, and the beginnings of new life paths are central parts of these changes. As she loops back through her life, Baker's mother moves beyond his grasp and leaves him to reform his self around the absence of her presence.

Letting Go of Life and Facing Death

A last developmental task of life is to let go of it and to grasp death. From an experiential, spiritual perspective, Stephen Levine, offers gentle, powerful insights into the dying process. Above all, Levine looks at death as a natural part of life, one that is absolutely predictable and completely safe. When we hold onto the form our selves and lives have taken, we fear death and the loss of what we have gained in life. Levine sees the tangible form of our lives as an arbitrary one; it is only a small part of a larger, universal oneness.

Like pain, death is a final experience of life that we put off as long as possible. Some of us run from death until it strikes us down. Most of us turn to meet it and make physical, social, psychological, and spiritual preparations for dying. As Jim told us in Chapter 7, preparing for death, our own or someone else's, involves grieving the losses anticipated. It means letting go of life while living it.

To die is to lose everything. Unlike earlier losses, death consists of letting go of our entire embodied existence. As we get closer to our own death, we realize that everything and everyone we love will be pulled away from us by the flow of life. Our task is to loosen our grasp on life and ourselves, to let something unknown come into existence—the selves we become when we cease to be.

In *Who Dies*, Levine (1982) helps us confront and work with the dying process. He brings us into the hospital beds and sickrooms of dying people of all ages and describes excruciating experiences of dying. Above all, these experiences raise the question of who we really are. Similar to his work with pain, Levine tells us to let go into death. Letting go of the selves we struggled hard to create and to make real can be difficult but freeing work. Death can be a teacher who opens us to the vastness of our being, a spaciousness that we never imagined when we were busy holding onto our importance and power in the world. When we stop trying to defeat death and let go of who we were, we can drop into unknown parts of ourselves.

When terminal illness has stripped us down to our frail bodies and our dependent selves, we have little left to lose. Caught in this weak self, we look out from our sickbeds at many parts of life. Lying helpless, we see the ways we have sought happiness by being what we should be, by reaching for physical pleasures, by avoiding our vulnerability, by trying to control life. If we can let go of our old selves, the ones that were not dying, we can rest more easily in our sickbeds. Dropping our preconceptions about life and death enables us to lie peacefully in the "nows" of life. When we open to ourselves and life, we can receive whatever comes to us. According to Levine, satisfaction is release from wanting. Satisfaction occurs when we shift from not having to having; it is accomplished by the fulfillment of desire rather than the possession of things. Happiness, then, depends upon our relation to desire and not on what we have attained or achieved (pp. 60-72).

If we trust ourselves and feel safe enough, we can use our impending death to experience the vast unknownness of ourselves and life. Realizing that we have already died, we can open to the wonder of life. Knowing that we will lose everything, we can enter into life, however it presents itself to us, in openness, wonder, and love. Levine (1982) explains:

> When we realize we are already dead, our priorities change, our heart opens, our mind begins to clear of the fog of old holdings and pretendings. We watch all life in transit and what matters becomes instantly apparent: The transmission of love, the letting go of obstacles to understanding, the relinquishment of our grasping, of our hiding from ourselves. Seeing the mercilessness of our self-strangulation, we begin to come gently into the light we share with all beings. Taking each teaching, each loss, each gain, each fear, each joy as it arises and experiencing it fully, life becomes workable. We are no longer "a victim of life." And then every experience, even the loss of our dearest one, becomes another opportunity for awakening.

If our only spiritual practice were to live as though we were already dead, relating to all we meet, to all we do, as though it were our final moments in the world, what time would there be for old games or falsehoods or posturing? If we lived our life as though we were already dead, as though our children were already dead, how much time would there be for self-protection and the re-creation of ancient mirages? Only love would be appropriate, only the truth. (p. 99)

Levine tells us that we have everything to gain by dying. If we are not ready to die, we are not ready to live. Rather than being a loss, death is a doorway into wholeness. When we are willing to face life's unknown vastness, both outside and inside ourselves, we soften and open. The truths of life become clear, and we are filled with love. Being open to all that we have been, are, and will be enables us to die in peace and balance. Then, stepping over the threshold of death, we enter the immensity of the universe and the original oneness of our nature.

PART III

❖

Intimate Relationships

In Part III, I look at human life through the lens of intimate relationships: those between parents and children, friends, sexual partners, ex-lovers, and extended friendship family members. In doing so, I loop back through the developmental stages discussed in Part II and look at interpersonal beginnings and journeys. I expand the contents and insights of a phenomenology of human development to include love relationships.

Loving and being loved preoccupy us throughout life. The relationships that are explored in Part III are personal and private, ones that include the deepest experiences of intimacy. They are the relationships that are closest to our hearts and through which we seek personal and interpersonal fulfillment. Some of them, like those between parents and children, are given at birth and develop between people of unequal status and age. Others, like friendships and sexual love relationships, are equal, mutually chosen ones.

Phenomenological descriptions of intimate relationships illuminate the experiential nature and the essential structure of different forms of intimacy. Each form of intimacy has its pleasures and problems; each brings us into the heart of human life and, often, face-to-face with disappointments that can transform our souls. We become ourselves in intimate relationships, those that continue and those that end.

Beginning with our interpersonal, emotional birth in the parent-child relationship, our developmental journeys are ongoing explorations in self-love and love of others: parents, friends, and sexual partners. Intimate relationships co-create and are co-created by us. Each schools us in essential aspects of intimacy: honesty, presence, sharing, commitment, freedom, vulnerability, trust, mutuality, generosity, desire, hope, loss, disappointment, loneliness, and emotional comfort. Starting with our parents, the people we love and by whom we are loved assist us to grow, change, and actualize ourselves. First, let us look at the nature of the relationship between parents and children and its shifts over time.

9

Parents and Children

As infants, we begin the longest relationship we will have in life, our relationship with our parents. This relationship is our first, and it continues long after our parents are dead. Initially, and throughout life, parents are the touchstone of our interpersonal selves, the place we began, and, often, the place to which we must return to truly know ourselves. As our first relationship, the parent-child relationship is foundational. It is here that we begin to be and to become ourselves. It is here that we have our first interpersonal experiences. These experiences last throughout our lives and thread through all other relationships.

Although most of us cannot remember ourselves as infants, we can imagine the beginnings of our interpersonal journeys. We can spend time with infants and rediscover who they are and how life must be for them. We can also watch our parents hold and talk to infants, and notice what qualities they treasure and what values they affirm and negate. In Western European cultures, we see infants as dependent, helpless, and vulnerable. These qualities draw us to babies, especially smiling ones, and make the most serious and aloof of us beam and soften. Babies blink back at us without protective coverings, hidden game plans, or ill intentions. Their openness, presence, and availability unwrap our hearts and draw us to them. Within this pleasurable experience, babies symbolize

new beginnings, unspoiled love, hope, and the possibility of satisfying intimacy. The baby within us, still searching for wholeness and
perfect love, is drawn to babies as beacons of hope.

Relationships between parents and children begin and end as unequal ones. In the beginning, parents must take care of infants and
children. Adult qualities of independence, protectiveness, and helpfulness complement the physical realities of infancy. A good parent
is attentive, resourceful, empathic, gentle, firm, kind, and loving.
Although parents receive many pleasures and joys from being
with infants, the relationship is asymmetrical; the parent cares for
and takes care of the infant without expecting reciprocation. Later,
as parents age and die, the asymmetrical relationship reverses.
Adult children may care for emotionally and physically frail parents. Then, children must be good parents to their parents and help
them embrace their dependence, vulnerableness, and helplessness.

Much occurs between these two extremes that brings us full circle
through life. First, let us look at the emotional requirements of infants and some of the things they need from parents to cultivate
their healthy being-in-the-world-with-others.

The Infant's Existential Birth

According to phenomenologist Ronald D. Laing (1959), our physical birth provides the possibility of our existential birth—our birth
as unique, active subjects in the interpersonal world. This existential
birth occurs when our parents welcome us into the world and love
us as special human beings. By being treated as a person, the infant
becomes a person. By being loved, an infant experiences himself or herself as lovable. Sufficient validation of the infant's spontaneous self is
necessary for existential birth.

With enough interpersonal validation, each of us experiences primary ontological security. This is a security of our most fundamental being. When we feel ontologically secure, we feel whole, real,
alive, continuous, and autonomous. Ontological security helps us
know that we have the right to exist. It enables us to feel that our
being-in-the-world is justified. When we are ontologically secure,
we rest in a protected place in the world and do not have to justify

our existence. Rather, we have the luxury of pursuing our desires and developing ourselves. Ontological security results in existential autonomy. Being existentially autonomous involves experiencing ourselves as separate, worthy people who are the responsible centers of our lives. When two people are existentially autonomous, they can experience each other as separate people, rather than as extensions of themselves. Thus, they can relate reciprocally and enter into each other's lifeworld without losing their own. Adults who are responsive, empathic, and respectful of infants during the first years of life cultivate their ontological security and existential autonomy.

With insufficient validation, infants develop primary ontological insecurity. This is an insecurity of their most fundamental beings in which they feel fragmented, unreal, in danger of emotional annihilation, discontinuous, and dependent. Ontologically insecure persons have fragile places in the world and feel unworthy of living. They feel existentially dependent because their very being needs validation from others. Until we are existentially born through interpersonal acceptance, we need and seek affirmations of ourselves from others.

As an ontologically insecure infant grows up, he or she develops a false self as a protection against debilitating anxiety and rejection. The false self is a self-for-others, a self that corresponds to the imagined expectations of other people. Validation from parents is so important that children learn to hide and deny who they really are so that parents will love them. But, as a child develops a false self, the hidden, real self feels unacceptable and unlovable. Problems arise when the false self makes it increasingly impossible for the real self to be seen, understood, and accepted (Laing, 1959, pp. 39-61).

Some of us go through our entire lives without revealing our real selves. Most of us use intimate relationships to reexpose rejected and insecure aspects of ourselves in hope that our real selves can be loved. Within the context of loving relationships, our real selves burst forth, sometimes in chaos and anger, to seek love, understanding, and the right to live.

Our first experiences of being loved for ourselves occur in the parent-child relationship. Our first confirmations of being unacceptable, bad, shameful, and unworthy also happen in our interactions with our parents.

If parents are ontologically insecure and existentially dependent, they pass these wounds onto their children. Self psychologists Heinz Kohut (1977, 1984) and Alice Miller (1981, 1983) discuss how this transmission takes place. It begins in the childhoods of parents, grandparents, and great-grandparents.

The Child's Interpersonal Needs

Each generation of children shares common needs for human acceptance and validation. All children begin life with a healthy narcissism, a self-centeredness that enables them to be totally engrossed in their own impulses, needs, and desires. As infants and children, we are spontaneously ourselves, without delays or modifications. We coo, cry, babble, scream, smile, grasp, poke, kick, wiggle, look, and sneeze without any thought of being rejected for doing so.

Parents who respectfully attend to all aspects of the spontaneous child, mirror and echo the child back to itself. With empathic response from parents, the child can connect these different parts of the self and form a cohesive self, a self that remains whole across diverse experiences (Kohut, 1977, pp. 65-139). Through expression of all parts of the self, the child connects experience with behavior, and feeling with response to that feeling. A child who is respectfully and lovingly mirrored and echoed shows all of his or her self, enabling the child to form a cohesive self on which she or he can rely.

Parents who feel comfortable with their real, emotional selves can be receptive and responsive to the spontaneous infant or child. They can remain attentive, loving, respectful, and accepting as they interact with and take care of the exuberant, greedy, upset, or messy child. Being connected with their own needs, they can tolerate the emotional needs of the child. They can witness and learn about each aspect of the child without feeling attacked or negated. When children can be all of themselves with someone else, they gain an inner sense of self. This enables children to be aware of experiences and feelings and to trust themselves. Eventually, they feel self-confident, emotionally independent, and self-loving.

Miller (1981) believes that a child who is allowed to be self-centered, greedy, and asocial long enough will develop spontaneous pleasure in giving and sharing. If needs, desires, and expressions are received and respected, the child, in turn, will respond to other people with consideration and altruistic interest. A child who is related to with genuine interest and empathy will feel validated by interactions with others. By being treated thoughtfully and attentively, the child will learn how to be genuinely considerate of and sensitive to others.

When we are empathic with children, we look, listen, and respond to them. We do not pretend to be present or to trick or force them to conform to our wishes. Instead, we notice them as people who are separate from us. We learn from them, about them. We strive to be ourselves with them and to discover who they are.

Being sensitive and responsive to a child does not exclude taking care of one's own needs. Often, we imagine a wild and domineering child when we imagine a child who has not been trained in obedience, constraint, respect, and selflessness. It is as if the power struggle reverses and, as adults, we are the powerless pawns of the child. If the child does not obey us, we fear that we will have to obey the child. Miller (1981, 1983) believes that this either-or thinking reveals the parents' emotional wounds.

Adults who have not received emotional support for their needs and desires during childhood continue to long and search for it. If they have not found it by the time they are parents, they will seek validation of their spontaneous selves from their own children. They do to their children what has been done to them. Having been loved out of their authentic selves, parents try to regain their emotional freedom and power by making their children obedient to their wills. Children raised by such parents are ultra-sensitive to parents' needs, wishes, and values. They give up their emotional freedom and, instead, become people who validate parents. They sacrifice themselves to heal their parents' wounds and, in the process, become wounded themselves. Thus the legacy of emotional hunger and deprivation is continued.

Children are vulnerable to taking on these duties because of their position vis-à-vis their parents. Parents are all-powerful people in the lives of children. They control vital life functions and define reality. Bonded to parents and learning about themselves and the world through their parents' eyes, children are gullible, pliable, and loyal. They subscribe to the emotional expectations of their parents and internalize these as reality. Parents remain unaware of the injuries of their own childhoods by idealizing their parents and believing that the negations they endured were for their own good. By doing so, they protect themselves from feeling the pain of their injuries and develop a reason they can live with for passing these wounds on to their children (Miller, 1981, pp. 3-39).

The way out of this multigeneration emotional holocaust is for someone, parent or child, to notice and acknowledge whatever negations they have endured. When wounds have been acknowledged, the first steps toward emotional healing have been taken. Noticing what has happened to oneself is a way to regain emotional vitality and freedom.

If adults are able to look at their childhoods, to see what happened to their emotional selves, and to feel sympathy for their disappointments, sadnesses, and angers, they can recover from the invalidations of the past. Experiencing grief over what happened, when we were too small to prevent it, puts us in rhythm with our emotional selves. In doing so, we stand with the sad, angry, and ignored children within us and give to ourselves the understanding for which we longed. Acknowledging and mourning our losses and wounds enables us to recover from them.

Miller, a psychotherapist, believes that what happened to us is not what harmed us. Rather, the harm comes from being unable to know our experiences and our true feelings about them. Facing the negations of our spontaneous selves, seeing how our parents loved us out of ourselves to fulfill their emotional needs, and speaking about the resulting feelings help us recover from these rejections. Emotional disaffirmations that are acknowledged, empathically remembered, and reexperienced eventually heal. It is possible, then, for adults to recover from their childhoods. If they do not idealize their parents and the childrearing practices that harmed them, and if they recognize the emotional wounds from their childhoods, they can regain their emotional vitality. Then they will be able to listen to and learn about emotional life from themselves and their children (Miller, 1983, pp. 247-276).

Parents who use the hardship stories of their childhoods to manipulate children out of their emotional disappointments are in danger of perpetuating disconnections from their emotional selves and from their children. Author Russell Baker (1982) catches himself in this dilemma with his son. He writes:

> Children rarely want to know who their parents were before they were parents, and when age finally stirs their curiosity there is no parent left to tell them. If a parent does lift the curtain a bit, it is often only to stun the young with some exemplary tale of how much harder life was in the old days.
>
> I had been guilty of this when my children were small in the early 1960s and living the affluent life. It galled me that their childhoods should be, as I thought, so easy when my own had been, as I thought, so hard. I had developed the habit, when they complained about the steak being overcooked or the television being cut off, of lecturing them on the harshness of life in my day.
>
> "In my day all we got for dinner was macaroni and cheese, and we were glad to get it."
>
> "In my day we didn't have any television."
>
> "In my day . . ."
>
> "In my day . . ."
>
> At dinner one evening a son had offended me with an inadequate report card, and as I leaned back and cleared my throat to lecture, he gazed at me with an expression of unutterable resignation and said, "Tell me how it was in your days, Dad."
>
> I was angry with him for that, but angrier with myself for having become one of those ancient bores whose highly selective memories of the past becomes transparently dishonest even to small children. I tried to break the habit, but must have failed. A few years later my son was referring to me when I was out of earshot as "the old-timer." (pp. 6-8)

Parents who have acknowledged what happened to them, have felt their feelings about it, and have been heard and understood by a sympathetic person, are apt to be emotionally responsive to their children. They will be capable of listening to the thoughts and feelings of their children and be willing to learn about emotional life in general. These are vital skills for parents. They become even more important as children become adolescents.

Parents and Adolescents

When children become adolescents, the inequalities between parents and children narrow and the relationship approaches an equal one. Normal adolescents expect to be more responsible, dependable, and independent than they were as children. Similarly, parents expect to give more autonomy to adolescents and to respect their privacy and integrity while, simultaneously, monitoring their responsible use of freedom. Adolescence is a transitional period from childhood to adulthood in which both adolescents and parents want the adolescent to successfully attain adult skills and status.

Adolescents face important life tasks. They are in the process of defining the persons they are and will become. They must firm up the values that will direct their lives and the aptitudes and skills they can rely on to form viable work and personal relationships. They must make commitments to careers and relationships. These major life transitions bring adolescents face-to-face with their fears, ambivalences, and vulnerabilities as well as their hopes, desires, and strengths. Being in transition from childhood to adulthood, adolescents are moving out of an old life and self and are not quite established in a new one.

As adolescents clarify their identities and life values, they separate from parents and launch into their adult lives. Optimal separation involves adolescents clarifying their own preferences, interests, and choices and, in doing so, noticing how these are similar to and different from those of their parents. The adolescent, through interactions with adults and peers, constructs a viable and resilient self that both stands out as unique and fits in as shared. A self realized together with others has a secure place and purpose in the world.

Parents experience changes in their selves as adolescents grow into adults of equal status. If they have been successful parents, adolescents stop being children, leave home, and form other primary relationships. Letting go of adolescents while simultaneously remaining present to them and assisting them to leave is a difficult emotional task. Parents must be able to tolerate being left and to experience loss. Often, middle-aged parents are also facing the realities of their parents' aging and nearing death. Anticipating the loss of the generations above and below them makes parents question the meaning of their lives and experience their own uncertainties, problems, and longings.

Many shifts in the relationship between parents and adolescents are necessary as children move through adolescence into adulthood. Qualities that once made parents good parents—taking charge, teaching, and deciding—must be set aside. Increasingly, parents of adolescents witness who their adolescents are as people separate from them. Now, parents must cultivate giving up control, talking with and learning from their children, and respecting their decisions. They invite adolescents to be their equals. Their relationship fares well if parents and adolescents can recognize their differences, seek to understand themselves and one another, and give, take, and learn from each other as they grow and change.

Parents often have to reexamine and draw their values back into their own lives as adolescents differentiate. The process by which decisions are made and actions are taken becomes as important as its outcome. During this transition period, parents and adolescents must increase their understanding of one another as they are, rather than how they wish each other to be. They see each other's faults and blind spots and learn to take these into account as they interact.

A psychoanalytic expert in adolescent development, Peter Blos (1962) believes that generational conflict between parents and adolescents is an important life span task. Conflict highlights differences in values, preferences, morals, interests, abilities, and habits. Experienced differences increase people's differentiation from each other. Conflict that is not so extreme that it severs relationships stimulates the discussion and negotiation of needs. Talking and reasoning issues out together helps people know their views and values. Speaking and listening to each other generates new thoughts and insights and enables generations to learn from and change with one another. All contribute to and profit from this: Parents can tell adolescents how life has been lived, adolescents can tell parents how life can be lived. Both views are necessary for a full understanding of life. A self, thought out and discussed with significant others, is existentially autonomous and dialectically relational.

In this transition to a more equal relationship, parents may need to guide adolescents and to provide a safe haven for regrouping and for ingesting new awarenesses. Optimally, parents serve as touchstones and sounding boards. They offer alternative perspectives and interpretations that help adolescents orient to life events. As adolescents mature into emotionally healthy adults, they use parents to solidify their selves and to gain confidence in their abilities to develop viable life paths.

Parents and adolescent children rebalance power and vulnerability in their relationship. If all goes well, they negotiate a mutually respectful separation that includes sharing their independent lives with one another. They share individuality and, in doing so, readjust the giving and receiving and the teaching and learning between them. Old roles are updated, current personal needs and preferences are clarified, and new forms for interactions are co-created. These changes enable parents and young adults to share strengths, to assist one another empathically with weaknesses, and to gratify rather than justify their selves and lives.

Adult Children and Parents

As adult children mature, they step into paths similar to the ones their parents were walking while they were growing up. These new developmental events add to young adults' understandings of life by giving them a view of it from their parents' perspectives. Earning a living, maintaining important relationships, and developing a family of one's own rotate adult children through worlds similar to their parents' and help them understand things from a lived-through perspective. Each life event shared by young adults and parents makes their relationship deeper and richer. It helps them develop truly empathic understandings of one another.

If parents and adult children have developed and maintained respectful, honest, and loving relationships, they can enjoy the fruits of their labors as they grow older. Being able to be themselves with themselves, they can be themselves together and live separate but connected lives. Parents and adult children who can be honest with one another can revitalize their relationship by risking being who they are and desire to be. Daring to face each other in love, they see themselves and one another. They incorporate changes into their relationship and take the action necessary to keep it alive and vital. Loving themselves, they reach out to love one another.

Many adult children, however, are engaged in emotionally limited relationships with parents. They continue to believe messages from their childhoods; loving parents means not disappointing them, making them proud, and living according to their values. If these messages persist, adult children hide their real emotional selves from parents. Usually, they do so through lies of omission. They are not willing to risk the love they do have by being honestly themselves. Not being truly known and, thus, loved for their whole selves, they fear rejection and abandonment.

Most of us live with unsatisfying love rather than risk losing what we have by being more truthful. When parents and adult children use routines and rituals to avoid unpleasant and unsettled issues between them, they reaffirm unspoken secrets that erode intimacy. Adult children are exquisitely attuned to the edges of unsafe areas that will upset, anger, disappoint, hurt, or sadden parents, and can automatically slip around them. Miller (1983) believes that adult children who do this are caught in a web of earlier emotional damage; they negate their emotional selves in order to protect the physical and emotional well-being of the parents. Once caught in this inauthentic, habitual relationship, it takes every ounce of courage to shift the relationship to a more honest and emotionally open one. The time is rarely ripe to do so.

Sometimes, crises and painful events help parents and adult children expand their capacities to love, to understand, and to accept one another. If pain becomes unbearable, honesty may not be as frightening. The first step to establishing open communication is to notice privately what has been hidden, what has been too frightening to talk about, what unhealed hurts are still there. These are also the first steps toward emotional healing. When we can experience righteous anger over the emotional injustices that robbed us of ourselves, we stand with ourselves in sympathy and support. By doing so, we give to ourselves what we desired from our parents. Standing with ourselves, we can grieve our losses. Grief helps us realize what happened to us, in all its past and present ramifications.

Authentic grief does not lead to blaming our parents or ourselves. Rather, it leads to forgiveness. If children talk to parents about these emotional realizations and are met with guilt and blame, the relationship remains stalemated in defensiveness and fear. This perpetuates anger and guilt and reaffirms helplessness and blunted awareness. Then sadness, forgiveness, sympathy, and empathy cannot be shared, and the relationship remains truncated in self-justifications and resentments. True recovery occurs when parents and children can forgive one another for the wounds they unwittingly caused. One of the saddest events of life is for parents and adult children to love one another, to long for acceptance and acknowledgement for each other, and to never dare to seek it.

No time is right for increased honesty and emotional risk between parents and adult children. Children procrastinate because things are in transition, things are stable, things are going well, things are not going well, their parents are healthy and happy, their parents are sick and in pain. Many adult children hesitate to speak honestly with parents because they wish to protect them. They fear that honesty will traumatize parents and cause physical illness and even death. Miller (1983) believes that these fears reveal the original wounds: that free and spontaneous children will hurt and even kill parents. Miller places the pain, however, back in the parents' laps. She feels that any attempts at honesty are better than robbing the relationship of its emotional vitality. It is not the child who causes the parents' deepest pain. The child who dares to be himself or herself shows parents that their lives, too, could have been more honest and free. For Miller, this is the true cause of the parents' sadness, grief, and anger.

Our task, then, as parents and adult children, is to reveal ourselves as the people we are and are becoming. Based in mutual care, we give and receive love by being ourselves together and facing ourselves and each other as we are.

Noticing and working with the pain of our childhoods enables us to see ourselves and family members in a new light. This is so for 49-year-old Elizabeth, whose father is an alcoholic. Elizabeth has realized the emotional ways her father damaged her. She says:

> My father wasn't an obvious alcoholic. He was dysfunctional in ways that were hard to pin down. On holidays, for example, he'd either withdraw or be totally obnoxious. You could never be sure which way it'd go. But he wasn't loud even when he was obnoxious. He'd say really

hurtful and negating things in a soft, quiet voice. To this day, he can't tell me I've done something right. There wasn't one thing I did as a child that pleased him or was good enough for him. There was, and is, always something wrong with me.

As she has healed her bad feelings about herself, Elizabeth's appreciation of her mother has grown. Without any work with Twelve Step programs, her mother has escaped from these negating maneuvers. Elizabeth explains:

My mother's done some incredible things in her relationship with my father. I don't know, in fact, that she's ever acknowledged he's an alcoholic or even knows it. But she's figured out all the things I've learned in Al-Anon and Adult Children of Alcoholics groups; she detaches from him and doesn't take any responsibility for what he does. She'll say something when he's really being obnoxious, but she won't rescue or protect him. She has her own friends and does what she wants to do, with or without him. Over the last twenty years, she's become a person in her own right, who does the things she wants and needs to do.

Elizabeth is beginning to see her mother, now aged 75, as a resourceful, politically involved, and thoughtful woman. Their relationship has become an equal one between people who like and love one another. Elizabeth talks about the qualities she treasures in her mother:

One of the things I'm drawn to and amazed at about my mother is how accepting she is of everybody. It doesn't matter who you are—the janitor or the dean, young or old, rich or poor, famous or unknown, black or white, straight or gay—it doesn't matter. From the time I was in college, she's always loved me unconditionally and made it clear that the only person I needed to do anything for was myself. Whatever she gives me, she gives unconditionally; she never asks for anything in return.

We have interests in common like the fine arts, new restaurants, women's rights, and walking. Her politics have shifted a lot in recent years. We go for long walks and talk about such current events as the Supreme Court abortion issue. I don't know if she calls herself a feminist, but it's clear that our politics are much closer together now than previously.

As she and her mother age, Elizabeth is gaining a new appreciation of her mother as a person, rather than as just a mother. Clearly, relational shifts like these are gifts. Parents and children must both be emotionally available and courageous enough to do this empowering work.

Adult Children and Elderly Parents

As parents age, the inequalities of the parent-child relationship shift. Sometimes, the shift is a mirror image of infancy in which the child cares for the parent. Sometimes, both parties remain in the same roles, with each becoming more gentle and emotionally available. Sometimes, parents go to their graves still locked in battle with their children.

As parents grow old and approach death, numerous opportunities arise to mend relationships, to acknowledge the love so long desired, to heal old wounds, and to forgive negations that were sustained. Some parents continue the emotional battles of their lives even after death. Others manage to leave enough change and love in the wake of the emotional destruction they have waged to help survivors heal. Still others leave hearts and lives filled with the love they have given.

If relationships between children and elderly parents are honest and loving, little is left to do but to enjoy the relationship until parents die. Changes must be adjusted to, but relationships that have been truthful and close are flexible and supple. As it becomes evident that a parent will soon die, most of us discover that we cannot imagine life without our mothers or fathers. Having always been there either as a loving, neglecting, or abusing presence, parents are part of the cellular fabric of our lives. Even though many of us have pitted our strength against our parents, we, like Russell Baker in Chapter 8, prereflectively think of them as invincible and everlasting. When we realize they are frail and breakable, that they will die, we confront our dependencies upon them and face desires for their love and acceptance of us. It is easier to let go of a dying parent when we have gotten all we wished for from them.

Our task, as children of parents who are increasingly vulnerable, dependent, and needy, is to not do to them what they did to us when we were in these unprotected states. If we have healed from the negations of our childhoods, we can be "good enough" parents (Winnicott, 1965, pp. 145-146) to our parents as they breath their last breaths. We can help them let go of life and accept death. We can acknowledge the ways they harmed us, thank them for the gifts they gave us, bear witness to their pains and accomplishments, and say the last things that will put the relationship to rest for us.

When parents die, no matter how close or distant, resolved or unresolved the relationship, the presence of their absence creates a large hole in our selves and lives. No matter how much or how little we retain from our relationship with them, we miss them as they were or as we wish they had been and continue to carry them with us throughout the rest of our lives.

10

Friendship

In addition to relationships with parents, we develop intimate relationships with equals. Friendships are usually our first experiences of equal, close relationships. All of us have friends of one sort or another. During grade school or high school, many of us long for a special friend. Some of us find this friend early in life. Others of us are adults before we have a best friend. For many of us, our spouse is our best friend. For others, our best friend is someone separate from our lover or spouse.

Friendships form differently from parent-child relationships. They are chosen when eyes meet, and points of interest draw us to one another. During a shopping trip last summer, I witnessed a child's first experience of friendship.

Helene, her 2-year-old daughter Sarah, and I were wandering through a toy store. Realizing that Sarah was no longer with us, we doubled back and found her at the swing set, standing several feet away from four children who were somewhat older than she. Sarah told us that she could not come with us because she was playing with her "fwens." This was the first time Sarah had used the word, and Helene and I were delighted enough to back out of sight and watch. Sarah quickly forgot us and turned her attention to the children who were pushing each other on the swing. She stood, with her finger in her mouth, watching them intently. She never moved toward the activity but was clearly involved in it. The children did not look at or speak to her. The lack of an invitation to participate with these friends did not dampen the friendship for Sarah. She remained absorbed, from a distance, until her mother and I led her away. Later that evening, Sarah spontaneously told her father about her "fwens" at the store swing.

When situations like this occur, adults often dismiss them as accidental associations of words and experiences and decide that they must have taught their children to think of such people as friends. Usually, they smile benevolently and secretly congratulate themselves on the superiority of their adult friendships. After all, their friends talk to and occasionally play with them. But the phenomenologist would believe Sarah; these children were her friends. Taking Sarah's spontaneous use of "friends" seriously, I thought about the truth of her statement—one she obviously believed, for half a day, with all of her heart and soul. I realized that Sarah's first friendship was similar to my own. Sarah and I, indeed, say similar things when we call people our friends. We each are referring to people we enjoy being around, who are engaged in activities and relationships we value, whom we want to have more contact with, and with whom we share common interests. The main difference that my 46 additional years of living seems to make is that my friends and I have interactional skills that enable us to weave our lives closer together.

In their developmental model of friendship relationships, researchers Robert Selman and Annie Selman (1979) have discussed early friendships. Even though Sarah is younger than the children they studied, she and her friends fit into their first category, momentary playmates. Momentary playmates are friends defined by proximity, whose viewpoint is assumed to be like one's own, and who are valued for their possessions and physical attributes. As I pieced Sarah's experiences together, "momentary playmates" seemed to capture it. Selman and Selman assure me that Sarah's later friendships will be increasingly relational, reciprocal, and respectful of other people as beings separate from herself. "One-way assistance," in which Sarah will value friends for what they do for her, will turn into "fair weather cooperation" that is reciprocal and mutual. When Sarah is about 9 years old, her friendships will become exclusive and include "intimate, mutual sharing." Finally, the teenage Sarah will have a number of autonomous, interdependence friendships that include different degrees of closeness and dependency (Selman & Selman, 1979).

It is nice to know that Sarah's friendships will become richer, both psychologically and interpersonally. But, as I remember her intent, absorbed expression, I am hard pressed to imagine a more satisfying experience with friends. Indeed, for a few minutes at 2 years of age, Sarah reached deeply into the realm of friendship.

My experience with Sarah brings up memories of my own early friendships. One memory, of a particular telephone conversation with my friend Martine, is especially strong. It is a steadfast part of my girlhood even though it grows dim and sketchy as I age.

It is evening, and I am sitting in the living room of my parents' home very close to where I had built my card table house. But, now I am 13. I am sitting with the telephone receiver to my ear. Martine has called, and neither of us is talking. We sit in long silences. The feeling inside me is a delicious one. Enough time is available for everything—for silence, for gossip, for giggles, for complaints, for homework talk, for side conversations with family members. Martine understands, too; she is always still there when I say nothing for minutes on end. Only one problem exists: This is rural upper Michigan in 1955 and our phone is on a party line. Occasionally, my mother's friend Elsie, who lives up the road, breaks in to ask if we are still using the line. More occasionally, my mother remembers that Martine called me and yells, with escalating intensity, for me to get off the phone. Martine and I are contentedly unruffled by these interruptions; we continue to sit in silence, holding receivers tightly to our ears.

It always strikes me that this memory has no end; it does not terminate with me eventually and dutifully hanging up and letting Elsie make her call. I am certain I did. But the memory, of friendship with enough time and space for me to be myself, goes on forever in my heart and mind. Now, in northern California in 1991, it does not matter that Martine and I have lost contact long ago. Our phone conversation of silent and perhaps mindless, thick closeness remains intact.

Other, more recent conversations are not as gripping even though I can remember the content more vividly. One is the surprise call in the 1960s, when Martine told me, in a rich southern accent, about her new life in Florida. Another is the pictures of her daughter, sons, husband, and home in Florida that her mother and I giggled and told stories over in upper Michigan. Two years later came a short note from Martine herself, thanking me for my sympathy card when her mother died. All of these pieces are fragments of the continuous but broken line of our friendship. We now live at opposite ends of the country, in lives that are completely different. I no longer call Martine my friend; other friends are closer. But no one can replace the essence of friendship that hangs in my memory on that upper Michigan telephone line. It nourished and still nourishes my soul; it is even a touchstone for my work as a teacher and as a psychotherapist. On our recent shopping trip, Helene and I may have witnessed the first steps toward something similar for Sarah.

During my graduate training, I discovered that Harry Stack Sullivan had sensitively portrayed the special friendship between Martine and me. Sullivan (1953) believed that intimacy, generally defined as a dynamic concern for maintaining interpersonal contact of one sort or another, was a central motivation in life. He stated that the need for intimacy is so great that people will endure great anxiety to maintain contact with other people. When we are infants, intimacy takes the form of being cared for by our parents. We are close with other people by being dependent, helpless, and fairly passive. During childhood, our intimacy needs take the form of wanting adults to act as an audience for our actions and performances. We want people to be close by, to attend to things that interest us, and to act as an appreciative audience for our accomplishments. As we enter grade school, peers of the same age and sex become the focus of our interpersonal attention. We want to belong to a group of peers, to be chosen and liked, and to cooperate and compete with equals.

A shift into Sullivan's stage of preadolescent development occurs when we develop an interest in one particular, special friend. Sullivan thought that this chum is the same age and sex as oneself and that the one-to-one closeness happens before sexual interest arises in adolescence. This special friendship serves vital developmental purposes; it enables preadolescents to correct anxiety-ridden misconceptions about themselves and to cultivate a heartfelt concern for someone else's well-being.

In the sheltered moments that preadolescents spend together, they can risk letting down protections against anxiety. Sullivan believes that different selves are formed from interactions with significant others. Our "good-me" includes the aspects of ourselves that have been met with tender cooperation from others. These are the qualities of ourselves that we feel most comfortable with and that we are sure others will value and like. Within American culture, all of us feel comfortable and even proud that we are clean smelling, hard working, kind, successful, cheerful, and self-sufficient. Our "good-me" is the part of ourselves that we feel most comfortable revealing to other people.

All of us have a "bad-me" as well. These are the self-attributes about which other people have consistently made us feel mildly anxious. Although families and subcultures differ, common disapproval can be identified in any culture. Within the United States culture, many of us feel a little anxious or embarrassed if people think of us as lazy, mean, self-centered, unsuccessful, downwardly mobile, dependent, anxious, or ashamed. Because anxiety is uncomfortable, we try to avoid it. We do not, therefore, often disclose these attributes to others. We disclose the things about which we feel insecure, anxious, or embarrassed when we feel safe, accepted, and cared for by someone special.

Our first friendships provide corrective experiences for the "bad-me." Friends who spend extended time together reveal more and more aspects of themselves. Protective barriers weaken, unresolved and vulnerable parts of the self are exposed, and "bad-mes" are shared. For Sullivan, these "mes" are organizations of meanings that are interpersonally constructed and altered.

When two people spend private, safe time together, they can risk talking about uncomfortable aspects of themselves and their experiences. Usually, a good friend sympathizes, reassures, and talks about similar or different insecurities. Sometimes, a friend disagrees with negative self-evaluations and offers, instead, positive views of these qualities. The most helpful consequence of exposing the "bad-me" to a friend is that the person develops a more realistic view of the self than prior to the disclosure. Also, when insecurities are shared, a person feels less different from and more like other people. This feeling enables people to develop empathic understandings of the human condition, of their own lives and the lives of others.

As they get to know each other and renew their friendship, preadolescent friends develop reciprocal care. Caring as much for someone else's well-being as you do your own is an important intimacy skill. Sullivan believes that our first important friendships give us foundational experiences in revealing ourselves, caring for someone else, and feeling cared for in return. Eventually, these experiences help us develop a relational orientation in living, one that facilitates mutual, close, loving relationships (Sullivan, 1953, pp. 245-262).

Even though I have no memories of deep, exposing conversations with my friend Martine, Sullivan's formulations reverberate through my early friendship. More than in other parts of my 13-year-old life, with Martine I could drop my barriers and just be. That is why the memory of silent intimacy is so precious. Within a girlhood that was filled with achievement and talking and knowing right answers, silly half sentences and mindless giggles were sustenance for my soul.

Since Sullivan's writings were published, social scientists have learned much about friendship relations. At first, they focused upon interpersonal attraction, on what first attracts friends to one another. They discovered that we form friendships with people who are physically attractive, like us, are close to us in age, are of the same sex as we, live close by, have values and attitudes similar to our own, and are different from us in valued ways. Attraction, interest, or attention begins on some mutually important common ground. A potential friend touches the self and whispers hope of self-affirmation and self-development. In the 1980s, social scientists turned their attention from initial attractions to understanding the nature of ongoing friendships.

Perhaps because of my early memories of friendship, I was one of these social scientists who knew that friendship relationships were more than variables that would predict friendship choices. Numerous life experiences drew me to research on friendship: the loneliness of psychotherapy clients who did not have close friends, a long-term friendship with another graduate student, a new and deepening friendship with a woman colleague. I wanted to give an inside view of important, adult friendship relationships. At the time, no descriptive, structural models of friendship relationships existed, and I wanted to provide one.

I developed a phenomenological, structural description of important friendship relationships for women based on in-depth interviews with two sets of most important women friends. In Chapter 4, I used a summary of one woman's descriptions to illustrate the kind of data that result from phenomenological interviews. In this chapter, I will present my descriptive summary of an 8-year friendship between two women, Maud and Rosaline. These women were college seniors when I interviewed them. They were 21 years old, Caucasian, heterosexual, unmarried, and from middle-class backgrounds. They both lived in the greater Pittsburgh area. I followed the procedures described in Chapter 4 to arrive at an understanding of the nature of most important friendship relationships for women. First, let's look at excerpts of Maud's and Rosaline's descriptions to bring us into their experience of their friendship (Becker, 1987).

Maud's Description of Her Friendship With Rosaline

Rosaline is my best and closest friend. Our friendship is primarily a feeling and surpasses any words used to describe it. I cannot hold onto it, but it is there and it can be trusted. Through the years, it has grown between us and enriches my very being.

Our friendship involves a knowing and caring in which my soul is permitted to be; to shine or remain dull. Similar illusions and realities are shared along with laughter, tears, distance and closeness. We do not always travel the same road at the same speed, but our rhythm in being is on the same level. We go to the same school and many of our friends are the same, but Rosaline moves one way and I move another.

When I think of our relationship, I see Rosaline and I drinking coffee and talking. For me, Rosaline's eyes reveal her sensitivity, shyness, and stability. She is pretty flowers, gentle meetings, chocolate covered strawberries, being settled, mystical experiences, needing help, and delicate feelings. Her living is a clear, gentle, and cautious pouring out of herself to other people. My caring for her includes a sensitivity to who she is, enjoying her strengths and helping her with vulnerabilities.

Rosaline allows and encourages me to be myself. Sometimes that involves listening to me or watching me be restless. At other times it consists of disagreeing with me, challenging me, or spending time away from me. She knows my usual tactics of hiding myself from other people, so that even when we are emotionally distant I experience her presence. Our closeness remains constant, despite disagreements and physical separations. (pp. 63-64)

Rosaline's Description of her Friendship With Maud

There are moments in the quiet of some days when I sit back and remember what we are. We are friends, and it has been this way for as long as I can remember. Where shall I begin? How shall I describe a friendship of eight years, whose sweetness I am just learning to taste?

Our friendship remains what it is. It is itself. Each gives to the other what is hers and, in this, the friendship has the freedom to move freely and grow. It cannot be manipulated, calculated, or measured. It is like an unplanned path that is developing as we walk. We do not know where the path is leading, but it does not matter because it is a nice place to walk. It has room enough for each of us to do and be whatever we want and still remain in the relationship.

The steady uneasiness in the state of being alive calls me to my friend Maud. Maud is October, while I am April. Being different, we come together over cups of black coffee, and quiet conversations. Maud, as October, has a maturity that I lack. She is fall colors; golds, browns, purples, reds, and oranges. Having only falling leaves and grey, cold days to look forward to, she is filled with a calm loneliness. She knows that her emptiness will remain for a long time.

April, on the other hand, is just coming out of the ground. She is yellows and pale blues. Covered with rain and reaching toward the warmth and sun of summer, her roots and buds hold hope of maturity and fulfillment. Her restlessness is a happy unfinishedness.

In our friendship, Maud and I live in the same cycle, sharing the other's world while remaining ourselves. (pp. 64-65)

These excerpts give us a vivid, experiential view of Maud and Rosaline's friendship. They evoke our own experiences with friends and make us think about our different friendship relationships. From such descriptions as these, I developed a general view of friendship. This view provides a structural description of its essential components (Becker, 1987). First, I will present this description. Then, I will discuss each of its aspects. I hope my definition of friendship will deepen each reader's understanding of this important everyday phenomenon.

A STRUCTURAL DESCRIPTION OF FRIENDSHIP

Described structurally, friendship is a loving relationship between two people that develops in a world created by them. It is an ongoing exchange based upon attributes of care, sharing, commitment, freedom, respect, trust, and equality. Friendship relationships enable people to engage in their own pursuits, their friends' experiences, and other relationships. As such, friendship provides a context for people becoming themselves personally and interpersonally.

Now, I will look more carefully at the parts of this structural description.

A Loving Relationship

As a loving relationship, friendship is focused upon a special other person. A friend, especially a very important one, is known and loved as unique and irreplaceable. When I think of a friend, I am present to what I value about her or him, what he or she means to me, and what we have lived through together. The relationship is more than the specific things we have talked about or done. It transcends these events. A cherished human being, my friend, is the main subject of friendship. Discussions and activities are important, but the relationship cannot be reduced to them. Being with a friend is what is important; what we do together is secondary. For some of us, as Rosaline said so well, friendship is primarily a feeling that is larger than the words we use to express it. When I love my friend, I care for and feel close to him or her. Explicitly or implicitly, my life is connected with my friend, and I feel with her or him even when we are not together. I want to share my life with a friend, to know and be known by my friend. In love, I include my friend in my life, hoping for and trusting in a similar invitation.

Between Two People

To be intimate with someone else, we first must be willing and able to be intimate with ourselves. Being with oneself is a foundational element of friendship. I must be on friendly terms with myself if I hope to be and have a friend. The more I know, care for, and am present to myself, the more I can bring myself into a relationship. If

I do not spend time knowing myself and understanding my wishes and priorities, I bring an absence from myself to friendship. Friendship depends upon the presence of two people, people who are intimate with themselves. Their close relationship can grow and thrive when both friends are cultivating their individual selves. Friendship's intimacy is constructed out of the selves of its participants. Without these two selves being present and strengthened, the relationship will be undermined. Paradoxically, people must remain themselves to cultivate intimacy, but they also become themselves through the relationship.

A friendship depends upon two participants, but it cannot be found in either friend; friendship is created between friends. Even though all of us know that love occurs between two individuals, most of us have difficulty executing this "between" aspect of intimacy. Getting the right mix of closeness, without being too close, and separateness, without being too far away, is an unending task of life. The fact that friendship happens between people is one of its exciting but frightening qualities. Neither friend possesses the relationship, and yet both are necessary for its creation and survival. Although one friend cannot control the relationship, each can shift, jar, or affect it. Because the relationship happens between myself and my friend, I can never completely predict its events and meanings. Although it becomes familiar and trusted as it endures, it is always ready to become alive in new and unfamiliar ways.

The World Created by Friends

Friendship begins on some common ground: in humor, understanding, joint interests, shared stresses, common activities, or similar backgrounds. New acquaintances enjoy themselves together and, upon this foundation, begin to be friends. Their separate worlds touch at valued points of mutual interest, and they get to know one another. As sharing deepens and expands, differences are acknowledged and become important parts of the relationship. Friends create a collaborated world of meanings and experiences from time spent together. The world created between friends is an intimate space. Over time, tones, words, topics, and meanings are increasingly understood, taken for granted, and built upon. This shared world of activities, discussions, and meanings enriches time spent together and nourishes the relationship. It enables friends to know one another in depth. When a friendship is an important one, the shared world created between friends is a treasured touchstone of life. It enhances life and enlivens future plans and hopes.

Friendship's Ongoing Exchange

Being and becoming friends is an ongoing process. As a friendship develops, it becomes established; as it is established, it develops further. An important friendship is a dynamic point of stability in my life. I expect it to be there, but I am never completely sure what I will find.

A friendship becomes a valued and vital part of myself when it lasts through many years and situations. I know that it is there and that I can depend upon it. The history that my friend and I have together, things shared and lived through with each other, permeates present moments and stretches into the future. The relationship is ever-present: I cannot imagine life without my friend being part of it.

The relationship is established but also developing. It is becoming more of what it already is; it is changing and growing. In an alive friendship, something new is always happening: intimacy is deepening, understanding is shifting, and people are growing. Experiences right now confirm, change, and reestablish the friendship. My evolving exchange with my friend opens up the limits and possibilities of our relationship. We and our relationship are developing and moving into an unknown future. As our friendship lasts through time, it is established and defined but continues to grow and change.

Essential, Interrelated Attributes

Care, sharing, commitment, freedom, respect, trust, and equality are essential characteristics of close friendships. All are necessary components of the relationship; one is insufficient to make it a friendship. These foundational elements are part of all particular friendships. When the relationship is a close and important one, these qualities are clearly visible. Particular friendships contain some of these seven attributes more prominently than others. In one friendship, freedom may be focal. In another friendship, commitment may be highlighted. Over time, all of these qualities are evident; they are essential components that make a relationship a friendship.

Friendship's structural attributes are interrelated and interdependent. For example, trust, care, and commitment are built through sharing and equal exchange. When I care for my friend, I want to show myself to him or her. My friend's gentle listening while I talk about vulnerable parts of myself makes me love her or him more than before. Also, it makes me want to listen with the same presence, care, and respect. Woven together, the essential constituents of friendship compose its integrated nature.

Care

Care is what we speak when we say, "I love you." When I care for my friend, I am concerned about him or her as a valued, special person. My friend's day-to-day and long-range welfare matters to me, and I want to share in and enhance his or her life. In care, I like my friend, want to know and understand her or him. I wish to share my life with my friend. Even though my care is focused on my friend, it is filled with myself. When I care, I bring all of myself with me and offer it, without restriction, to my friend. I want to be good for my friend, a positive addition, an affirming and enriching presence.

My friend's well-being is important to me, as important as my own. When his or her life is troubled or pained, I feel it, too. I want to make my friend's sorrow disappear. But I cannot always do so. The ache of loving a friend who is in pain can be more excruciating than dealing with my own stress and sadness.

Usually, care is a positive, desirable feeling. When I care, my heart opens, and I am involved with and connected with someone I love. But care can also be a difficult emotion. I can care too much. I can be beside myself with grief, anger, or worry when the friendship is not working smoothly or when my friend's life is troubled. Care opens me to aspects of life that are out of my control. In care, I am there and vulnerable to life's unexpected twists. Care for my friend implicates me in the pains, as well as the joys, of someone else's life. Although I can sometimes help, more often I can only be present, listen, and try to understand.

Sharing

Sharing between friends gives the relationship its detail, depth, and breadth. As friends get to know one another, they talk over and live through increasingly important aspects of their lives. Friends define the range and the limits of their closeness through the topics discussed and the activities undertaken. As the relationship continues, the boundaries of the relationship are reaffirmed or expanded.

When people bring more of themselves into the relationship, they extend the world they share and intensify the relationship. As trust deepens, sharing expands. Rather than running out of things to say and do together, good friends find more and more to say and do together.

Friends reach behind social convention as they are honest and reveal personal opinions, meanings, feelings, memories, and hopes to one another. Whatever they do and say defines and cultivates their personal relationship. Friendship does not deepen without risks being taken. Even in well-established friendships, sharing more personal and vulnerable aspects of oneself is risky. A risk that some part of oneself will be rejected, judged, or devalued is always possible. Fears of rejection recede as risks succeed and the care between friends is affirmed. A shared assumption of open and honest exchange is taken for granted, trusted, and treasured as the friendship grows and endures.

Commitment

Commitment, lived through and talked about, is a vital part of friendship. At some point in the relationship, friends experience their importance to each other. They speak about their pleasure in being friends and express hope that the friendship will continue. When they acknowledge and validate their relationship, friends establish an interpersonal tie upon which they can depend. For friendship to thrive, the participants must say yes to it and each other. They must promise to nurture the relationship by setting aside time together. When I commit to a friendship, I make it a priority in my life and pledge to stay with my friend through hard, as well as easy, times.

Commitment, given freely and with love, is a gift that cannot be controlled. My own or my friends' commitments cannot be mandated, they happen between us. Although each can influence the decision to be friends, neither can form the relationship alone. Our commitments to be friends are priceless precisely because they cannot be manipulated or earned; they are gifts that extend beyond our efforts.

When I agree to be someone's friend, I reach beyond myself and link my life with hers or his. Our mutual agreement, that we are friends, situates us in the interpersonal world and establishes a place we belong. Reciprocal commitment cradles and complements our individual lives. By saying that we are friends, my friend and I agree to be and become ourselves together. In doing so, we experience one of the deepest pleasures of life: being a friend and having a friend with whom to share life.

Freedom

Freedom is also an essential part of friendship. No matter how close and committed friends are, freedom is always a part of friendship. Along with commitment, freedom is equally essential to the relationship. Whereas commitment highlights the importance of two friends joining together, freedom emphasizes the importance of the separateness of friends. Friendship depends upon the participants remaining themselves and living lives that are independent from the relationship. In friendship, people are themselves, together.

Ideally, close friendships provide enough room for the participants to be and to become themselves. Within the boundaries set by commitment and care, the development of each individual strengthens the relationship. Being free, friends come to, but also go away from, one another. When friends know that their relationship is a strong and primary one, they are more apt to not try to hold onto each other. Acknowledging and confirming each friend's freedom nourishes the friendship. As friends evolve and grow, they bring these changes into the relationship. They rechoose to be involved with one another, renegotiate the limits and possibilities of the relationship, and reassess its meaning and importance in their lives.

Although good friends know, anticipate, and depend upon each other, they are never completely within each other's grasp.

No matter how long-lasting and secure the relationship is, it remains a breakable creation between them. Each friend is always, implicitly or explicitly, free to not be a friend. This freedom gives the relationship a fragility for which the friends must care. Even though its strength increases as it endures, friendship remains a vulnerable co-creation. Neither friend can make it invincible, but both can contribute to its endurance and vitality. A treasured friendship rests upon freedom, as well as commitment.

Respect

Respect between friends is based upon their separate selves and lives. In respect, friends recognize and value each other as individuals. Friends who respect one another value their differences, as well as their similarities.

Realizing that they cannot live a friend's life for them, friends learn about and bear witness to each other. They attend and adjust to each other's opinions, values, habits, strengths, and problems. Each attempts to understand the other on her or his terms and to see the integrity of choices and actions. Even though friends may disagree, they do not interfere or intrude upon one another. Implicitly believing in each other's integrity, friends give support to each other wherever possible. They disagree, when necessary, to preserve their own integrity. Respect involves finding the right balance between support and truth, presence and advocacy, challenge and care.

Trust

Trust lets friends feel safe with one another. When they trust each other, friends let down protective barriers and relax into being themselves. As they feel safe and expect emotional support, friends are able to be themselves together. They can show vulnerable aspects of themselves because they can depend upon kindness and gentle understanding. As trust builds, the freedom to be one's self expands. Being certain that I can count on a friend encourages me to trust him or her even more than before. As friends live through both troubled and fun-filled times, they believe that their relationship will last. Increasingly, friends depend upon the friendship being there for them and are confident of a safe haven within which they can rest from life's stresses. Trusting one another, friends call upon each other in times of need. They ask for help and expect their interests and causes to be upheld. As trust builds, friends can take for granted mutual support, acceptance, benefit, and help.

Equality

Equality is the last essential attribute of friendship. Being equals, friends are peers upon important dimensions of life. They are matched in their ability to make valuable contributions to each other's life and development. When friends are equals, they are in comparable places in the progression of their lives. Based upon who they are, they offer something of importance to one another. If they are at different developmental levels, their strengths and needs are complementary. Each gains something of worth from the relationship.

Friendship's equality is evaluated experientially. What may look like an unequal relationship to an observer may be experienced by the participants as one of mutual benefit. Over time, friends experience a balance of giving and receiving. In contrast to less personal, more utilitarian relationships, the give and take between friends is not carefully calculated and tabulated. Friends give to one another openhandedly and trust that their generosity will be appreciated and eventually returned. Acceptable exchanges, balanced over time, sustain the friends' reciprocal commitments and care. They assume that the relationship is a mutually enjoyable and beneficial one.

Personal and Interpersonal Enrichment

Friendship relationships provide a loving context for personal and interpersonal development. The love that friends have for one another nourishes and affirms individual lives and heartens involvement in the lives of others.

The personal benefits of friendships are many: feeling special, being accepted and cared for, knowing someone is interested in understanding your pain, as well as your dreams. Within the supportive environment of a friendship relationship, people can appreciate and validate themselves. They can gain the encouragement to be themselves and to risk becoming whom they wish to be. A close friendship is self-affirming; it returns people to themselves and their own growth process.

Individual lives are also expanded and deepened through friendship relationships. My friendships are heart connections to other people; they provide me with interpersonal anchors in life. My care for a close friend motivates me to stretch beyond my self-centered concerns so that I can be with her or him. When someone else's well-being matters to me, I try to stand with and assist her or him. By participating in a friend's experiences, interests, and concerns, I broaden my perspective and gain a different view of life. Traveling into another's lifeworld changes and enriches my life. I gain a sense of myself as loving and giving, as well as someone who is treasured for who I am.

Close friendships are intimate without limiting involvement in other kinds of intimate relationships. Although prioritized, friendships are not exclusive. In friendship, people remain separate people. The relationship can be a touchstone for exploring other relationships, those with sexual partners, parents, and children. Important friendships renew hope in satisfying intimate relationships that affirm the participants. If satisfying and successful, friendships open people's hearts to love.

11

Friendship Families

Even though we rarely talk about it, friends can be important members of our families. When we say that someone is "family," we mean that, symbolically or literally, our connections are deep and lasting ones. We inherit blood ties and cannot choose to make or break them. But we also develop relationships based upon emotional preferences and mutual choices, those with spouses and friends, that are as or more intimate than those with biological family members.

Loving someone and being loved back is a dream all of us work to actualize. Even when we find a primary sexual partner, the person who is "the one for me," we need a community of people who love us. This community, this family, is a support system that enables dyadic intimacy to thrive and last. Most of us have an inner picture of our dream family, a family that lasts through time and makes life worth living. Although loneliness, loss, and disappointment can never be completely outdistanced, the longing to love and be loved, to be part of a loving family, is at the heart of life.

As people leave their families of origin, move to new areas of the country, fall in and out of love, make and maintain friendships, commit to life partners, and birth and raise children, they create lasting interpersonal ties. These networks, which include friends as often as

AUTHOR'S NOTE: The author expresses appreciation to *The Humanistic Psychologist* for premission to reprint this chapter that was originally published as follows: Becker, C. S. (1991). A phenomenology of friendship families. *The Humanisit Psychologist, 19*, (2), 170-184.

kin, are vital mixtures of intimacy. Based upon mutual commitments and care, these families of people who love one another are sustained by emotional preferences and tacit agreements that enable members to be and become themselves.

In this chapter, I explore one such intimate group: friendship families. Looking more closely at friendship families will illuminate the essential qualities of the experience of family. First, I introduce you to two women and their friendship families. One woman, Claire, has numerous families of friends. The two that we meet are the Brunch Bunch and the Lunch Bunch. The other woman, Elizabeth, who told us about her renewed relationship with her mother in Chapter 9, will invite us into a work-centered friendship family and a friendship family consisting of an ex-lover and a couple who supported Elizabeth and Kristin through the ending of their lover relationship. Second, I discuss the essential components of friendship families.

As you read through the descriptions and essential components of friendship families, ask yourself the following questions: Are these experiences like mine? How do my experiences of friends as family differ from what is here? How is intimacy with friends similar to and different from that with biological families? Do friendship families differ for men and women, people of different ages, racial and ethnic backgrounds, sexual orientations, and life-styles? These questions will help you use what I present to know more about friends you consider family. Your answers will help you formulate the central components of intimate relationships with parents, children, friends, and sexual partners.

The working definition of friendship families I begin with is as follows: A friendship family is a group of people who give each other emotional support and sustain one another through important life events. They have made commitments to developing, maintaining, and renewing their relationships over time.

In that their relationships are not primarily sexually focused, members of friendship families are not lovers. They also do not include people from biological family groups.

I begin the exploration of friendship families by looking at an event in Claire's life.

Claire's Friendship Families

A DREAM THAT CAME TRUE

It is a sunny June morning in Hayward, California. Just 1,000 graduates, plus their loved ones, are gathered to witness each graduate's walk across the outdoor stage to receive his or her degree. An old woman wearing a tiara instead of the usual mortarboard rises from her wheelchair and, with the help of a cane, walks forward to receive her bachelor of arts degree. The young man next in line whispers something to the announcer, and "Claire is 74 years old" booms across the crowd. In a standing ovation, 10,000 people rise to cheer Claire.

This in itself was a special moment. But for those people in the audience who knew Claire personally, it was filled with many layers of meaning and celebration. For her sister, children, grandchildren, and a number of friendship families, Claire's graduation was a spiritual triumph in the face of death.

An hour before Claire received her diploma, JoAnn, her friend for 41 years, had given Claire a gift box with the tiara inside. As Claire stood gasping at the jewels sparkling against the red velvet, JoAnn said, "Put it on. You've earned it. No more stars. Only diamonds and pearls now."

JoAnn and Claire had talked about stars for decades. During one of Claire's many hospitalizations for hip surgery, JoAnn, a Catholic, told Claire, a Jew, to think of her pain as another star in her spiritual crown of glory. Through the years, as Claire had a hysterectomy, a double mastectomy, asthma, angina attacks, a heart attack, an appendectomy, and broken bones from a car accident, JoAnn's refrain of "another star in your crown" became a way for them to talk about the pain and love between them. When Claire was diagnosed with leukemia, in the same month that her husband, Saul, was diagnosed as having Alzheimer's disease, Claire told JoAnn, "Enough is enough. No more stars. I'm seeing stars."

The tiara was a symbol of all the pain, hope, and love that had passed back and forth between the women and their families over the years. It was also JoAnn's celebration of Claire's triumph in earning a much-longed-for college degree.

THE BRUNCH BUNCH

Claire's dream of a bachelor's degree became a concrete plan when her medical doctor told her to get involved with something she had wanted all of her life, as her reward for coping with leukemia and Saul's illness. At the age of 69, she registered for fall classes at the community college near her home. She enrolled in freshman English and a women and society class. The women's studies class was where she met the group of friends who sustained her through her associate of arts and her bachelor of arts degrees.

This group of five women that was eventually named the Brunch Bunch has been a friendship family for 5 years. The group began as a study group for the class midterm. Class lectures, assignments, and pressures acted as the foundation for the group. Then the women found other connecting points among their diverse lives. After the class ended, they met once a month for brunch, at first rotating through each person's home and then meeting at restaurants.

For Claire, the other women in the group, all in their late 20s and 30s, are stimulating additions to her usual relationships with family and friends. She was the last of them to finish her bachelor's degree, and the Brunch Bunch was there to witness and celebrate with her. Ann, who now lives in Illinois with her husband, flew in for Claire's graduation. Jessica, who divorced and came out as a lesbian while finishing her undergraduate degree and entering graduate school, was there with her lover. Gretchen, who had begun and ended a difficult business partnership with her husband's best friend during those 5 years, came with her husband and children. Samantha, now in her second year of veterinary school, came to town for the day. Each member of the Brunch Bunch had shared deep parts of her life with the others. All of them had helped each woman become a little more of who she wanted to be.

The Brunch Bunch formed an intergenerational family that supported and encouraged each woman as she actualized her educational dreams. As a diverse group, the women benefited from their different ages and life-styles. They solved common and individual problems, traded personal wisdom they had acquired through life experiences, and played together. They surrounded each other with a circle of commitment and care. Claire summarizes the meaning of this friendship family in the following way:

> The Brunch Bunch fills a void in my life. It takes the place of my older friends who have stagnated. I feel stimulated, on a par with them even though we're very different ages and have diverse life-styles. None of us has many members of our nuclear families living in the area. We fill in for the lack of those relations.
>
> Over the years, we traded knowledge, did homework, went to Tahoe together, gambled, talked about our children and our parents. There have never been any judgements about our differences and everyone has always had a right to her opinions. We do everything anyone could do to help—we sympathize, empathize, support. Then, we accept and respect whatever the person decides or does. We don't judge each other for who or what we are; we concentrate on how much we love one another and how we can express, deepen, and expand that love.

This friendship family has helped each woman accomplish her educational goals. In the process, the women have woven bonds that seem strong enough to sustain their family ties as each continues on her individual life path.

THE LUNCH BUNCH

A second friendship family, the Lunch Bunch, also attended Claire's graduation. The Lunch Bunch is another group of five women that has been together for 25 years. All of the women were members of the city choral group when Claire went to audition. She heard a familiar Boston accent in the alto section, and with "You're from Boston." "So are you," the friendship between Dalia and Claire began. All the women were married when they met. Three—Dalia, Estelle, and Violet—are black, and Dorothy and Claire are white. Eastern, Southern, and Western regions of the United States are represented among them. Their religious affiliations are Jewish, Catholic, Lutheran, and Baptist.

The friendship among these women began during breaks in choral practice when they kidded and laughed about Dalia's and

Claire's accents. Then they talked about their husbands and children. When Estelle and Dalia had babies, Claire knitted blankets for each baby and was a stand-in for geographically distant grandmothers. Once a white, Jewish woman had been accepted as the grandmother of black, Catholic, and Baptist baby boys and girls, differences among them were never a barrier. As individual members left the chorus, the women made a commitment, regardless of what was happening in their busy lives, to meet for lunch on the second Saturday of each month.

Initially, their involvements in the city chorus and their families gave them a common denominator. As their history together grew, it expanded to include more and more aspects of themselves, their loved ones, and their lives. The group talked of problems with children, career stresses and changes, and illnesses. Eight years ago, they instituted an event in December to which their spouses were invited. When Violet's husband got promoted while she was in Europe studying voice, they gave him a party. When Claire needed a ride to the hospital at 3 o'clock in the morning, Dalia took her. When Estelle wanted to talk about a problem with her son, they listened and offered advice. When Saul was in the last stages of Alzheimer's disease, they discussed euthanasia. They have continued through the thick and thin of life, to talk and to be there for one another. Claire explains:

> We talk about everything. We get into hot discussions about lots of things, but nobody gets offended, nobody gets insulted. Everyone is a grown-up and has a right to her opinions and beliefs. If I need help, or I'm doubtful about a decision, I bring it up and we talk about it. Everyone expresses themselves and we leave it open and give the person the room to decide what they want to do. All the problems stay in the group. After talking for so many years, we're usually in agreement about many things. But our differences remain. And each of us knows that the others can be called upon for anything at any time.

The Lunch Bunch is a group that is closed to outsiders. No one, no matter how close they are to one member, can come to lunch more than once. Their common beginning in the chorus group stands firm and no one can catch up on their shared history. While they tell each other everything, everything they say also stays in the group. In addition to the regular monthly lunch, some members meet separately.

But, there are no secrets among them. The friends' caretaking extends to spouses and children, but the relationships among the women remains central.

Elizabeth's Friendship Families

The second woman we meet is Elizabeth, a 49-year-old lesbian who lives in a small, picturesque, New England college town. Elizabeth is a carpenter and an artist. She invites us into two important friendship families: a work friendship family, and a friendship with a lesbian couple.

THE WE'LL TRY ANYTHING COMPANY

The We'll Try Anything Company is an independently owned small construction and renovation business. The owner, Karen, as well as its two employees, John and Elizabeth, are gay. All are in their late 40s. Elizabeth has worked with the company for three and a half years; it has become one of her important families. A number of things have made Elizabeth, Karen, and John a friendship family.

Their shared gay identity draws Elizabeth, Karen, and John close to one another. They spend at least 40 hours a week together and, during that time, all of them can stop worrying about protecting themselves from homophobic stereotypes. They can be spontaneous, open, and easy with the details of their everyday lives when they are not being careful about their sexual orientation. Elizabeth explains:

> Nobody has to think about what they're saying because we all know we're gay. We spend more time together than we do with our partners, so we really get to talk a lot.
> We get to talk about the immediate problems of our lives, all day long, everyday. They're the people who are there for me every single day to listen to all the little things, to talk about what I'm going to do now, or to make suggestions on a day-to-day basis. We probably know more about each other's lives than other friends, who we talk in greater depth with, but only see occasionally.

This work family is a support network that is available on a consistent basis.

The members of the We'll Try Anything Company work efficiently and smoothly together. They all have the same amount of life experience and skill and are well matched in the pace at which they work. Their areas of expertise complement each other; Karen is the organizer, John is the electrician, and Elizabeth is the carpenter. But they all know a little about each other's area. This knowledge enables them to talk out and think through problems together. They act as a resourceful team without challenging each person's area of authority. Because they all love to learn from solving problems that provoke creative solutions, all of them are, indeed, willing to try any job. Each member is flexible, versatile, and resourceful.

John, Karen, and Elizabeth help each other through the horrendous parts of their work by making terrible jobs fun. Cleaning out and repairing student apartments is one of the staples of the company, and they encounter unimaginable horrors. Finding ways to joke and make games out of the work eases such tasks as taking water drenched, moldy sofas to the dump; cleaning mustard paintings off walls; and emptying apartments filled with abandoned personal possessions. The friends build enjoyment by imagining the circumstances that resulted in the conditions they have to correct. They offer emotional support to each other through their use of imagination and humor. As they joke, they work efficiently with synchronized divisions of labor that do not have to be spoken or planned.

All the members of the We'll Try Anything Company can tolerate not knowing what the next job will be or exactly how long it will take. The employees are salaried, and neither John nor Elizabeth worries about whether they are working more hours than they should. But, they also know that Karen will understand when they have to be late for work. Karen gives and they give; it all balances out over time. Recently, Elizabeth broke up with her lover, and when Karen heard that she needed a place to stay, the first words out of Karen's mouth were, "You can stay with me. Don't worry about it." If one of them needs something that the others can help with, they will give it. All of them have done and will do that for each other. Elizabeth cannot imagine life without daily contact and conversations with Karen and John.

THE ELIZABETH, KRISTIN, DIANNE, AND RACHEL FAMILY

Another of Elizabeth's friendship families is a group that consists of her ex-lover, Kristin, and a couple, Dianne and Rachel, who have been their friends for 10 years. Elizabeth and Kristin were lovers for 8 years. They broke up 2 years ago. Now they are settling the final details of the properties they owned jointly. They are definitely not lovers, and, as ex-lovers, Elizabeth and Kristin are not yet friends. They are, however, still family to one another. Elizabeth considers Kristin, along with Dianne and Rachel, part of a small family group. She explains:

> Since Kristin and I stopped living together and being lovers, we don't have the same expectations of each other. We do what we want and don't try to control one another. That helps us let go of the angry, painful tugging that was so prominent near the end of our relationship. Now we come together in the places where things were good between us. As ex-lovers, we even argue better.
>
> Now that Kristin and I aren't lovers, our lives are diverging more and more. But we've been a family, and I want to salvage that bond between us. We've shared so much of ourselves with each other and have lived through so many crucial events together. It's very important for me to stay connected to that.

The two couples shared a two-family brownstone in New Haven during the first 5 years of their relationships. Dianne and Rachel are the only close friends who have managed to stay friends with both Kristin and Elizabeth during their breakup. This in itself is reason enough for Elizabeth to consider them close family members. She says:

> Rachel and Dianne are the two people who have consistently stayed with Kristin and me over the two years it's taken to complete our breakup. When we were in the middle of feeling really hurt with each other, Dianne and Rachel could talk with both of us. Sometimes they had to talk to us separately. Sometimes they could spend time with us together. Dianne, especially, was good at helping me see my piece in what I was upset about. At the same time, she didn't put either of us down.
>
> Rachel and Dianne both made it very clear that there were no sides and that they wanted to remain in both of our lives. When it became less and less possible for us to continue as lovers, they refused to get caught

in the middle. They said, "We love you both. We want to stay close to both of you." And they have. It was so important that they did that. They knew us both and could help us hold onto the relations among the four of us.

In the years before Kristin and Elizabeth separated, the four women supported each other through a number of losses. During those 8 years, Elizabeth's grandmother died, both of Kristin's parents died, Kristin almost died from an emergency appendectomy, Rachel's oldest son was killed in an automobile accident, and Dianne's father died and her mother entered a nursing home with Alzheimer's disease. Having lived through so many tragedies together, the women have deep bonds with one another. They have gone through and discussed some of the hardest parts of life together. Elizabeth reminisces:

> The four of us really bonded together through those crises. We talked and acted in ways none of us had ever done before. I learned to talk about and listen to feelings. We could be depressed and be together, and it was all right to do that. We created a safe place for each other. Just yesterday, Dianne called to ask if I wanted to go with her to visit her mother in the nursing home. There aren't many people she'd ask to do that.
>
> These women are going to be there for me no matter what happens. They're people I feel that I can say whatever I need to say to; they're not going to disappear from my life if I get angry. It's clear, too, that whatever I say doesn't get repeated. Those things are not as clear with my mother and my sister. I feel safe with Kristin, Dianne, and Rachel around feelings, and know that they accept me as I really am.
>
> Dianne, Rachel, and Kristin are all people that I could ask to do something for me if I needed it. They might say "no," but it's still okay to ask. I know they'll do the same. We don't count who does what for whom, it all balances out. We all get back as much as we give.

Besides experiencing major losses together, Elizabeth, Kristin, Dianne, and Rachel are interconnected in other important ways. All of them own and love dogs. They have spent hours talking about dogs, and they love each other's dogs as much as their own. They take care of each other's animals and can travel with greater ease knowing that their dogs are getting loving care and attention.

The four women also have wonderful fun together. They all love to camp and travel and have stayed in some beautiful places together. Each woman has been an avid reader since childhood, each reads constantly, and they exchange books and discuss them. Rachel has published several books, and the friends have edited and critiqued each of them. Elizabeth takes special pleasure in finding a book that she knows all of them will like and looks forward to everybody reading and discussing it.

In addition to sharing many interests, the friends are good at being in the same place and doing different things. Elizabeth gives an example:

> Dianne owns a cabin in Maine, and the four of us often spend a week there. It's a small cabin, so it would be easy for us to get on each other's nerves. But, we're really good at doing separate things while we're together. I might be working on a sculpture or a drawing; Rachel might be editing a book; Kristin might be playing music; Dianne might be reading. That feels really special to me. We're very at ease being with ourselves and not talking to one another when we're together. There aren't a lot of people I can say that about.

This friendship family has witnessed the hardest parts of life together. Through it all, they have held onto their relationships with one another and have constructed a family that, it seems reasonable to expect, can last through anything life can offer.

The Essential Components
of Friendship Families

A friendship family is a dependable group of people who care for one another and have made commitments to maintain and develop their relationships. These relationships have lasted through difficult periods of life and have been a source of comfort and strength to each person in times of need. Friendship families are nourished by collective memories of irreplaceable life events and personal changes that have been experienced together. Reciprocal generosity, steadfast support, and equivalent and synchronized growth and change are essential qualities of friendship families.

I will look more carefully at each part of this essential structure.

MUTUAL CARE

Friends who are family to one another have close, intimate relationships that they have constructed out of emotional preferences and personal choices. They love and appreciate each other as special people. Through mutual care, they have established heart connections that make them primary in each other's lives. Their connections, through love, place them in each other's lives, to fill voids, to unearth longings, or to actualize dreams.

Through care, lives become intertwined. Friendship family members are concerned about each other's well-being and life events. Mutual care matches love with love, giving with giving, and asking with asking. In care, friends open themselves and their lives to each other and hope for comparable invitations. Caring for one another, they witness and enrich life together.

Experientially, I bring all of myself to my friends and offer it, without restriction, to them. My friends do the same. Being a family of friends, we care for one another by expressing feelings and exchanging affection. We take care to caretake in loving ways, in ways that assist and strengthen each other. This interconnects the pains and joys of our lives. Care ties me to a network of supportive and loving relationships that helps me live through the unexpected, painful twists of my life. But it also leaves me vulnerable to the grief and worry that enters these people's lives. In care, friendship family members are available to one another, to celebrate life's joys and to endure life's pains, surrounded by their love for one another.

PRIORITIZED COMMITMENTS

Friendship families are based upon promises to maintain and develop relationships with one another. Commitment involves saying yes to these particular people. As friends, we say yes to knowing each other and to being in each other's lives. Members of friendship families make room in their lives for one another. They pledge to invest in and nurture their relationships with emotional and physical participation. They agree to do this in dialectical ways, matching levels of investment and involvement.

When friends commit to being family to one another, they honor what they have shared together and affirm desires to be present in each other's future lives. Implicitly and explicitly, they agree to preserve and protect their relationships in the face of life's pressures and intrusions. They promise to work with problems that arise so that their relationships remain honest, clear, and dependable points of contact. Mutual commitments involve letting oneself be seen and known. Family members agree to let each other enter their lives and to know their settled and unsettled evolving selves. They cultivate an honest, nonjudgmental, and safe place to be and to become themselves.

By making prioritized commitments to one another, friends create bonds that tie them together and hold them close. Further, these commitments construct a boundary between themselves, as a group, and other important people. This boundary not only defines the group and helps it coalesce, but it separates it from and links it to each person's social world. Within the group, the friends' commitments to each other include respectful acceptance of each person's commitments outside the group. By association, the important players in each person's life are part of the friendship family. Members honor each other's important involvements and do what they can to enhance these life commitments.

COMPARABLE GROWTH AND CHANGE

Friendships begin in aspects of life that are mutually salient to the participants. On this common ground, friends begin to weave their lives together. Sharing interests and values enhances important parts of individual lives. It also builds a common life among friends. As they complete valued projects and accomplish personal changes together, friendship family members solidify their loyalties to one another. Together, they wake up to themselves, others, and life.

Although close friends do not have to be involved in the same dimensions of life, they do have to be equally involved in learning and growing into themselves and the lives they have chosen. Across their differences, they are matched explorers of life. If all of them are engaged in life in ways that are mutually respected and valued, this comparability enables them to accompany each other as partners. Being equally engaged in growing and learning, they can assist and support each other.

Individual growth and change are normal parts of healthy intimate relationships. If each friendship family member is actively involved in her or his life, the relationships among them remain vital. Being active participants in their own lives, they bring personal insights and problems to the friendship.

SYNCHRONIZED MOVEMENTS

Evolving in comparable ways, friends keep in step with one another. They stop, turn, return, and move forward together. Being reciprocally responsive, they share the movements of their lives. Shared rhythms of resting, remembering, exploring, risking, and reaching settle them into the depths and expanses of their lives.

Moving through life together, friendship family members return to themselves as they circle through each other's lives. Wanting to accompany one another, friends move into uncharted territory and come to the edges of themselves. In love, they reach beyond where they are, to be with, to see, and to understand each other. In love, they become bigger than they imagined they could be. Being with one another, they step off their edges into their becoming selves. Seeing, they respond. Responding, they see. Seeing, they become. Becoming, they are themselves. In rhythm, family members rest and stretch together and, in doing so, enter inner chambers of their beings.

Friendship family members adjust and readjust the rates and rhythms of their individual growth and change together. They respond to and are stimulated and encouraged by the developments in each other's lives. Bringing their individual growth and change to the relationships, friends encourage each other to become who they want to be. They inspire one another to develop potentials, to work toward valued goals, and to actualize dreams. Based in mutual care and commitment, friends keep pace with each other as they grow and change.

Together in synchronized rhythm, friends build their lives and actualize and transform themselves. Successes, celebrated together, hearten them and reverberate through their shared and separate lives. Losses and defeats, survived together, bring them to the depths of their beings and school them in essential lessons of life.

LOOKING LIFE IN THE EYE TOGETHER

Friendship families have weathered life's tragedies together and have come to know themselves and each other in these raw and vulnerable parts of life. They have witnessed pain and sorrow and turned to one another in times of need. Being family to one another means knowing who will be there to assist and to be with you when life gets difficult. Asking for help cuts through social amenities and separates out those people who come through for us. People we can depend upon, whom we can reach out to when we feel most dependent, helpless, and desperate, are the ones who stand closest to our hearts and are our treasured companions in life. These are the people that we know truly care for us.

Living through hard times with others enables us to see who they are in times of great pressure and crisis. We see who sticks with us, who reaches out to help, who is empathic enough to be gentle and giving, who remembers our pain and anticipates ways of comforting us. We see our own needs and desires; we see our inabilities to ask and receive comfort. Life's pain clarifies people's characters and values. It reveals how present to ourselves and to others we are; it shows our emotional and spiritual strengths and weaknesses. Painful life events bring us down to the quick of life, they illuminate our unresolved issues and enable us to look clearly and deeply at ourselves and one another. Our vulnerabilities, as well as our strengths, become visible.

The eye of life glows with wonder and tragedy. Those who have walked with us through the wastelands of life are the ones with whom we celebrate its joys. The high points of life, its welling up in laughter, in a sun-filled breeze, in a feast of celebration, are those we share with friends who are family. We bask in our accomplishments, we enjoy the fruits of our labor, we rest after hard work. People who are family share with us most intimately and deeply the highs and lows of life. They are the people on whom we can depend to help us master and survive life.

When we look life in the eye, we see that it is larger than ourselves. We see its power and its beauty, and we experience our small but active place within it. Witnessing life, friendship families grow wise together. With one another, they learn more and more about the mysteries and meanings of being themselves and living life.

RECIPROCAL GENEROSITY

People who are family to one another are reciprocally generous. Based upon their care for and commitment to one another, friendship family members face each other with open hands and hearts. They welcome one another into their lives to share its pleasures and resources. The fullness of their beings overflows outward, toward people they love. In generosity, they offer the abundances of their lives and selves to each other. The plentifulness that is me flows forth to the people I love.

Generosity is based upon respectful awareness of our own and our friends' limits, values, and struggles. In generosity, we invite friends to join us in our lives, to come closer, to let us see each other at close range. Our invitation is openhanded, without restraint or obligation. We invite friends to share, to be, and to discover the ways our lives can touch and grow together. In generosity, I share myself with others without emptying myself for them.

When friends are thoughtful about me and my needs, I carry their responsiveness with me and look for opportunities to reciprocate with equal, empathic timing. In gratitude, I want to return the love. I want to make a call or send a card that is just right, to offer support that fits smoothly into their lives, to search out their pleasures as I explore the world. In this way, they accompany me in my life. I anticipate the pleasure of delighting them. I anticipate the delight of celebrating their wishes and desires.

In reciprocal generosity, family members trust the fullness of care and presence among them. They need not tally the flow of giving and receiving. They know that each will give as much as she or he can, without reservation. They learn to trust that what is given does not carry hidden obligations. People who are family open themselves to one another, believing that they are matched in kindness and in openheartedness.

COLLECTIVE MEMORIES

Important life events that have been lived through together are the bedrock of friendship families. The past, where lives touched and intertwined, is the place friends return to and treasure. Shared memories contain the story of how their individual lives joined together to form a family.

Families of friends reminisce together. They celebrate the magic of meeting and joining lives. They witness, often with wonder and gratitude, the gift of their relationships and the irreplaceable place they hold in each other's lives. Their shared past is given, it cannot be earned or achieved. No one can catch up with it. It is something they have created together and now can hold, treasure, and enjoy. Retrospectively, they see the order of things, the place they created together, the mutual benefits of their associations. They witness who they have been to each other, the ways they have influenced each other, the gifts they have reaped from meeting. They see the meaning of random life events and how these have coalesced into close family bonds.

SHARED TIMELESSNESS

Experientially, friends who have become family to one another feel ever-present in each other's lives. They know that they can call on each other in times of need, and they experience the interlinking of their lives. Living separate but interconnected lives, friendship family members experience their individual lives surrounded by bonds of love. These bonds anchor them in their own life paths while simultaneously tying them to kindred spirits. Once established, a circle of friends surrounds each person and accompanies him or her through life. Friends find it hard to imagine life without this intimate presence.

Relationships among friends who are family seem timeless. Life cannot be imagined without these relationships. Once established, they seem as long-lasting as oneself. Having gone through the most difficult of life circumstances, the participants trust their relationships to endure. They know that their commitments to one another have prevailed in the past and expect them to do so in the future.

They trust they will continue to be part of each other's lives. A sense of the timelessness of their relationship is based upon the depth to which they have shared important parts of themselves together.

Friendship family relationships are dependable and reliable touchstones of support. Our friends are constant and steadfast. We expect them to always be a part of our lives, to share life with and to be available to discuss ourselves and our concerns. They are so much a part of us that we cannot imagine ourselves and our lives without them.

Enveloping each other in care and kindness, friendship families construct an envelope of love that holds their lives. They weave a safe place to be and to become themselves. Shared life events, meanings, and promises tie their lives loosely but strongly together. Together, they reach out to catch the full force of the life wind that stretches their egos taut, to the point of transformation. Together, they endure the life forces that shake their beings and shatter their protective structures. Together, they raise their glasses in celebration, glasses filled with spiritual and emotional vitality, to witness life and to honor the intangible but awesome power of love.

12

Sexual Love Relationships

No love is as awesome as sexual love. Whether it involves a first love, a brief encounter, or a lifelong relationship, experiences of sexual love are a staple of dreams of completion and fulfillment in life. Most Americans have been raised to long and even live for a relationship that is emotionally and sexually satisfying. Often, men are socialized to focus on the sexual side of sexual love; women's socialization emphasizes the emotional part. To all of us, however, sex and love are central aspects of our selves. Relationships that include sexual loving and loving sex can generate complex and, often, difficult interactions that, in turn, can transform the participants' very beings.

A phenomenology of sexual love extends our discussions of intimacy into the realm of the body, the flesh, and sexual desire. When sexual desire is an essential part of a relationship, it intensifies the pleasures and problems of intimacy. As we will see, phenomenologists approach sexual love in different ways: some highlight sexual desire, others illuminate love, still others focus on verbal disclosure and trust, as well as envy and jealousy.

Like parent-child relationships, sexual relationships are primary and formative ones that are infused with social prescriptions. Intense feelings surface in both of these relationships because we seek personal and interpersonal fulfillment through them. We can be deeply affirmed or wounded by parents, children, and lovers who are close to our hearts and play central roles in our lives.

Unlike relationships between parents and children, sexual love relationships are equal ones between people who choose to be close to one another. Relationships with kin come to us ready-made. Sexual love relations are chosen. These elements of mutual preference and consent make sexual relationships intensely hopeful and potentially disappointing. They evoke our greatest dreams of intimacy, happiness, and wholeness, especially if our relationships with parents have left us emotionally hurt and hungry.

Friendships are an important developmental bridge between these two emotionally passionate relationships. In friendship relationships, we gain valuable skills for constructing close, equal relationships. We learn how to notice and talk about thoughts and feelings and to work together to solidify shared intimacy. With friends, we uncover our own and other people's difficulties with closeness and differences. Friendship relationships give us experience with important aspects of intimacy without the added intensities and vulnerabilities of sexual love. Adding sexual intimacy to a relationship extends intimacy into uncharted emotional territory. Often, this terrain is filled with pleasure and happiness. Just as often, it contains hidden wounds that we never knew were there.

Throughout the world, sexuality and sexual intimacies carry diverse taboos and meanings. Most cultures subscribe to a double standard of sexual behavior. This double standard gives men greater access to their sexuality; it is more acceptable for men to have and express sexual desires. Women are expected to be sexual, too, but not too sexual. If women are too free sexually, they risk negative evaluations. Sexist restrictions upon female sexuality make it clear that women and their bodies are dangerously powerful. Otherwise, these stringent and almost universal rules that control women's rights over their own bodies would be unnecessary.

Most of us live in patriarchal and heterosexist societies in which heterosexual love relationships are preferred and considered normal. In the United States, many liberation movements burgeoned in the 1960s: sexual liberation, the civil rights movement, the women's movement, the lesbian and gay liberation movement. All of these movements made people question their preconceptions about human rights and human freedoms. They helped people begin to overthrow stereotypes and to struggle with moral, racial, gender, and sexual orientation differences.

Issues raised by these social changes still reverberate through our sexual love relationships. As people rethink and transform their lives, relationships with lovers and spouses are less predictable and more vulnerable. In the early 1970s, for example, lesbian and gay life-styles were declared as healthy as the heterosexual life-style by the American Psychiatric Association, as well as the American Psychological Association. Beginning in the 1960s, many women and men defied their gender roles and crossed over into each other's social and psychological realms. A positive outcome of these changes is that people have had to reexamine their own experiences in order to understand sexuality and to choose their preferred ways of being sexual.

Sexuality

When we try to define sexuality, in a strange and restricted shorthand, many of us discover that we equate sex with orgasm and further equate orgasm with heterosexual intercourse. We can confirm this generally shared definition of being sexual by asking any adolescent to tell us about sex. When they recover from their surprise, most of them will probably explain to us that sex is "doing it." If they feel particularly safe with us, they may even tell us that sex means "fucking." Pressed for details, our informants may be reduced to vague hand gestures and an embarrassed, "You know." The rolling of their eyes will tell us to stop before we are considered complete idiots. Persisting past this barrier will expose an array of experiences that is difficult to put into words.

Even those of us who feel more sophisticated than our adolescent contemporaries find it difficult to articulate bodily and sexual experiences. The trouble lies partly in the prereflectiveness of the phenomenon. Cultural and family taboos also teach us not to talk about sex. Even today, we can hear religious leaders tell us that sex is sinful and that we should discipline and deny our sexual desires. A legacy of shame and guilt has resulted from many puritanical religious traditions. And sexual experiences are usually private and intimate ones that we want to protect from public exposure. All of these factors make it hard for us to talk about sex.

In a deep existential way, our sexuality is inseparable from our being. From birth, we are bodily beings in the world and our bodies are sexual ones. Although most contemporary social scientists do not subscribe to Freud's beliefs that the child is driven by sexual urges, they do agree that, with puberty, sexuality is an important aspect of healthy development and relationships. When we pay close attention to our experiences of being sexual, we discover that sex touches all aspects of our beings and lives; our sexual selves are grounded in reflective and prereflective intentions.

Reflections on our everyday sexual selves reveal our bodily selves interacting with particular others. Being sexual means engaging in activities that arouse and express our sexual selves: touching and being touched, caressing and being caressed, kissing and being kissed, stimulating and being stimulated. Even thinking about these moments can stir our bodies and open up sexual desire. But sexuality is much more than mere physiological arousal and release, it includes many thoughts, feelings, values, and desires. At its most gratifying, being sexual fulfills our need to be fully in our bodies, and, in doing so, to love and be loved, to pleasure and be pleasured, and to explore our spiritual, as well as our sensuous, selves. For some of us, the height of sexuality is exploding in orgasm. For others, it is being exquisitely tender. For still others, it is daring to act on fantasies and desires. Usually, each of us experiences all of these aspects of sexuality. To be sexual is to be our bodies in ways that touch and gratify our spirits.

As we explore and discover our sexual selves, we learn about our intentions and desires in life. We wish to feel young, attractive, alive, desirable, irresistible, lovable, special, lucky. We wish to feel happier than we ever imagined, to attain the ecstasy that our movie star heroes and heroines enjoy. We even wish to live happily ever after. As our sexual selves evolve, we often discover that the painful disappointments of our sexual relationships help us discover and heal ourselves. In anger, hurt, jealously, and envy, we discover the deeper levels of our existence.

From a phenomenological viewpoint, we are our bodies, and our bodies are sexual. Sexuality permeates existence just as existence permeates sexuality. But this is not to say, as Freud does, that all of existence can be reduced to sexuality. Rather, sexual life is a part of life that has a special relationship to the affectional and erotic (Merleau-Ponty, 1962, pp. 157-159). While it is coexistent with life, sexuality, like existence, is open-ended. Merleau-Ponty (1962) explains:

> The same reason that prevents us from "reducing" existence to the body or to sexuality prevents us also from "reducing" sexuality to existence: the fact is that existence is not a set of facts . . . capable of being reduced to others or to which they can reduce themselves, but the ambiguous setting of their inter-communication, the point at which their boundaries run into each other. (p. 166)

> Existence is indeterminate in itself, by reason of its fundamental structure, and insofar as it is the very process whereby the hitherto meaningless takes on meaning, whereby what had merely a sexual significance assumes a more general one, chance is transformed into reason; insofar as it is the act of taking up a *de facto* situation. We shall give the name transcendence to this act in which existence takes up, for its own purposes, and transforms such a situation. Precisely because it is transcendence, existence never utterly outruns anything, for in that case the tension which is essential to it would disappear. It never abandons itself. What it is never remains external and accidental to it, since this is always taken up and integrated into it. Sexuality therefore ought not, any more than the body in general, to be regarded as a fortuitous content of our experience. Existence has no fortuitous attributes, no content which does not contribute towards giving it its form; it does not give admittance to any pure fact because it is the process by which facts are drawn up. (pp. 169-170)

Like human nature, human sexuality is the expression of an intentional, meaning-giving person. An experiencing, sexual person is at the heart of the dynamic interplay of existence and sexual life.

According to Merleau-Ponty (1962), sexuality is ever-present as an ambiguous atmosphere that coexists with life and is interfused with it so that it is impossible to label a decision or act sexual or nonsexual. As such, it is an intentionality that follows the general flow of existence and yields to its movements. Our sexual bodies include our sexual physiognomy, orientation, and common and unique erogenous areas. As sexual beings, people co-create sexual worlds that appeal to their erotic and affectional desires. This world is first of all a prereflective one, a world that is lived before it is reflectively understood (pp. 156-169).

A discussion of sexual love necessarily involves elaborating upon Merleau-Ponty's idea of the body subject that we first learned about in Chapter 2. Merleau-Ponty (1962) uses the terms *body subject* and the *phenomenal body* interchangeably. The body subject is permeated with subjectivity and is connected intentionally with others and the world. Merleau-Ponty compares the body subject to a work of art; it is "a focal point of living meanings, not the function of a certain number of mutually variable terms" (p. 151). To be a body means to be affectively present in the world as an intentional, intelligent subject. Merleau-Ponty says:

> [O]ur body is not an object for an "I think," it is a grouping of lived-through meanings which moves toward its equilibrium. Sometimes a new cluster of meaning is formed: . . . our natural powers suddenly come together in a richer meaning, which hitherto has been merely fore-shadowed in our perceptual or practical field, and which has made itself felt in our experience by no more than a certain lack, and which by its coming suddenly reshuffles the elements of our equilibrium and fulfils our blind expectation. (p. 153)

In some areas of life, our bodies learn about and know the world before reflective understanding occurs. This is so with sexuality. Often our bodies alert us to the sexual aspects of interactions. Van den Berg (1972a) gives an example of a young woman's body responding to a sexual look:

> A girl of about sixteen enters the room in which her elder brother is talking to a few friends. When his friends see who is coming in, they stop talking and look at her. For the first time in her life, the girl notices that she is being seen through male eyes. She blushes. . . . Her brother's friends are looking at her in an unmasking way; they are looking through her clothes. Their eyes are trying to undress. As a result, the girl is robbed of her body; to a modest degree, her body turns into a body of her brother's friends. But this estrangement of her own body is not all. Also, for the first time in her life, she finds that she desires to possess this different, newly shaped, body. She becomes a woman entirely. Later, in a less surprising moment of her own choice, she wants to *be* this body. (pp. 70-71)

The complexities of our bodies and ourselves are revealed in this example. It shows a bodily comprehension that is inherent in our sexuality. Further, it clarifies our wish to be sexual in ways that develop and satisfy larger dimensions of ourselves.

Sexualized looks, movements, and touches can invoke the body as a subject or the body as an object. Another's gaze, for example, can create the most tender aspects of modesty, desire, and love. Or a look can bring immediate embarrassment, shame, and feelings of objectification. In discussing the difference between the body as subject or object, van den Berg (1972a) emphasizes that the phenomenal body must take center stage in everyday life and in sexual interactions:

> The medical student who is caressing his girlfriend's hand makes a mistake if, in his mind, he simultaneously goes over his anatomy. His girlfriend's hand has no blood vessels, muscles, nerves or bones. He is caressing another hand—which is indeed soft and hard here and there and has a number of features (even throbbing vessels) that cannot be found in his anatomy book. Even the physiologist knows that it is not correct, that it is not fitting at a festive dinner table to speculate on the fate of the food he is eating with other people. No chemical processes are taking place in his stomach: he notices that he becomes satisfied. Prereflective life, that is, life as it is lived in our day-to-day existence, has no knowledge of physiology. Eating, one becomes stomach, just as one becomes head, studying—head to such an extent that the hungry stomach does not exist, nor do the tired, crossed legs under the table. In the sexual act, it is not the sexual organs, objects, that are made available to one another, two subjects jailed in their bodies; the mere thought makes the sexual act impossible. In the sexual act, man and woman become creatures of sex, even sexual organs—a change about which the anatomist and the physiologist can establish nothing at all. (pp. 51-52)

Sexuality occurs within this dialectic of objectified bodies and phenomenal bodies. Each embodied person is vulnerable to objectification, to being treated as a thing that fulfills someone else's desire. But our bodies are also the vulnerable, vibrant cores of our beings. As bodily selves, we long to be honored and rekindled as subjects. In lovemaking at its most satisfying, lovers seek, find, and dwell within body subjects. Many of the contradictions of love can be traced to this dual body—a body that can be both subject and object.

The nature of passion adds to this paradoxical intertwining of body as subject and body as object.

The power of passion, be it sexual desire or all-consuming love, is that it takes over our bodies. It comes upon us from somewhere beyond, above, or below our experiential selves. Experientially, our passion is outside ourselves, often in the one desired or loved. Sometimes, it comes from the dark depths of ourselves, carrying ancient longings and wounds. At other times, it seems to come from lofty parts of ourselves that contain hopes of a future self. The body is a willing instrument of passion's power. Passion takes control of our bodies. It draws us away from self-centeredness and self-groundedness and leads us toward unknown experiences. In this way, we are "beside ourselves" with love.

In discussing the Greek god Dionysos, psychologist Bernd Jager (1979), tells us that passion is not a reflective decision. Rather, we experience passion as a yielding to seduction or to fate. Experientially, it is something that we find ourselves already living; it comes to us ready-made from beyond ourselves. In passion, we are drawn outside our instrumental bodies, beyond areas of comfort, competence, and mastery. It leads us toward the communal, peripheral, and wild.

Passion happens to a person; it is not something that can be completely orchestrated or willed. As such, we suffer passion. It transports and transforms us. Because all passion draws us away from our centers, it brings us suffering, as well as pleasure. In the sense that passion draws us out of ourselves, it leaves us with no grounding in ourselves and our lives; it leaves us without a foundation. When we experience passion, we are taken over by strong feelings. We become these feelings and are pulled, changed, and transformed in the process. Although passion is often ecstatic, it always, eventually, leads us into pain. By its very nature, it announces upheaval and draws us to the edge of life and death (Jager, 1979, pp. 218-222).

A phenomenology of sexuality illuminates a complex intertwining of existence and sexuality. Sexuality plays within the dialectical union of self and body, revealing the body as both subject and object. This interplay of subjectivity and objectification continues in the following explication of sexual love relationships.

Sexual Love Relationships

Two prominent phenomenologists, Jean-Paul Sartre (1956) and
Maurice Merleau-Ponty (1962), have developed contrasting views of
sexual love relations. Sartre emphasizes sexual desire and sees love
as self-focused. Further, he says that love is filled with internal contradictions and is doomed to fail. In contrast with Sartre, Merleau-
Ponty describes the intersubjective world of love and sees it as
altruistic. He stresses the benefits of love and its ultimate success.

Sartre helps us understand the difficulties and obstacles of sexual
love. For Sartre, love begins in sexual desire that draws the person
down into the body in search of bodily pleasure. Sexual desire is,
thus, self-centered; it begins and ends in bodily desires for gratification. Sexual desire pursues satisfaction by enchanting and fascinat-
ing the other person, by luring her or him closer and capturing the
other in a sensuous net of bodily delights.

When I desire someone, I want him or her to desire me, too. My
pleasure is not enough; I want the other to be bodily, sexually, and
emotionally close to me. I want the other to give herself or himself
freely to me. For Sartre, sexual desire's deepest longing is to possess
the other. When I desire someone sexually, I want him or her to be
mine. Here lies the internal contradiction of sexual desire; I want the
other to be mine, but to give herself or himself to me freely. If a lover
truly becomes my possession, desire wanes because the other
loses subjectivity; he or she becomes an object that I possess. Desire kindles and burns only when the other remains free, desired,
and slightly outside my grasp.

This internal contradiction—that desire seeks to capture the free
subjectivity of the other—dooms love to an unsuccessful ending.
With an invisible slight of hand, the other is perpetually too free or
not free enough. Love is the inherently impossible attempt to capture the other as a person. As such, it creates a domino effect of subject-object interactions in which both self and other are alternately
reduced to possessions and rebirthed as persons. The perpetual dis-
satisfaction of love comes from this subject-object dance. Because
each lover is vulnerable to being reduced to an object of the other
person's pleasure, love is incessantly insecure. Finally, shame hov-
ers around love's edges because each person, in her or his human-

ness, is inadequate and unprepared in some way (Knee, 1990; Lapointe, 1974).

Sartre's structural descriptions of sexual love relationships are, indeed, sobering. Even the most romantic of us knows the truth of his insights. Even the most jaded of us believes, or at least wishes, that the reality of love is more than just this. We can find the other side of love in the writings of Merleau-Ponty.

Merleau-Ponty (1962) illuminates another experiential view of sexual love. He asserts that sexual love is an interaction in which subject faces subject, exactly what Sartre says is impossible. Gone is objectifying grasping. In its place is an encounter of being with being, self with other self. For Merleau-Ponty, love is an affective atmosphere and a manner of relating that surrounds the lover and is based in reciprocity. To love is to be called forth from one's self, toward another living presence. Love illuminates the loved one as a special and lovable being. It penetrates the person's qualities and looks into the other's essence, into his or her very being. In the other's being, one finds a kindred spirit, one that heartens the self and encourages the subjectivity of both lovers.

From this perspective, love is a profound experience of intersubjectivity in which self and other co-create each other and, in turn, are co-created. Lovers enter into a "we" that expands each person and increases individual freedom. Participants change and are changed by the newly constituted, dynamic union; they transform and are transformed by sexual love. Lovers, together, become more than they were as separate individuals. Reciprocal love affirms and enhances each individual. It co-creates lovers in the fullness of their beings. This fullness is only accessible with someone else.

For Merleau-Ponty, sexual love is inherently other-centered; it calls people out of self-serving concerns to be for and with the other. Although desire, that wish to possess the other as mine, is part of love, altruism triumphs. Authentic love reorients desire. It transforms self-serving intentions to possess the other into loftier goals of being and becoming. The subjectivity of the loved one motivates a lover to be present for and with the other. Together, in trusting tenderness, lovers help one another be and change. New aspects of each emerge as they enter shared, uncharted explorations of themselves.

When I enter into a sexual love relationship, I am seeking bodily, sensuous pleasure, but I am also seeking contact with another person. This contact is simultaneously sexual and spiritual; it is a reaching out for and to the other and a reaching in for and to myself. In knowing myself and the other in our embodied existences, I learn about both of us. In dialogue, in giving and receiving sexual pleasure, we fulfill our spiritual, as well as our bodily, beings. As I become acquainted with a lover's body, it becomes a special body, one that becomes "the theatre of a process of elaboration" of myself and someone else. In our intersubjective, body dialogue, we discover our intentions, as well as our connections with the world (Merleau-Ponty, 1962, pp. 352-354).

According to Merleau-Ponty (1962), sexual love is a bodily dialogue of intersubjectivity. As such, it rests upon the freedom of both participants and, ultimately, seeks to enhance mutuality and freedom. Gestures of affection and passion weave a single "we," and lovers become more than their individual selves. Through reciprocal movements and expressions, each grows and changes. Lovers stretch beyond their previous limits and co-create one other. Love such as this is a rediscovery of oneness with self and with the beloved. It involves communion and communication of whole selves, which brings lovers to new heights of self-actualization. This love, which Merleau-Ponty calls authentic love, is more free than the freedom of preserving egocentric autonomy. It is a freedom to be and to become, with and for a beloved other. Illusory love is concerned with preserving independence and focuses upon attributes rather than being-to-being contact. When these concerns are cast away, freedom expands into a symphony of intersubjectivity (Merleau-Ponty, 1962, pp. 352-361).

For Merleau-Ponty, to love is to be able to see the other become new before my very eyes. Although this is often a delightful experience, it also can be a shattering and self-transforming one. In Merleau-Ponty's (1962) words: ". . . when I say that I know and like someone, I aim, beyond his qualities, at an inexhaustible core which may one day shatter the image that I have formed of him" (p. 361).

Sexual love relationships are dynamic. If they are healthy, they change as the partners evolve. When one member of a couple changes, the other member must also do so. Thus good communication is essential to the well-being of a partnership. The ability to talk together and share self-knowledge with a lover or spouse is an important intimacy skill. Humanistic psychologist Sidney Jourard has been a pioneer in researching self-disclosure and its impact upon sexual love relationships. He extends the phenomenology of intimacy into self-disclosure, privacy, and change.

Self-disclosure is a vital part of healthy sexual love relationships. Mature love involves knowledge of and care for one another. It enables lovers to respond to and respect each other's needs and idiosyncrasies. For Jourard (1971), healthy relationships between two people are characterized by mutual respect and open communication. These qualities enable lovers to feel safe while being honest and unguarded. A good sexual relationship depends upon a loving person-to-person relationship, one that includes commitment, honesty, respect, and emotional closeness. To live, one must be willing to disclose oneself (pp. 46-47).

To disclose means to show or manifest yourself. We disclose ourselves to people we perceive as trustworthy, people who have goodwill toward us, people who are willing to reciprocate with equal honesty and openness. This healthy behavior helps us feel connected with ourselves. It promotes psychological integration. When we disclose ourselves to others, we grow and change in their presence. To disclose ourselves to others, we must know ourselves or at least be attempting to do so. This takes work and courage. It also takes trust, trust of oneself and of others. To disclose oneself to a loved one is to bring the truth of one's being into the relationship.

Privacy is an important complement to self-disclosure. To show ourselves to someone else, we must be with ourselves. Being alone is a necessary part of being with and knowing ourselves. Because being in an ongoing relationship carries an implicit promise to be as one has been, being alone is vital to staying centered in one's changing self. When alone, we can notice new thoughts, feelings, and meanings without the pressure of others' expectations of us. Knowledge of our changing selves is necessary to strong, dynamic intimacy.

Privacy is important in another way in sexual love relationships. Especially when revealing our bodily/spiritual selves, a safe interpersonal space that protects confidences is important. We need privacy with a loved one. We also need our lover to keep vulnerabilities within an intimate, nonpublic relationship. Privacy with a lover builds trust. When we trust, we can be ourselves without guard and protection. Privacy, both alone and with an intimate other, helps us be fully ourselves and cultivate intimacy in all of its depth and expansiveness. Privacy helps us actualize our personal and interpersonal selves. In discussing the structure of privacy in intimate relationships, phenomenological psychologist Constance Fischer (1971) says:

> Unlike other privacy, in intimacy the *prevalent* style of being in relation is always openness, never task analysis, escape, or whatever. What unfolds through a style of openness in intimacy is a rediscovery of at-homeness with a particular something. The unfolding is a coming into expression of unarticulated aspects of one's centrality or essence. The unfolding is then a very personal one, whereas privacy sometimes involves unfolding of an object as object more or less in its own right. As in privacy, the unfolding may be interpersonal as well as personal, but here both participants sense the personalness, share to some extent the meanings within it and the usually unspoken acknowledgment that it is somehow a route to the existential center of at least one of them. (pp. 154-155)

By helping actualize each person's being, privacy strengthens the intimacy of sexual love. It nurtures love within a boundaried, protected realm. This protective nurturing, however, also promotes change and growth that, in turn, threaten the status quo of sexual love relationships.

The deepest way to protect sexual love relationships is to expect that they will change. Change is part of any person, and it is inherent in a relationship that remains alive and vital. Jourard believes that most of us marry an image of our lover, one that is co-constituted in a romantic haze. The marital task is to break through this image and to know the other as a real person. In a healthy, committed sexual love relationship, trouble is normal and even desirable. It helps crack the role-playing pictures both partners have constructed and enables lovers to know one another in their different values, needs, and goals. Although couples are terrified by change, boredom is even more lethal. Both spouses must grow to preserve a satisfying, dynamic relationship.

Jourard believes that stagnation, boredom, and dishonesty will sour a couple's love and lovemaking. Love is best cultivated with actions that foster the growth and happiness of both participants. Coupled with laughter and spontaneity, love begets good sex; sex that encompasses much more than physical pleasure. Jourard (1971) defines the sex that is part of healthy sexual love as an expression of *joie de vivre*, a sharing of the joy of life. This sex is full of life's wholeness. *Joie de vivre* comes from fully experiencing oneself, one's beloved, and life (p. 43). It involves following commitments but letting go into the unknown and witnessing what life brings to us. Often, saying "I love you" begins a self-transformative journey.

When we say "I love you," we say many things. Here is an example from Jourard (1971):

> I love her. What does this mean? I want her to exist for me and to exist for herself. I want her alive. I want her to be and, moreover, to be in the way that *she* chooses to be. I want her free. As she discloses her being to me or before my gaze, my existence is enriched. I am more alive. I experience myself in dimensions that she evokes, such that my life is more meaningful and livable.
>
> My beloved is a mystery that I want to make transparent. But the paradox is that I cannot make my beloved do anything. I can only invite and earn the disclosure that makes her transparent. I want to know my beloved. But for me to know, she must show. And for her to show her mysteries to me, she must be assured I will respect them, take delight in them. Whether the mysteries are the feel of her flesh against mine—something I cannot know until it happens—or what she is thinking, imagining, planning or feeling.
>
> If I love her, I love her projects, since she is their source and origin. I may help her if she wants my help; or let her struggle with them unaided if this is meaningful to her. I respect her wishes in the matter.
>
> If I love myself, I love my projects since they are my life. If she loves me, she confirms me in my projects, helps me with them, even if the help consists in leaving me alone. If she tries to control me, she doesn't love me. If I try to control her, I don't love her. I experience her as free and treasure her freedom. I experience myself as free and treasure my freedom. (pp. 52-53)

Within the commitments of a sexual love relationship, lovers witness themselves being and becoming who they are and want to be. Loving involves being willing to change and to be available to reinvent the relationship. It means reexamining lives, tracing back to where persons withdrew or lost touch, and sharing the feelings and consequences of these events. Sometimes, the most loving thing to do with one another is to dissolve the relationship, to separate and to go on alone. As we will see in the next chapter, even this ending involves the relationship continuing in some form, either in measured time and space or experientially, within the historical continuity of our lives. Life and love are open-ended and unpredictable. Some surprises are joyful. Others are terrible and painful.

Structural Components
of Envy and Jealousy

Along with love's bliss, painful problems confront us when we love. Especially in sexual love, our failings and insecurities can be highlighted. Some of us experience such dark emotions as anger, envy, jealousy, and guilt. These passionate feelings seize us and turn us upside down and inside out. They shake the very foundations of ourselves and our relationships. Phenomenological psychologist Peter Titelman provides insights into the structure of two powerful and disconcerting emotions that are often woven into sexual love— envy and jealousy. These structural descriptions help us situate envy and jealousy within our lives and help us recover ourselves in and through them.

Titelman (1981) illuminates the experience of envy and compares it to jealousy. Both envy and jealousy are painful interpersonal experiences. Envy occurs between two people; jealousy involves three people. Similar to traditional analyses of envy and jealousy, Titelman characterizes envy being about possessions or personal qualities, while jealousy concerns special people.

Envy begins in an interpersonal situation in which I experience someone else having what I want and lack. The object of envy may be anything: a car, a house, a suit of clothes, a ring, a pen. I can even be envious of someone's personal qualities, skills, or luck—their good looks, quick wittedness, ease in social situations, or luck in the lottery or in business transactions. When envy surfaces in sexual love relationships, it may be focused upon the person I love or upon someone who is like me, only better off.

What I envy is something I want, feel that I can and even should have, and, unjustly, do not possess. The person envied is similar to me. I can imagine being in his or her life and enjoying the envied possessions and qualities. This imaginary crossing over into the envied state sharpens envy's sting because it widens the gap between my undesirable self and my envisioned one. The difference is insurmountable. I feel defeated by someone already having what I am so far from attaining. Caught in my deficiencies, I blame others and life conditions for the incongruency between my immobilized and desired selves. This casting of blame increases further the distance between myself and the actions that will bring me the envied qualities or possessions. I am off center, lacking, blocked, and unable.

Lovers can envy each other's possessions or qualities. When envied objects are perceived as giving the other person relational advantages, envy can turn into jealousy. Envy is only resolved when the envier is able to achieve what is desired. Then, the decentered state is dissolved and paths open between the present self and the imagined, future one. As envy dissipates, the envier experiences herself or himself as able, and envied objects move within reach. Envy, then, is an inauthentic way of achieving a goal. Its inauthenticity lies in the envier's disengagement from himself or herself as an effective force in the world, one that promotes important, prioritized desires and, where possible, transforms possibilities into probabilities (Titelman, 1981, p. 190-193).

In contrast with envy, which usually occurs between two people and is focused upon another person's qualities or possessions, jealousy occurs when a third person becomes a threat to a dyad. Jealousy involves the loss or the impending loss of a relationship that one wants to hold onto, a relationship that is vital to personal fulfillment and claimed as one's own. The jealous person often becomes frenzied in mind and body and tries to hold onto the loved person, defeat the intruder, and reclaim the relationship. A jealous lover is consumed by suspicion and is self-protective by being vigilant and ever-present. She or he blames the rival and puts forth superhuman efforts to preserving "what was" against a foreboding "what could be." The jealous lover is driven by previously unknown passions—competition, rage, longings for unconditional love, abandonment.

Loss of love is at the heart of jealousy, and everything possible is done to prevent it (Titelman, 1981, pp. 194-203).

Even more than envy, jealousy shakes the personal and relational foundations of a person's life. Fear, hurt, loss, sadness, and betrayal are among the tattered spoils that jealousy leaves in its wake. Lovers who wish to salvage their relationship from jealousy must acknowledge and heal these feelings. They must clarify commitments, speak honestly about unhappinesses, and listen to and reassure one another. Fears of abandonment must be reconnected to earlier losses of love, and emotional safeguards must be developed that anticipate and ward off future traumas. If these emotional issues are dealt with, jealous feelings can be transformed into healthy awareness of attractions that are potentially threatening to an ongoing relationship.

Sexual love relationships touch deep into our emotional beings. When they end, the pain that results from this loss travels through every fiber of our selves and lives.

13

Breakups

Love relationships end even though we would do anything to make them last. With greater numbers of heterosexual marriages ending in divorce than ever before (Santrock, 1989, p. 323), many of us have experienced or will experience the ending of a relationship with a lover or spouse. The most common and painful endings of lover relationships are those in which one person wants to end the relationship and the other wants to continue it. Regardless of how or why a lover relationship ends, both partners experience loss. Even the person who leaves feels loss. Faced with the pain of a breakup, most of us ask, What went wrong? What could we have done differently? How can I avoid this sort of tragedy in the future? Sometimes it takes a lifetime to answer these questions. Some of us will die still searching for the answers.

Because sexual love relations are our most intimate ones, the pain and loss stirred up by their endings can reverberate through all aspects of our lives. A breakup is usually the first major loss we experience in intimacy. As such, it can open up unknown parts of our emotional selves and teach us valuable lessons in intimacy. As it is happening, a breakup seems horrible and unbearable. Later, we can see that it brought us valuable opportunities to grow and change.

In 1988, I published a phenomenological study of lesbian breakups (Becker, 1988). The project involved interviewing self-defined lesbians who had experienced a relationship that ended. I wanted to discover the varied life events that occurred when lovers separated. Further, I wanted to show how people recovered from the ending of a lover relationship.

I studied lesbian breakups for a number of reasons. Two years before the study, I had experienced the ending of my own 5-year lesbian relationship. Even though I had sat with lesbian friends and clients while their partnerships ended, the loss of my own relationship cut me loose upon an uncharted sea of pain. Once I recovered, I wanted to write about the process I had gone through. Nothing had been written about lesbian breakups, and I wanted to begin developing a literature that would help lesbians weather this painful life event. And too, lesbian and gay communities have prescriptions for ex-lovers. Unlike their heterosexual counterparts, lesbians often are expected, and expect themselves, to become friends with ex-lovers. I wanted to know whether ex-lovers' friendships did, in fact, develop.

I call the period in which a partnership ends—before, during, and after the breakup—the ex-lover transition. I collected stories of this transition from 40 lesbians who ranged in age from 24 to 66 years. The majority of women were white; 25% were women of color. They came from diverse class and religious backgrounds, and their professions and political attitudes were wide-ranging. I asked these women to tell me what they experienced when their lover relationships ended and encouraged them to elaborate upon whatever relationship and events they recalled. I wanted to know why they broke up, what helped them recover from the pain and loss of the ending of their primary relationship, and the kinds of ex-lover relationships they constructed.

Although relationships and breakups are as unique as the people involved in them, some patterns emerged from the life stories told to me. Of course, these patterns apply most accurately to the women with whom I spoke. But my book tour gave me opportunities to talk about these trends with many men and women throughout the United States. These people confirmed the insights I present here. Heterosexual undergraduates who have read my book have found more similarities than differences between their experiences and those of my research subjects. As you read this chapter, notice what is similar to and what is different from your life experiences. The main purpose of the chapter is to help each of you understand his or her experiences of losing an important lover relationship.

Reasons Lovers Break Up

The lesbians whom I interviewed ended their lover relationships for five distinct but not mutually exclusive reasons. These reasons were as follows: (a) affairs that irreparably traumatized the relationship, (b) polarized differences that were irresolvable and with which it became impossible to live, (c) passive withdrawal from a dissatisfying relationship by one partner, (d) persistent crises and chaos, and (e) circumstantial changes that caused a weak relationship to come apart. Although all of these factors occurred in some relationships, for other couples, one of them was enough to make a lover relationship fail. Most breakups were long and complex processes.

Alice, for example, described how her lover, Melissa's, affair eventually ended their relationship. Even though Melissa ended her affair, they were unable to repair the trust between them. Alice explains:

> I was really hurt. I never felt that way before, and I didn't trust her. I couldn't get over it. I used to think, "I really have to get over this. It's not a big deal. She left. She's back. I love her. I trust her." But I never got over it. (Becker, 1988, p. 29)

Melissa's affair irreparably damaged Alice's ability to trust Melissa and to be open and vulnerable with her. Eventually, Alice fell in love with someone else, and Alice and Melissa began the long and painful work of becoming ex-lovers and remaining friends.

Another woman, Louise, found that differences between herself and her lover, Fran, polarized them: Louise talked and Fran did not, Louise expressed feelings and Fran did not. The relationship was comfortable, but Louise became lonely and unhappy. She wanted more from it than she was getting. Fran was depressed and rarely wanted to talk or to make love. Louise needed more from the relationship—emotionally, verbally, and sexually—than Fran gave her, and ended the relationship when she realized that Fran was not going to change. Even though Louise was the one who left, she was overwhelmed with ambivalence and guilt. She says:

> It was horrible. I felt hopeless, like I was a failure. I remember going in and crying on the bed. I went back and forth in my mind—"You wanted this. No, I didn't. But you were the one who started this. You're letting her go." Part of me knew that she would stay if I said it was okay. But it really wasn't okay. When she wasn't able to make the changes, I felt rejected—like she didn't love me. (Becker, 1988, p. 26)

In the relationship and during its ending, Louise felt abandoned by Fran. Louise was strong enough, however, to let go of the relationship and to search for one that affirmed important parts of herself.

Passive withdrawal by one lover can also end a relationship. Withdrawal begins and continues as a way of avoiding differences; disagreements are sidestepped. Paradoxically, this easy way out of difficulties can end up becoming painful and explosive. Susan describes what happened between her and Carla:

> A kind of movement started, a kind of separation even though we were still living together. I started bagging things. Certain differences would come up and, rather than fighting about them, they sat and stirred inside of me. The more I didn't talk about things, the less I risked talking. Pretty soon, I felt like I was walking around on crushed glass. (Becker, 1988, p. 42)

As tension built, smaller and smaller difficulties irritated Susan. Soon, there was little about Carla that she liked. The relationship finally ended in an explosion of angry accusations.

Long-standing patterns of crises also can erode a love relationship. In a crisis-oriented couple, one partner is usually overwhelmed by crises and the other one resolves them. For a while, emotional polarization can work well for a couple. It can, however, escalate, and one or both partners can become exhausted and discontented. One couple, Ellen and Rachel, lived through many emergencies. Rachel was the victim and Ellen was the rescuer. As one trauma was replaced by another, Ellen sought comfort and pleasure outside her relationship and soon found a more satisfying lover.

Changes in circumstances also can cause lover relationships to end. Circumstantial breakups are the least painful because they occur when emotional commitment between lovers is weak. External changes can end a relationship when lovers have not made commitments to it or have gradually neglected the relationship and its development. Then, a shift in situational factors, a job relocation, the breaking apart of a shared household, or admission to graduate school, can occasion a breakup. Circumstances end relationships when partners are looking for a convenient exit from them.

Recovering From A Breakup

In retrospect, the ex-lovers with whom I spoke found that recovering from a breakup contained many tasks. The emotional work described below is essential to the recovery process. Each part of recovering from a breakup can help us manage pain, heal, and grow and change.

Letting Go of the Relationship

When we find that we cannot prevent the ending of a lover relationship, work shifts from preserving it to letting it go. Acknowledging and accepting the end of a lover relationship can be a multileveled and extended process. Each member of a couple often oscillates between acceptance and disbelief.

Letting go of a lover relationship is the first step to recovering from the pain and loss of its ending. Not being lovers changes the couple's shared life and reverberates through each individual's emotional and social worlds. Even broken love lives on, and it is paradoxical to love someone and leave him or her. Because letting go of close, loving bonds is complex and difficult, it helps to identify events that mark the ending of a lover relationship. Marker events, whether they are internal shifts or external events, help lovers identify a new relational reality. For the women I interviewed, two external events, uncovering a partner's ongoing affair and breaking up a shared home, were clear marker events. Any event can be ambiguous; experienced meanings determine an event's effect.

Events that signal the ending of a relationship can also be ones that have happened hundreds of times. Precisely because they symbolize what is wrong with the partnership, they can be focal points of change. Hannah had such an experience with her lover, Robin:

> We were going to our therapy session; I was upset and feeling far away from Robin. Since we were early, we went for coffee before the session. We were sitting on a sunny patio at a cafe, and Robin picked up a newspaper and started reading it. All of a sudden, I realized that this was it. No more walls, no more newspapers, no more trying to make it better.

It was over. I ended our relationship in therapy that day. (Becker, 1988, p. 39)

For Hannah, her relationship ended when Robin raised the newspaper. For Robin, the relationship ended at a different time, the psychotherapy session or days later when she and Hannah separated the shared household.

Once a person acknowledges that she wants to end a relationship, she needs to talk about it and to act upon her decision. Then the breakup becomes a reality. Realizing, speaking, and acting are important pieces of letting go of a relationship. It is possible to let go of a relationship on one level and to hold onto it at another. When desires are acted upon, decisions become real. Separating material possessions can bring all the unresolved issues of the relationship and the pain of its ending to a head. Nina tells of her experience when she moved her belongings out of the house that she and Tess shared:

> The day I showed up to get my things, Tess told me I had two hours to get all my things together and get out. I hadn't been able to get in to pack my things; I told her it would take as long as it took.
> I started throwing things in boxes and giving them to my friends to put in the truck. When I got to the camping equipment I couldn't decide what to take. Tess had never been camping or fishing before she met me, and I doubted that she'd ever do it again. I took the equipment that been given to me by my family. I also took some of the things we'd bought together, and left her some tools and kitchenware that were mine.
> My friends advised me to move fast. We made a chain; I handed them things and they ran upstairs and put them in the truck. It turned out that as they were putting things in the truck, Tess was taking them out and putting them in the garage. We started screaming and yelling about what belonged to whom and who would use the stuff the most. (Becker, 1988, p. 62)

When lovers dismantle the physical ways their lives have been joined together, emotions flair and painful decisions become realities.

Returning to Yourself

When a lover relationship ends, ex-lovers are left facing themselves. These selves are often filled with emptiness, abandonment, pain, and loss. Feeling the feelings that result from a breakup is an important part of recovering from it. Like the death of a loved one,

no one can prepare completely for the meanings and emotional reactions of such a major loss. Feelings that surface in a breakup are
wide-ranging: hurt, sadness, guilt, anxiety, anger, relief, shame, fear,
distrust. All feelings are important to recovery; none of these feelings
are easy to withstand.

Once feelings are available, it is helpful to experience and work
with them. This is hard to do because they are uncomfortable and
arouse unresolved issues. Any relationship is filled with many feelings. Sometimes feelings arise that we never knew we had: hate,
envy, hopelessness. Sometimes breakups help us express feelings
better than ever before. In a second breakup, Louise discovered that
she was feeling and expressing anger in new ways. She explains:

> When Vicki and I were lovers, she was the one who got angry and
> yelled and screamed; I was the one who listened and cried. I have a
> hard time saying mean things. When I got angry at Vicki, I held it in and
> handled it myself.
>
> Then, when Vicki left me for another woman, I got a lot of encourage-
> ment from my therapist and my friends to tell her how angry I was. I
> thought, "Why should I turn it inward? I don't have to say anything
> bad, I can just keep saying that I'm angry." I think that really helped;
> getting my anger out in a healthy way so that I didn't feel bad about it
> the next day.
>
> Sometimes I would get overwhelmed with rage. I even called her at
> work a couple of times, just to yell at her. Then I'd hang up before she
> could yell back. Sometimes she'd call me and try to talk it out and I'd
> say, "Fuck you. Shut up. I'm pissed." Then I'd hang up on her. It felt
> great. After two months of doing that, I began to feel better. (Becker,
> 1988, pp. 89-90)

One of the best outcomes of this breakup for Louise was that she
learned how to express anger in ways that affirmed her feelings and
enabled her to stand up for her emotional rights. This expressive-
ness corrected her previous tendencies to take care of the other
person's feelings and to ignore her own needs and desires.

As ex-lovers acknowledge, experience, and integrate their emotional reactions to a breakup, they find that these feelings are connected with older, unresolved issues. The ending of a lover
relationship often involves a reliving of emotional problems with
parents, siblings, or previous lovers. A number of women experienced grief over the earlier death of a parent. This previous grief had

been truncated and became available again when they felt abandoned by a lover. In these instances, breakups provided second
chances to resolve hurt and sadness. Corine explains what happened to her:

> When Jessie and I broke up, it helped me to concentrate on what I was
> really grieving about—my mother's death. Once I was convinced that
> my intense feelings were about losing my mother, it took some time and
> work to get over it. It was hard work, but it was my work to do—it
> wasn't something that someone had done to me. It gave me something
> to focus on—for me.
>
> During that time, I went to a retreat on dying with one of my sisters.
> I don't remember thinking about my ex-lover, it was more about my
> mother. But it is one of the main things that helped me heal from break-
> ing up with Jessie.
>
> One of the most powerful parts of the retreat was a film of Stephen
> Levine in which he talked about losing your identity when someone
> dies. He said that was one of the main things you were grieving. I
> realized that when my mother died, I'd died as a daughter; when Jessie
> and I had broken up, I'd died as a spouse or lover. Going through that
> experience with one of my sisters really helped me understand that I
> was grieving those lost parts of myself. (Becker, 1988, pp. 165-166)

Corine's breakup uncovered the old pain that needed to be healed.
Once she had grieved her mother's death, Corine was less devastated over the loss of her relationship with Jessie.

It is important to talk to other people about breakups. Talking
about painful experiences helps us feel less alone. We name feelings
and clarify their meanings by talking about them. Feelings that are
shared are easier to endure. Other people knowing about our experiences also gives us support, allows us to put our reactions into a
larger perspective, and gives us feedback. Susan talks about what
she gains from talking to friends during and after a breakup:

> I always feel that I lose my sense of reality around a breakup; of what
> happened and what the other person thinks happened. There are always a
> lot of accusations about what you said and what they said; it's a crazy
> time. So it's nice to talk to people, and find out their impressions; to
> either find out that you're right, your ex-lover is right, you're both
> right, or you're both wrong and it's something else entirely. It helps me
> put the story back together in some kind of integrated way that's
> grounded in other people's perceptions as well as my own experiences.
> (Becker, 1988, p. 71)

Sharing our raw emotional selves with trustworthy, honest, and caring people helps us become strong again.

Rebuilding Your Life

As ex-lovers let go of the old relationship and notice the feelings that arise from this loss, they have to face an empty hole in their lives and their selves. The best recovery fills that emptiness by focusing upon oneself rather than upon other people. Spending time alone is an important part of rebuilding your life around yourself versus someone else. This solitude gives you the room to notice your likes and dislikes, the parts of yourself and the relationship you will always treasure, the content and source of pain and sadness, what was lost and gained through the relationship, and what was lost and gained in the breakup. It enables you to become acquainted with both positive and negative parts of yourself, as well as old and new strengths and weaknesses. Sue discovered opposite sides of herself six months after she and Silvia stopped living together:

> Some friends invited me to visit them on the spur of the moment, about six months after Silvia and I stopped living together. I said "Sure," and jumped in the car and started the four-hour drive to their cabin. On the way up, I had the greatest sense of freedom. I realized that it was because I wasn't in a relationship; I didn't have to discuss what I was doing with a lover before I did it. On the way home, I had the opposite feeling. I thought, "What if I have an accident? No one's waiting for me at home, it could be weeks before someone would know I was hurt or dead." I felt alone and scared; there was no one who cared for me in a special way. (Becker, 1988, p. 88)

It was helpful for Sue to get such vivid experiences of these opposite parts of herself: her enjoyment of freedom and her fear of being alone in an uncaring world. Experiencing both sides eventually enabled her to integrate them into her life.

Knowing how to nurture yourself in times of emotional need is an important emotional skill. It requires awareness of needs and a desire to discover what makes you feel better. Finding ways of comforting and caring for yourself involves developing new personal and interpersonal habits. It also involves taking emotional risks and exposing vulnerable parts of the self. Taking personal needs and desires seriously, breaks self-negating habits.

As people rebuild their lives, they clarify values and emotional preferences. They learn what not to do next time and gain insight into complex relational problems. They learn how to take care of themselves and to take the next step necessary for personal and relational growth. Lillian tells what she did after yet another lover relationship ended:

> After I cut off contact with Marge, I knew I needed to get in touch with myself. There was something missing in me; I wasn't comfortable with myself and I didn't like myself. I had lived alone, but there was something else that I'd been avoiding—I didn't know how to be with myself. I was determined to get to know myself and to learn how to be comfortable with myself.
>
> I was feeling more identified with the things that I needed around me. I saw them as *my* things, rather than just things that I didn't care about. I got more comfortable being at home, and even liked it after a while. I put a lot of effort and money into fixing up my house; I remodeled the kitchen; I painted; I added a hot tub and deck; I replaced the fence.
>
> I'm so thankful for those years I spent alone, making my home exactly as I wanted it to be. After I finished, I remember sitting in my living room one night feeling how much I enjoyed what I had. I was thankful that I'd reached that place—that I consider normal—of being able to be alone and feel whole and at peace. I had always had an empty lack of completeness inside of me that I kept trying to fill with other people. Now I felt complete in myself. I liked myself and felt gratified by my own company. (Becker, 1988, pp. 84-85)

Once Lillian had reclaimed and filled up her own emptiness, she was able to stay present to herself while being intimate with a lover.

Reshaping Social Relationships

When a couple ends their relationship, the ending resounds through their social worlds. Relationships intertwined with a shared life are shaken and changed by a breakup. The effects of the breakup upon relationships with family members and friends must be understood. In a certain way, each social relationship needs to recover from the loss and change of a partnership ending. When lovers have gone separate ways, social networks must be reshuffled and rebuilt. When friends and family remain integrated, loyalties have to be clarified. Some ex-lovers need people close to them to chose sides and cut off contact with a former spouse. Others are helped by friends and family members remaining in contact with an ex-lover.

For the women I spoke with, friends and relatives were important sources of support during and after a breakup. These people listened, talked, witnessed, and got involved in helping ex-lovers manage the ending. After a breakup, a family network that includes kin, as well as friends, is an important source of emotional and social support. If a person has not understood the importance of maintaining close relationships with relatives and friends while also being in love, she can gain this awareness during a breakup. A family that complements, is involved with, and supports a lover relationship is crucial to its well-being and survival.

During and after a breakup, people learn to reach out to nonlovers for comfort and care. For some, this is a new experience in developing multiple, varied relationships based upon care and reciprocity. Ideally, ex-lovers find a community of people who serve as a loving family, one that surrounds and assists them with the emotional issues of the breakup and lives through the first year of holidays, birthdays, and anniversaries with them.

Having Contact With and Being Away
From an Ex-lover

An individually crafted balance of contact with and separation from an ex-lover is helpful in recovering from a breakup. Both contact and the lack of it help emotional healing, but the timing and amount cannot be prescribed. It must be worked out by attending to what makes the ending real and what facilitates resolving the feelings and the trauma.

Contact with an ex-lover provides information about what is resolved and unresolved about a breakup. Women in my study often felt that they were finished with the emotional problems of an ending only to discover, when they were face-to-face with a former partner, that they were still in the grips of anger or sadness. Seeing an ex-lover provides an emotional update, it gives realistic information about the work completed and the work left to do. Louise had such an experience when she spent time with Fran after not seeing her for six months:

> I felt angry during my first visit with Fran. I didn't blow up or anything like that, but I was angry and confused by feeling so much anger. When I saw Fran, I wanted to curl up with her. But I also wanted to yell at her.

I wanted to love her and I wanted her to show her love for me by talking to me about her feelings.

I left there feeling unsatisfied; I hadn't curled up with her, yelled at her, or told her that I loved her. As usual, she hadn't talked to me about her feelings. I felt that she didn't love me and I was furious; I didn't feel that I could do or say anything about it. (Becker, 1988, pp. 113-114)

Louise was surprised by her ambivalent feelings. She realized that she still expected Fran to be her primary source of comfort and that she had not let go of the relationship. Louise saw that she continued to hope Fran would love her as she wanted to be loved. These awarenesses eventually helped Louise let go of Fran and find non-lovers who affirmed herself in ways that Fran had not provided.

Spending time away from an ex-lover can be beneficial as well. Physical separation facilitates emotional separation. It makes emotional losses real and opens up the resulting emotional wounds. Not having contact with an ex-lover leaves you facing yourself, unmoored from the coupleship and surrounded by the work of rebuilding your life. Not seeing an ex-lover gives you the time to get reacquainted with the new you: to acknowledge how you have been changed by the relationship, to appraise the emotional healing that needs to be begun, and to face loss and loneliness. Getting to know yourself apart from the lover relationship is an important piece of recovery.

After spending time away from a former lover, contact enables you to see whether a mutually satisfying friendship can be built. When people are no longer lovers, their perceptions of one another can shift. Some ex-lovers realize that they once loved but now do not even like each other. Hannah talks about her experience of meeting Robin for coffee and seeing her in a new light:

Robin and I met for coffee seven months after she had moved out. It was awkward, but it broke the ice to see each other and talk. Both of us were nervous and tried not to show it. It took a few minutes of superficial chit-chat for us to relax. She talked about her new lover; I talked about mine. We sort of caught up on each other's lives. We didn't talk about any of the issues in our relationship. In fact we've never talked about what happened or our feelings about it. I expressed myself in the relationship and now there's nothing left to say. I think we both realize that there's really nothing to talk about because there is such a difference in values between us—we're just different.

Since that first meeting, Robin and I have met three or four times. Our conversations aren't close ones and I don't think we'll ever get back to talking on an emotional level. The care and trust we once had for each other is gone. I feel that Robin is a person I don't even know, which is sad in light of the four years we spent together. I'm not angry at her like I was in our relationship and I don't feel like she's my enemy. I just feel like I don't know her. Now, I wouldn't get involved with her in the first place. In fact, I wonder how I did—what the attraction was. (Becker, 1988, p. 116)

Other ex-lovers found many things they liked and loved about each other. This mutual care and respect provided the foundation for a friendship.

Relationships With New Lovers

Relationships with new lovers help people recover from breakups in several ways. The pleasure and excitement of new love gives people hope that their love lives are not over forever. Loving and being loved heartens people. New love heals some of the wounds of a breakup, brings forth the person's best qualities, and revitalizes the person. New parts of oneself blossom with new lovers, and old parts arc reclaimed and revived. Love lightens pain, sadness, and even the most difficult losses. When lover relationships end, one partner may already be involved with another lover. As they recover from a breakup, ex-lovers eventually become involved with new lovers.

A number of women in my study ended their relationships because they had fallen in love with others. These new relationships motivated them to end unhappy relationships. It helped spouses clarify unmet desires, and it motivated them to begin the difficult work of untangling their partnerships. Judy tells how her involvement with Myra motivated her to end her relationship with Tammy:

Before I met Myra, I had started withdrawing—emotionally, psychologically, and sexually—from Tammy. As I got to know Myra, and realized that I was falling in love with her, I knew that I had to end my relationship with Tammy quickly and kindly.

The joy and excitement of being in love with Myra sustained me through the trauma of telling Tammy that I wanted to separate. It felt wonderful to be in love again; I don't think I've ever felt so in love. For the first time in my life, I felt like my lover was my equal—I felt safe and relieved. After Tammy moved out, my relationship with Myra helped me set limits with Tammy and kept me from getting caught up in taking

> care of her. Knowing that I had to finish my relationship with Tammy
> before I could fully develop my relationship with Myra enabled me to
> make the necessary changes as fast as possible. (Becker, 1988, p. 101)

Her relationship with Myra renewed Judy emotionally and sexually and enabled her to do what she had wanted but had been unable to do.

New lovers facilitate fresh work upon old problems. Although most
new lover relationships appear different and better than old ones, problems usually occur as the relationship develops. It is particularly disturbing to see the problems that ended a previous relationship reoccurring
with a new person. This realization, however, clarifies our part in relational problems and enables us to see their origins in our selves.
Contact between ex-lovers can provide insights into the part we
play in relational problems. Julie's contact with her ex-lover, Dana,
helped her see the patterns each of them brought to sexual love relationships. She explains:

> We both wanted to get over our bad feelings about our breakup. It took
> a long time. It took watching Dana go through a couple of relationships
> and seeing that she kept getting involved with women like me, only
> worse.
>   I started to see the things that had happened between us happen with
> other lovers. At first she'd say, "It's different, I realize this and this."
> Then she began getting into the same patterns; getting angry with her
> lover and letting the anger interfere with their sex life. I told her, "Your
> karma is to get involved with somebody like me, only worse." She really
> got caught up in some horrible relationships. . . .
>   In the meantime, I got involved with someone who was just as judg-
> mental of me as Dana had been. Dana had been critical of trivial things;
> my new lover, Sara, was judgmental of my fundamental values. It was
> even more earth-shaking for me to face that kind of negation and it was
> the same damn thing that I had hated about Dana. (Becker, 1988, p. 120)

Seeing old patterns reoccur with someone new can be discouraging,
but it can help us change them.

What Helps Ex-lovers Become Friends

When possible, remaining in contact with an ex-lover has its advantages. Pieces of ourselves have developed with former lovers,
and large chunks of our histories have been shared with them. Re-
taining contact with ex-lovers gives emotional and social continuity

to our lives. It provides social continuity that bears witness to our change and stability over time. Contact between ex-lovers helps them decide whether they can be friends.

Once they are no longer lovers, former partners must appraise honestly what they like about each other. Personal attributes and interests enjoyed together form the foundation of a nonlover relationship. As she resolved some of the difficult problems between her ex-lover and herself, Judy became reacquainted with some of Tammy's qualities that she valued. She says:

> Tammy has a very sharp wit; she enjoys humor as much as I do. Each of us appreciates the other's way of laughing at things that come up. She's a little kinky too—she does things in an off-the-wall way that follows a crazy logic. When it's not infuriating, it's absolutely pleasurable.
>
> Tammy's bright, dependable and responsible. I know that if I was really in crisis and needed something from her, she'd do it. That's a nice feeling. Tammy's work involves caring for people—she's very competent and gives people wonderful care. I really respect and love her for that; we have similar values about what's important in life. (Becker, 1988, p. 151)

Each ex-lover, however, must be ready and able to develop a friendship that is not a lover relationship. Whatever changes in meanings and actions are part of the shift from lovers to friends, these changes must be mutually agreed upon and accepted. Ex-lovers are often out of step with each other; one person is ready to be friends when the other is not. To be friends, ex-partners must like each other, want to be friends, be willing to work at making the transition, and be ready to do these things at the same point in time.

When ex-lovers try to be friends, they have to work through or set aside such difficult feelings as anger, betrayal, and guilt. Honest talking and nondefensive listening are sometimes all that is necessary. Feelings that cannot be resolved interfere with a trusting and respectful friendship. When ex-lovers can see the part they played in the ending of the relationship, be honest with one another, accept each other as they are rather than how they wished they could be, and let go of old hurts and expectations, they have a better chance of becoming friends. Differences can be taken less personally between friends than between lovers. This new attitude can enable ex-lovers to be at ease with and accepting of differences between them. Sue explains how much easier it is to experience the clashes of values with her ex-lover, Silvia, now that they are living separately:

> There were a lot of class differences between Silvia and me. When we were lovers, I got enmeshed in her values. Now, I feel more separate and don't get caught up in them.
>
> When we were lovers, Silvia would have to buy something for the house every week. I'd say, "I'm saving money; I can't afford it." I felt uncomfortable living with debts, but she didn't mind it. Now, the same thing goes on, but it's over there—at her house. Often, when I go over there, she'll have bought something new. I don't have to feel panicked while she's telling me how much money she saved by buying it. We're still doing what we used to do, but we're in separate houses and I'm not hooked into it. (Becker, 1988, p. 152)

Because friends expect to be more separate than lovers, ex-lovers can negotiate difficulties more easily than previously. Ex-lovers who wish to be friends are more tolerant and accepting of each other as separate people than they were as lovers. Like friends, they are apt to accept one another and to adjust the possibilities and limitations of the relationship to their real selves.

Emotional and sexual boundaries must be renegotiated when ex-lovers try to be friends. Former intimacies can be a strong basis for mutual sharing, love, and respect. While some ex-lovers have difficulty finding the common basis for a friendship, others have problems distancing from intimacies that are no longer appropriate. If ex-partners still feel sexually attracted to each other, they must develop mechanisms for redirecting this magnetism between them. Shawn recounts what happened between her and Teresa:

> I had broken up with Teresa; both of us knew our relationship wasn't working even though we still were very sexually attracted to each other. Because both of us were ambivalent, we decided not to see each other. But, since we lived on the same block, we were always running into each other. At first we tried saying hello, but that always led to a conversation. Then, we tried waving. That worked for awhile, but then we were having intense fights every time we saw each other. (Becker, 1988, pp. 55-56)

Shawn discovered that passionate fighting soon led to sexual involvements with Teresa, and she had to find new ways to structure their time together. Playing catch finally helped them change their sexual attraction into something that could be part of a friendship. Shawn explains:

> I didn't know how to be friends with Teresa after we first broke up. When we'd been lovers, there had been an enormous amount of passion and intensity; we'd never just spent peaceful time together like friends do. So, there we were with all of our sexual feelings and no basis for a non-sexual relationship.
>
> Both of us liked to play sports, so we developed a routine of going to the park and playing catch. Doing something physical while I was with Teresa really helped me deal with my sexual feelings. We'd play catch for a while and then we'd sit and talk. Our talks were intense and diffi-cult; I kept waiting for her to get involved with another lover and to stop being jealous of my relationship with Sandy. (Becker, 1988, p. 128)

When Teresa became involved with a new lover, it helped Shawn and Teresa let go of the old relationship and develop a friendship that was comfortable and enjoyable.

Emotional closeness also must be readjusted when ex-lovers try to be friends. New limits must be set and the relationship must take second place to new relationships with lovers. If ex-lovers do not clarify their new friendship status, their relationship can threaten new lovers and, in turn, make a friendship impossible. Ellen re-mained emotionally primary to her ex-lover, Rachel. Then, her new lover's birthday, which was the same day as an anniversary she had always shared with Rachel, made her choose between them. Ellen remembers the turmoil this forced choice caused her:

> The classic triangle, where I felt pulled between my commitments to Rachel and to my new lover, Donna, took place during the first year that Donna and I were lovers.
>
> Rachel and I had a tradition of spending April 25 together—the day her father had died. Every year, we'd go to movies, one right after the other, all day long. I'd said to her, "No matter what happens between us, I'll always do this with you." "I won't abandon you," was the con-scious message; "No one's going to love you better than I do," was the unconscious one.
>
> After Donna and I had been together for a couple of months, I asked her when her birthday was. When she said that it was April 25, I broke out in a cold sweat. I went into therapy and talked about it; pleasing everyone was something I took pride in and I felt completely torn.
>
> It turned out that I spent the day with Donna and didn't see Rachel. But, on my way over to Donna's, I dropped a card off at Rachel's house

that said I remembered this was an important day to her. All day, I kept reminding myself that I had chosen to be in a primary relationship with Donna and I had to stick to it. I didn't know if Rachel would be okay without me. . . .

Rachel was devastated when I told her that I couldn't spend the anniversary with her. Two days later, I was devastated when I found out that her new lover, Sandy, spent the day with her. I'd had this fantasy that she'd been alone and suicidal because I wasn't with her. It was hard to find out that I was so easily replaceable; Sandy went to the movies with her and it was fine. It made me realize how invested I was in taking care of Rachel. (Becker, 1988, pp. 140-141)

Reprioritizing loyalties can help people correct dysfunctional ways that they love and can enable ex-lovers to cultivate respect for each other's autonomy and resourcefulness.

Satisfying friendships between ex-lovers maximize enjoyment and minimize conflict. One of their benefits is the emotional and social continuity they provide in people's lives. When the traumas of the breakup have been resolved, ex-lovers have a wider and wiser view of how being lovers and breaking up fit into their growth process. Contact between ex-lovers can cultivate these understandings. Wendy talks about the usefulness of her relationship with Jody:

The thing that ties Jody and me together is that we met at a junction and created a crisis with each other. We pushed a lot of each other's buttons, but it wasn't bad. The way I see it now, we weren't meant to be lovers forever but we were meant to run into each other. Our pain wasn't useless—it was our stuff and we each had to do something different and apart to heal ourselves.

For me, it meant putting an end to fixing people, to trying to bring my mother back to life, and to feeling responsible for other people's lives. It meant dropping the appearance of being unambivalent about making commitments. For Jody, it involved looking at how she could fix herself rather than finding a lover who'd do it for her. It meant trying to nurture herself.

In a way, we're more compatible now than when we were lovers. She's more introspective; I'm more relaxed. We both feel much more alive than we used to feel. Now, we giggle about what a mess we made together and how we both managed to get something good for ourselves out of it. (Becker, 1988, pp. 147-148)

By maintaining contact, ex-lovers can gain empathy for themselves and each other. They can see the overwhelming pressures they were managing and understand previously obscure dynamics.

Personal growth and change is validated by contact with people who have known us over time. In a less emotionally charged friendship relationship, ex-lovers can continue working upon essential intimacy skills. They can help one another learn how to love themselves while loving someone else, negotiate differences, make commitments, recover from disappointments and betrayals, and continue their personal integration while cultivating close and lasting relationships. Continuity of contact with old and new lovers can enhance awareness of habits that strengthen and weaken intimate relationships. In this process, difficult relational patterns can be changed, and new awarenesses and skills can increase the possibilities of lasting and satisfying intimate relationships.

PART IV

❖

Helping Relationships

Unlike intimate relationships, helping relationships are task focused and asymmetrical relations. In the helping relationships discussed in Part IV, professionals, whether psychotherapists or doctors or nurses or teachers, provide services for a fee. These trained authorities in their fields agree to suspend mutuality and reciprocity and to be there to serve others: to listen, to understand, to assist, to heal, and to empower. Each professional assists people with aspects of themselves— their hearts or souls, their bodies, or their minds—and enables them to take up their everyday lives with increased power and freedom. These relationships continue until the task is accomplished, and then they end.

In Part IV, I look at the similar and different natures of psychotherapy, medical helping, and teaching. Being task focused, these relationships can become so concentrated upon cure or empowerment through knowledge that the participants neglect the relational, person-to-person components. Much can be gained, however, from a phenomenological approach to professional helping relationships, one that increases awareness of and sensitivity to experiencing people. A phenomenological view of psychotherapy, physical illness, and teaching opens them to include real people and their concerns by illuminating people's experiences, desires, intentions, and lifeworlds. Knowing more about the relational

nature of helping can increase its effectiveness. All of the helping relationships discussed in Part IV strive to empower the
helpee: by unraveling emotional blocks, by healing physical
problems, and by sharing specialized knowledge. All of them
seek to enhance effective living and, in different ways, to help
people realize their potentials, possibilities, and freedoms.
The shared goal of these diverse relationships is to connect
people with their resources and enable them to be and become
dynamic centers of life who change and grow within a community of humanity.

14

Psychotherapy

The psychotherapy relationship is established for the explicit purpose of one person, the psychotherapist, being helpful to another who needs help, the client. Psychotherapy is like all other helping relationships, and yet it has mystifying and magical qualities. Because it is a private, confidential relationship with which few people have personal experience, much joking and fantasizing about it occurs. And too, psychotherapy can make us uneasy because its specific purpose is to deal with the unresolved wounds of life.

Psychotherapy that is based upon mutual trust and a sincere desire to change involves intimate sharing similar to and often greater than that with friends and spouses. Passionate feelings of all sorts—love, attraction, anger, hatred, betrayal, gratitude, envy, anxiety—occur within its boundaries. Unlike the other relationships we have discussed, psychotherapy is an intimate but also a professional relationship. It takes place outside of the everyday world, in a room of its own and in its own hour. Precisely because its place and time are so small, private, and safe from the real pressures of life, the psychotherapy relationship can be transformative. Its magic is based upon human presence, honesty, and care. These qualities are fundamental parts of everyday life.

All of us give and receive help. During the course of our lives, each of us will need assistance. People needing help share common experiences and meanings; they feel vulnerable and helpless; they want and need resources that are unavailable to them. Being in need can be painful. We can feel embarrassed and ashamed. But being in need also enables us to receive kindness from others. It can help us receive gifts that really matter.

Our needs are easy to identify when we need food, shelter, or money. When our needs are emotional, psychological, and interpersonal, they are harder to name and champion. Our own experiences of needing help enable us to understand other people's experiences of needing and receiving help.

People often ask for help when they are at the end of the line, when they have hit bottom, when things have gotten so bad that they can no longer avoid the issues. A problem has become an emergency, a crisis is in full bloom. People are brought to the psychotherapist's office by a clear problem or a vague desire to live more happily and fully. They need or want something they have not been able to find by themselves. In a way, people who come to a psychotherapist are forced to seek help. Implicitly or explicitly, they may subscribe to an ethic of self-sufficiency and independent resourcefulness that makes it difficult to ask for help. This ethic can make many of us feel ashamed, weak, and unworthy when we are dependent, in need, or without sufficient resources. We are afraid of what will happen to us if someone else sees how vulnerable and helpless we feel. In fact, we can be frightened by these parts of ourselves. When we cross over the threshold into the psychotherapist's realm, our pride is usually shattered, our willful control of life has crumbled, and we are stripped down to a vulnerable state.

The Therapist's Understanding
of the Client

An easy-to-understand example of phenomenological thinking about a patient's problems is given by J. H. van den Berg in his small book, *A Different Existence* (1972a). Van den Berg describes a composite patient who enters the consultation room in visible distress. The patient is Dutch, 25 years old, and speaks with great difficulty and hesitation. Van den Berg describes their initial meeting:

Even the first moments showed that he was in great difficulties. He looked at me with a mixture of distrust and shyness, and when he shook my extended hand, I felt a soft, weak hand, the hand of a person who doesn't know a way out and, not being in control of himself, lets himself drift. Stooping uncertainly, he sat down in the chair which I invited him to take.

He did not relax, but sat on the edge of the chair as if preparing to get up and leave. His right hand, which he had held under his unbuttoned vest when he entered, and which he had removed from there in order to greet me so unconvincingly, was immediately replaced in its original position. With his left hand, he drummed the armrest of the chair uneasily. He did not cross his legs. His behavior created the impression of a man who has been tortured for a long time. (pp. 5-6)

The story of this man's life confirmed the extent of his psychological torment. A university student, the man had not attended classes for months because he could not leave his room during the day. The last time he went out during daylight the houses looked grey and decayed and he felt they were about to fall down upon him. People looked unreal and far away, even those who passed quite close to him. Overcome by anxiety, fear, and loneliness, he returned to his room where he felt safer. Here too, however, fears and discomforts disturbed his tranquility. Both in the street and in his room, his heart beat irregularly and he held his hand over it to support and control it. Sometimes, in public settings, his heart beat so furiously that he was certain it would burst. Because his heart was quieter in his room, he rarely went out.

The man felt best when alone in his room, studying scientific texts. A few select friends who talked exclusively about scientific matters were allowed to visit him. News of daily events and social talk increased his discomfort, and his beating heart made it necessary to end these conversations. His heart was normal only when he and his friends unrelentlessly criticized women. Then he felt almost like his old self, and even laughed.

The man's heart first began beating so violently when a woman he had been dating left him. She had suggested they become engaged, he had laughed at her, and she had left the relationship. He never dated after that. Instead, he preferred prostitutes whom he enjoyed humiliating without touching. His main pleasure in life came from criticizing women, as well as his parents (van den Berg, 1972a, pp. 5-18).

From the client's description of his lived world, a world becoming increasingly constricted and emptied of people and happiness, van den Berg develops a descriptive portrayal of the existential themes of the patient's self and life. Van den Berg listens to the man's experiences, takes them seriously, and illuminates their lived meanings. Like many phenomenologists, van den Berg organizes his understanding around fundamental structures of world, body, others, and time. These formulations show important dimensions of the client's world and enable the therapist to enter the client's experiential world.

Phenomenologically oriented psychotherapists such as van den Berg want to understand the other's experience from inside his or her lifeworld. These experiences, filled with intentions, feelings, and meanings, are expressions of the client's active subjectivity. No matter how dysfunctional and distraught the person is, the phenomenologist believes that the client remains the intentional co-creator of meaning and is living as best as she or he can. The therapist seeks an understanding of the unique, lived meanings of each person's life. These experiences are found in the world, in the sensuous textures of objects, in feeling tones of interactions, in meanings of events. Understanding comes from exploring the meanings richly present in the patient's difficulties and concerns. The phenomenologist asks: What must it be like to be experiencing this? Where must the person be standing to be seeing this? What existential dimensions of life are problems for this person? This experiential, foundational picture of the person's life helps the therapist know where and how the client dwells and where and how the client can be contacted.

When the client is ill, his or her world is ill. The client finds her or his experience *in* the world, in a self embodied in time and space and living relationally with others. The meanings of a person's self and life can be found in these dimensions of experience. Taking his client's experience seriously, van den Berg finds a man bereft and alone in the world, without a past or a future life that supports his present existence. The world is, indeed, closing him out and threatening to collapse upon him. His body feels incapable of supporting him; his legs are on the verge of crumbling, and his heart is about to explode. People seem farther away each day, and pleasure is nearly beyond his reach. As he listens for the meanings and themes of the man's experiential world, van den Berg hears a man who lives in an interpersonally empty, unsatisfying, and untenable world. He is alone and lonely. His loneliness results from his experiences, meanings, perceptions, and life goals being unshared. He is isolated from a viable interpersonal community and, each day, his life becomes less viable.

Unlike most conventional therapists, van den Berg understands that the patient's illness is his inability to contact people in his present life. It is not the other way around, that the patient's past causes his present difficulties and that he cannot contact people because he is ill. For van den Berg, the patient's inability to contact people *is* his difficulty. Phenomenologists believe that the real problems are the present ones. The therapist intervenes by seeking contact with the patient in the present. The past and the future can be understood and changed when the client is understood as she or he is now, in the present. If the therapist succeeds in standing with the client in her or his experiential world, the client is less alone than before, and they have begun to build a shared, empathic world that surrounds and supports the client.

For phenomenologists, the co-created interpersonal world between therapist and client is focal to treatment. Within this relationship, the intentional lifeworld of the client is revealed. All the problems in the lifeworld outside of psychotherapy can be found also within the walls of the therapy office. The client can do nothing else but bring all of himself or herself into the psychotherapeutic relationship. The here and now of the therapy hour is rich with all of the client's life.

Van den Berg (1971b) has looked at the historical and sociocultural meanings of mental illness and has seen that the psychological problems that bring clients to psychotherapy change with historical and cultural shifts. According to van den Berg, when a society neglects or negates an aspect of life, a person loses that aspect of the self and must find a way of returning to it. In Victorian society, for example, sexuality and aggression were taboo parts of life. Freud's psychoanalysis underscored the importance of these life themes and helped clients reintegrate them into normal living. The psychotherapist assists the client by knowing about lost aspects of the self, by standing in for the emptied sectors of life, and by bringing these vital parts of life back to the client. Because the therapist embodies an integration that the client lacks, the psychotherapy relation brings these aspects of life within the client's reach. In this sense, the therapist is the client's "yet to become" self.

Whereas psychotherapy patients of Freud's day brought problems concerning sex and aggression, the contemporary client brings different symptoms to the therapist. Similar to van den Berg's composite client, the modern psychotherapy client suffers from loneliness in a society that is not cohesive and has lost a sense of community. Being alone and afraid, people seek their rightful place in the interpersonal world, one that can be the stable ground for their lives. Van den Berg believes that contemporary people have lost pride in their right to be unequal, to have unique talents, deficiencies, interests, and goals. Without a sense of their "rightful inequality," people strive for an unrealistic equality and togetherness. The therapist's job with such a client is to facilitate a return to uniqueness; to help the client find her or his special position on the ladder of society and life. Seen in this way, the therapist stands for what is missing or out of balance in the client's life. She or he embodies, speaks for, and brings these aspects of life back to the person, making it possible for the client to reintegrate them and to be whole.

Other existential-phenomenological psychotherapists have approached their work from within the philosophical understanding of human living and relating discussed in Part I. Founders of existential-phenomenological psychotherapy such as Ludwig Binswanger (1963) and Medard Boss (1963) discovered a useful therapeutic framework in Heidegger's philosophy of human existence. They developed clinical understandings of mentally ill people based upon a view of people as active subjects, co-creating meaning and living intentionally. Rather than focusing on past events as causes of emotional illnesses, for example, they saw that clients did not have a viable present or future life and that their relations to self and other had failed. Existential-phenomenological psychotherapists reconstructed the client's life history around fundamental themes of existence: how the person lived in time and space, the embodied self, his or her perceptions of the world, and relationships to others. Descriptions of these existential a prioris, these fundamental aspects of existence, enabled Binswanger and Boss to see the lifeworlds of their clients and to enter into these lifeworlds with respectful understanding. Boss's existential-phenomenological formulation of mental illness, called daseinanalysis, was based upon Heidegger's explications of people as *Dasein*. Beginning within the depth psychology first developed by Freud, daseinanalysis offered a larger view of human possibility and freedom than psychoanalysis. Daseinanalysis took as its foundation a view of the person as an intentional, reflective, free person-in-the-world-with-others. A recent special issue of *The Humanistic Psychologist* edited by American phenomenological psychotherapist Erik Craig (1988) summarizes daseinanalysis as a psychotherapy for freedom and shows its current clinical insights and applications.

Still other existential-phenomenological psychotherapists applied understandings of such existential themes of life as freedom, responsibility, anxiety, the search for meaning, loneliness, commitment, and death to their work with clients (see Yalom, 1980). One such theme, existential guilt, was seen as a core issue in emotional suffering. Existential guilt results from human responsibility, freedom, limitation, and finitude. It arises when a person does not fulfill his or her potential and is not all that she or he could be.

When I hesitate or shrink back from myself and my life out of fear or insecurity, for example, I evoke existential guilt. I am guilty for being limited, fearful, and less than I can be. Existential guilt can also arise in my relationships with others. Experiencing the effects my misunderstandings, insensitivities, or self-absorptions have upon myself or another calls me back to myself and to the other. My guilt, deeply and viscerally reverberating within my body, shakes me from my fears or self-absorptions and calls me back to myself and my human community. Contemporary philosopher and psychotherapist Maurice Friedman (1991) defines existential guilt as real guilt, a guilt that calls people back to their responsive responsibility and interpersonal answerability. Real guilt occurs in the interhuman world and shows me that my response has been inadequate or untimely (Friedman, 1991, pp. 518-519).

Faced and accepted, existential guilt can clarify values and ground us in commitments by which we can live with self and others in a shared world. Ultimately, it enables us to face ourselves and others with integrity, to stand with human values we can live by, to stretch beyond the confines of our personal concerns, and to join hands with like-hearted people. Facing existential guilt transforms it from a limitation into a strong basis for interhuman living.

A final example of a phenomenological approach to psychotherapy is one developed by psychotherapist Robert Romanyshyn (1990). Romanyshyn creates a depth phenomenology that owes much to psychoanalysis. This phenomenological view of psychotherapy recontextualizes psychological life as a metaphorical reality. Romanyshyn finds the roots of this depth phenomenology in psychoanalysis. He explains:

> Psychoanalysis attunes us to this dramatic landscape where human experience matters insofar as it is a believable story. Indeed, the storying of experience to which psychoanalysis introduces us indicates that human life as we live it in the world with others—that is, before we philosophize about it and before we reduce it to the level of our explanations, whatever they may be—is less a matter of what we know and more a matter of what we believe and can believe. The *what* of experience is as much, and perhaps even more, a matter of the faith of the human heart than it is the knowledge of the human mind. (Romanyshyn, 1990, p. 243)

From his phenomenological view of human life, Romanyshyn sees that remembering our lives is a dynamic process of re-membering ourselves within the context of the present, as well as the past. As such, we create our lives in the process of returning to, facing, and understanding ourselves. Psychological life is metaphorical in that it is identical to and different from the facts of life. In the interplay between events and meanings, psychological life is created and witnessed. We create from our lives what truly matters to us, as we are now and as we hope to be. Romanyshyn (1990) calls this process of working with the metaphorical character of life *storying.* He states:

> We *remember* the past precisely because we *re-member* it. We *preserve* what was precisely because we *transform* it. We *discover* the past precisely because we *create* it. And this work of re-membering, of transforming, of creating is a matter of what is believable and as such bearable. Truth, understood psychologically, is a matter of what one can believe.
>
> This storying of experience suggests that human life is a work of making, a *poesis* in the root sense of this term (see Romanyshyn, 1987). This work of storying indicates that in living in the life-world we are en-

gaged in a poetic history, in a making of what is already made, whether
that be the givenness of the present or the past, or the givenness of the
other, the world, and one's own body.

In a sense we have come nearly full circle insofar as the storying of
experience has led us toward the recognition that human experience is
a given to be made. (Romanyshyn, 1990, p. 244)

Romanyshyn (1988) understands psychotherapy as a creative process that includes "landscaping, figuring, and storying" experience.
Each person who comes to the therapist with problems or symptoms
brings her or his story of life to the therapist. In the first exchange of
words and gestures, the story that *is* the client and his or her world
begins to unfold. By carefully attending, the therapist can see and
hear the person's story and recognize the figure of the client within
the landscape of the story. According to Romanyshyn (1988):

> In re-membering the past the patient in psychotherapy is engaged in the
> process of re-shaping the given of his or her life into a vessel which
> contains it. And that vessel . . . is nothing less than the story which is
> told, a story which preserves the past by re-shaping it. . . . The story
> through which the patient re-members (transforms and preserves) the
> past is . . . a way of seeing, a guide, something which shows the way of
> his or her life. It is the manner, guise, or appearance of things, the way
> in which the things and events of one's life are revealed and preserved.
> It is the form or shape of these things of one's life, the way in which they
> are held and contained. And as such and in all these ways the story
> through which the patient re-members his or her life, the story which is
> the creation of psychotherapy as a creative process, is a kind of wisdom.
> (pp. 43-44)

The therapist's work is to be a present and understanding witness
who helps the client articulate her or his story. A story told and
heard can be a vehicle for reclaiming a life.

A client's story begins with a sense of what is not right in life. The
problems that brought the person to therapy contain the parts that
need to be re-membered. These problems, along with the client's
struggle to make sense of and to find a way through them, are the
work of therapy. Participating in this process, the therapist often is
privileged to sit with a person who has courage: to face pain, to return to disowned parts of life, and to speak a story for which he or
she does not as yet have words.

The self-knowledge that results from psychotherapy etches out a fullness and a roundness of life that is always larger than impersonally applied therapeutic techniques and linear, logical summaries of causes and cures. The psychotherapist's work is to stand in and with life's wholeness and complexity, and to make it available as a personal resource to the client. Romanyshyn (1991) explains:

> In an age and at a time overtaken by linear and programmed thinking, by obsessions with the bottom line and the straight path, by a passion for straightening things out and straightening them up, whether they be the messes of the environment or the perturbations of the human soul, we need, perhaps even desperately so, to remember the complex, twisted character of psychological living. Messes, individually and culturally, arise not because of the complex-ity of human affairs. They arise, individually and culturally, because of the illusory belief that such complex-ity is somehow wrong headed and in need of reasonable solutions. It is the denial of this complex-ity and not its presence which is problematic, the denial of soul in mind and not its presence which is the difficulty. We need, then, to remain twisted, soulful, in a linear world if we are to allow the circuitous path of psychological gnosis to find its way. We need to remain so in order to allow soul to twist itself between fact and fiction, reason and dream, the classroom and the therapy room, to weave and stitch its myth and poetry between them. If, individually and culturally, we are to make myths instead of symptoms, we need to preserve the complex character of our ensouled involvement with the world. We need to spare a place for the dream of our reasoning when, individually and culturally, we are about the work of inventing the events of our lives and those of the world. (p. 28)

The successful client leaves psychotherapy much more whole and ensouled that he or she was before entering the therapist's office. She or he is much more at home in the landscape of a unique life that is lived with understanding and purpose.

The Process of Psychotherapy

Psychotherapy takes place in back-and-forth talking and listening between therapist and client. The client talks about salient aspects of his or her life, and the therapist tries to understand the client on her or his terms, within a lived world orchestrated by intentions, memories, desires, and meanings. The phenomenologically oriented psychotherapist seeks to join the client in the lived world, to understand the figure of the client within this landscape, and to be with the client in such a way that the client can re-member his or her self and relationships. Because the client is understood as the intentional, co-creative center of meaningful engagement in life, a person who is responsible to tell a story, the therapist is primarily concerned with listening and being present. Understanding the client precedes intervention strategies; a shared search for the meanings in the client's life is valued over solving the client's problems. The client's position in life as an active subject who co-creates a story is central to the therapeutic work. Effective understanding must recognize the client's freedom and responsibility to craft a unique life.

Therapeutic techniques are employed within a respectful responsiveness to the client's being and becoming. Techniques used by phenomenologically oriented therapists draw upon the client's experienced knowledge in arriving at solutions to problems. One example of such a psychotherapeutic technique is a process developed by phenomenological psychotherapist Eugene Gendlin (1981) called *focusing*. Focusing is a way of accessing the wisdom of the prereflective body. It involves simple actions: being quiet, asking a general question about something in yourself or your life, paying attention to the "bodily felt sense" that arises in response to the question, and finding a word or image that expresses it. Gendlin has used focusing to help people change habitual ways of talking to and at themselves. Rational problem-solving techniques are suspended, and the person attends to the bodily, whole sense of something. This bodily sense is often unclear. It is usually ignored as we hurry to understand and solve a problem. We access preunderstandings of meanings and solutions of our intentional bodies when we focus; attending to the "whole felt sense" of something uncovers new insights and awarenesses. Focusing consists of six movements:

1. Clearing a space to attend to an inward bodily sense of the problem
2. Getting a bodily felt sense of the problem
3. Letting a word or image emerge from this felt sense (its handle)
4. Checking the word or image with the felt sense

   5. Querying the felt sense and its handle to adjust the fit between them
   6. Receiving and experiencing what comes from this process (Gendlin, 1981, pp. 43-70)

If focusing is successful, the person experiences a body shift that feels like a release. This body shift feels good even if it reveals difficult aspects of the problem. Focusing involves letting go of thinking and giving prereflective understandings room to emerge. Focusing opens us to the intentional body and its global, intuitive sense of life.

Like any psychotherapy, phenomenological psychotherapy aims at increasing the client's understanding of and power over the problems that brought her or him to the therapist. Entering into the client's lifeworld, the phenomenological therapist looks for salient existential themes, for the figure of the client within a unique story, for the person's lived intentions, concerns, losses, and desires. A touchstone of the work is the person-to-person relationship between therapist and client, a relationship that is created between them as they sit together and talk. If the client experiences the therapist as supportive, all interactions, even those in which the therapist errs, are helpful to the client. Useful insights are ones filled with feelings that occur within a relationship experienced as trustworthy. Van den Berg (1971b) explains:

> If by insight we understand the purely intellectual recognition of a connection which is logically sound or not easily refutable, then insight is not helpful. If, on the other hand, by insight we understand the emotional confirmation of a connecting link which seems sensible and practicable—and not only on logical grounds—then insight will help indeed. It has become increasingly clear in the course of the last 50 years that these nonlogical grounds include *the person of the psychotherapist.* More emphatically put: The reason which moves the patient to confirm the existence of a meaningful connecting link is above all the good relationship he has with the therapist. Expressed by a simple formula we might say: Insight is more a matter of communication and of interpersonal relationship, than that of knowledge. The patient's insight is to such an extent a matter of communication that only such insight will help which is *supported by understanding,* that is, *supported also by the therapist.* If the patient has a warm relationship with his therapist, then the therapist's insight is in principle right, no matter how small and insignificant, no matter how insufficient this insight may be. Is the relationship unsatisfactory or insufficient? Then the therapist may have a

completely worthy insight into the problems of his patient and the patient will not accept this insight and consequently will not profit by it.

Thus wisdom can harm and stupidity can do good in the realm of this
curious profession which is called psychotherapy. I do not wish to contend, of course, that a wise psychotherapist should not be preferred
above a stupid one; but the rule is, that an elementary trust between
psychotherapist and patient must be imperative. (pp. 331-332)

Successful psychotherapy, then, happens between a therapist and a
client who trust one another enough to open themselves to the
client's problems and to bring all of their resources to bear upon these
problems.

Trust between a therapist and client is built over time. It begins
with the client risking talking about difficult and painful matters
and, in this way, inviting the therapist to join in the problems. The
therapist listens to the client with respect, empathy, and awareness.
She or he cultivates a place that welcomes the client's experiences
and makes room for the client to explore feelings about life events.
When the client feels understood and supported, he or she can stop
defending the self and focus upon felt concerns. With the therapist's
support, the client can believe, with increasing certainty, that her or
his concerns are important ones and can explore important experiences, feelings, and meanings.

The therapist cultivates attentiveness to and presence with the client, instead of impersonally applied methods and solutions. The
therapist joins with the client and assists without taking over. He or
she helps by being with the client and expressing interest in his or
her life difficulties. Together, they explore the meanings, historical
context, and alternative approaches to the client's problems. Once
the problematic knots of the patient's life are loosened and unrav-
eled, the client gains access to other possibilities and connections.
If the therapy works well, an atmosphere is co-created within the
walls of the office that enables the client to face himself or herself in the presence of a nonjudgmental, knowledgeable,
concerned, resourceful, and empowering other person. The therapist witnesses, supports, guides, responds, and celebrates the client as she or he reclaims a real self in the world with others.

The therapist must enter into the client's experiential world while
simultaneously staying grounded in his or her own experience. This

dual movement results in the therapist being with while also being separate from the client, standing alongside while also standing and facing the client. By entering the client's world, the therapist transforms it into a shared world. When the client's meanings, experiences, hopes, disappointments, and longings are shared, they are more available than previously to the client and can be more readily integrated into a larger self.

As a phenomenologically oriented therapist, I bring various attitudes and values to the psychotherapeutic work of creating a shared world with the client. I approach the client with respectful attention, wanting to hear and understand the other on her or his own terms. I believe that the client's experience contains valuable insights into the person's difficulties. Even before meeting a particular client, I have cultivated a respectful openness to people's everyday experience, seeing this experience as the situational context for the essential intentions and meanings of a person's life. Important themes of life are richly embedded in the person's lifeworld, and I can understand them by listening to what the client spontaneously says. In his or her silences, actions, and words, the client reveals an intentional self, one actively engaged in co-creating a world with others. I greet each client with an implicit belief in her or his power to reclaim a desirable life in the world with others.

When I work as a therapist, I join the client by listening, by waiting, by talking, by sympathizing, by questioning, by suggesting, and even by disagreeing. But above all, I refrain from acting as though I know how the client should live. I do not find answers to the client's problems even though I sympathize with the suffering and take seriously the difficulties that have stalemated the client. Sitting with the client, listening attentively, and offering genuine responses, I become a supportive and stable person who is present in the client's world. I am not just there, I am actively engaged. I am all of myself, speaking what I really think and expressing genuine concerns and feelings. I am even ready to face aspects of the client's self from which the client flees. In addition to using my professional skills and knowledge, I bring my more personal human qualities to the client as resources that enhance the work. A spontaneous laugh, a genuine sound of sympathy, a word or image that resonates with the client's experience, a gesture of welcome, a kind touch, or a truthful response shows the client that I am there as a whole person.

Besides being present for and with the client, I must remain centered in my own experiential world. I can enter the client's world only if I remain grounded in my own world and self. While listening to the client, I listen to my emotional and intellectual responses; the feelings, thoughts, and images that are evoked by the client's story. I offer a selection of these reactions to the client, using them to further explore the client's experience. Grounded in a wide understanding of human nature, relationships, and development, I probe, as well as empathize. I strive to be gentle but honest, caring yet daring enough to touch the pain the client wishes to hide, supportive yet respectful enough to expect the client to stretch toward the next step of emotional growth, insightful yet dedicated to empowering the client's ability to live life without my help. I use whatever wisdom I can draw upon to reveal diverse aspects of the client's self and life so that they can be understood and integrated.

An important part of my healing power comes from my genuine presence as another person, one who is not the client. As an other who is separate and different from the client, I not only respond and empathize but also question and suggest. Doing so within the context of commitments to the client's well-being, I truly join the client and create a shared world of psychotherapeutic work. When I can be with a client in this way, the client is likely to experience permission and even encouragement to be himself or herself. Then, the client can draw upon a priceless experience—one of knowing that she or he will be seen and heard by someone whose care and understanding is insightful and constant.

The paradox of the psychotherapeutic relationship is that the therapist helps the client fix his or her problems by doing nothing to or for the client. This is, however, anything but a passive and disinterested presence. Precisely because the therapist is engaged and cares, she or he does not manipulate or objectify the client. Together, the therapist and client witness the client's anger, hopelessness, fear, dread, loneliness, abandonment. Together, they bring these difficult and unwanted aspects of the client's existence back into dialogue with a larger, dynamic self.

Successful Psychotherapy

In its simplest form, the goal of helping is to resolve contact difficulties, to help an objectified and truncated self return to full potential, possibility, presence, and freedom. Successful therapy returns the client to his or her experience and behavior. The client who is free to know what she or he thinks and feels, who can acknowledge a wide range of wishes and intentions, who is increasingly in touch with a comprehensive and integrated self, and who can be spontaneous and genuine with other people is relating to himself or herself as a Thou in Buber's (1985) terms. When a person is a Thou, it is possible for that person, who is self-present, to be fully present with others.

Beginning with a client who has lost a viable interpersonal context for life, the psychotherapist helps return the client to a sense of self that can act as a starting point for fulfilling relations with others. Quoting German existential analyst Hans Trüb, Maurice Friedman (1991) explains the process and end point of successful psychotherapy:

> The analyst must see the illness of the patient as an illness of his relations with the world. . . . The roots of the neurosis lie both in the patient's closing himself off from the world and in the pattern of society itself and its rejection and nonconfirmation of the patient. Consequently, the analyst must change at some point from the consoler who takes the part of the patient against the world to the person who puts before the patient the claim of the world. This change is necessary to complete the second part of the cure—that establishment of real relationship with the world which can only take place in the world itself. . . . The psychotherapist must test the patient's finding of himself by the criterion of whether his self-realization can be the starting-point for a new personal meeting with the world. The patient must go forth whole in himself, but he must also recognize that it is not his own self but the world with which he must be concerned. (p. 520)

The end result of successful psychotherapy is a dynamic one that is achieved but never finished. Existential philosopher Helen Merrell Lynd (cited in Friedman, 1991) explains the reciprocal relation between being oneself and being with others. She says:

> The ability to enter into relations of intimacy and mutuality opens the way to experiences in which the self expands beyond its own limita-

tions in depth of feeling, understanding, and insight. One's own identity may be ... strengthened by the meaning one has for others in one's group and by respect for those other persons as distinct individuals. ...

Openness to relatedness with other persons and the search for self-identity are not two problems but one dialectical process; as one finds more relatedness to other persons one discovers more of oneself; as the sense of one's own identity becomes clearer and more firmly rooted one can more completely go out to others. It is not a loss of oneself, an "impoverishment," but a way of finding more of oneself when one means most to others whom one has chosen. Nor must complete finding of oneself ... precede finding oneself in and through other persons. Identity is never wholly realized. Love is never perfect. Strength to apprehend love that is beyond anxiety, beyond desire for power over others is never complete, but may grow throughout life. Like identity and mutuality with others it is a lifetime process of discovery. (p. 400-402)

Successful therapy returns clients to the power of their unique selves. It enables them to experience themselves as co-creators of life, as people with emotional and interpersonal rights, who can know their meanings and desires, and who can exercise situated freedom in the interpersonal world. Phenomenological psychotherapy enhances the client's desire and ability to be all of himself or herself with other people. Being truly present to self and others, the client lives life in realistic, self-fulfilling, and interpersonally validating ways. Ultimately, the successful client takes up her or his life differently, more centered in self-awareness and in personal rights than before beginning psychotherapy. This usually enables the client to live with satisfaction, emotional freedom, and personal vitality and power.

Phenomenological psychotherapy cultivates the existential birth or rebirth of the client's self. This seems simple enough, but in reality it is a complex and fragile endeavor. When it succeeds, it is a dialectical, responsive, creative, and empathic process that touches both therapist and client with its wonder and force.

15

Helping the Physically Ill Person

In contrast with the psychotherapy client who brings intangible problems such as anxiety, sadness, unhappiness, and hopelessness to the therapist, the physically ill person takes concrete illnesses to the doctor. These illnesses—a pain in the knee, an ache in the stomach, a sore that will not heal, a pain in the chest—can be shown to the doctor, and the person, now the medical doctor's patient, can expect the doctor to do something to relieve them. In many ways, the physically ill patient can sit back and let the doctor solve the problem. Of course, the patient must cooperate by taking the prescribed medicine, following doctor's orders, and giving the body adequate nutrition and rest. In a number of ways, however, the physically ill patient steps aside so that the doctor can heal the illness.

The Nature of Medical Helping

The medical doctor's help is both similar to and different from that offered by psychotherapists. Both professional helping relationships are intimate ones. Sometimes these professionals know more about the secrets of the person's life than loved friends, spouses, and relatives. Like psychotherapists, medical doctors enter the patient's life only at specific hours and for brief time periods. They are excluded from the patient's normal, everyday life but can be closer to the patient's private, existential concerns. Both physicians and psychotherapists are experts in the dreaded and dreadful parts of life—loss, anxiety, pain, sadness, fear, and death. Patients come to both doctors at their most vulnerable—suffering, defeated, and needing help. Unlike more intimate, day-to-day relationships, ones with professional helpers are stripped of the burdens of mutuality and reciprocal responsibility.

Within Western medicine, physically ill people approach medical helpers in a manner much different from the psychologically ill. Physically ill people bring sick bodies to physicians; emotionally ill people bring sick souls to psychotherapists. Differences in these two forms of helping are visible even in the language; the person in need of medical help is always a "patient," while the person in need of psychotherapy is often a "client." Each form of helping has a particular way of approaching the person seeking help. Medical patients are treated, taken care of, and made better by the doctor. Psychotherapy clients must be actively engaged in their healing.

Medical expertise is based first and foremost upon technical information and skill. It is aimed at the patient's body, a body that has been objectified, cut open, dissected into its parts, and grafted and sewn. Pills, injections, and procedures are its remedies, and these demand only consent and minimal cooperation from the patient. Healing can occur outside of the patient's self, in the realm of the patient's objectified body. The competent doctor or nurse knows, of course, that the patient's intentions and experiences are the context for the effectiveness of the remedies and engages these aspects of the patient. Medicines or operative procedures, rather than the relationship between doctor and patient, are the pivotal aspects of treatment. Medical expertise is so sophisticated precisely because the body has been separated from the person.

Medical helping is task focused in a way that does not depend upon the personal meanings and intentions of the patient. The medical helper takes over for the patient, assumes responsibility for treatment, intervenes in the medical crisis, and resolves it. The doctor works outside of the patient's experience and understanding by monitoring the functioning of vital organs and body fluids. Illness and treatment occur in physical reality, in observable and measurable aspects of the patient's body.

Doctors and nurses are expected to help physically ill patients by taking over, by acting upon patients, and by healing them. Within Western medicine, medical personnel are expected to make symptoms go away and to remove illnesses from patients' bodies. Physically ill patients can come to physicians with even greater expectations than they bring to psychotherapists. Unlike people who are emotionally and interpersonally distraught, physically ill people rarely feel responsible for or ashamed of being sick.

The medical doctor's role is an authoritative one. He or she is master of the technical, physical matters of life and death. In the face of death, the meanings of life and death are overshadowed by the physical struggle against death. Only when death has been defeated or has won a permanent place in the patient's life do medical personnel step aside and make room for experts who are skilled in death's meanings. For the physically ill person, however, the meanings of an illness are the most real and gripping aspects of being sick.

Within the world of medical helping, a phenomenology of the sickbed (van den Berg, 1972b) illuminates the meanings and experiences of being ill. Although medical helping can bypass the patient's experience, it is not wise to do so. The great doctor and the exceptional nurse execute their interventions in a personal manner that is sensitive and responsive to the whole patient. The great doctor treats the patient's soul even though she or he is prescribing medication for a small realm of the patient's physical body. As professionals, doctors and nurses need to understand the personal meanings of their patients' illnesses. They need to assist a patient's family members and friends to understand the issues that confront an acutely or chronically ill patient.

Although physical illness involves the entire person, the experience of becoming physically ill is one of being called back to the body and, in many ways, of being reduced to a body. When we find ourselves becoming physically ill, however, we discover the signs of illness in our selves, our bodies, the surrounding world, other people, and our experience of time. Let us look at an example from my everyday life.

The Experience of Becoming Ill

It is a crisp, cold, sunny, November morning in northern California. As I leave for work, I pause at the front door and mentally try on a suit jacket that goes with the slacks I am wearing. Thinking that the rising sun will soon warm the day, I leave my jacket hanging in the bedroom closet. During my first class, I notice that time stretches on and on. I feel strongly about the topic, but I cannot seem to muster my enthusiasm. Students are quieter than usual. It is as though they are, and are not, present. They sit farther into the backs of their chairs and bend closer to their notes. After my lecture, the free time between classes does not give me the usual energy and excitement. I sit listlessly at my desk, mentally noting all the work I could finish. Each phone call and knock on my door emphasizes my tiredness. I am grateful and somewhat amazed that I give students what they need from me. Even though these are unusual experiences, two sneezes are my first hint of an approaching cold. Still, I am not sure. My breathing is easy and my nose is not running, so how can I have a cold?

After class, my briefcase weighs more with each step I take, and the parking lot is farther away than it was at 9:00 a.m. The crisp, sunny wind penetrates and chills my body. Inside my car, the passionate opera that I listened to in the morning has turned thin and pale and, even in its present state, is too demanding of me. Instead, I think of the steam room at my health club and the soft, warm comfort of my bed. Gradually, almost silently, in these changing experiences of myself and the world, I realize that I am catching a cold.

The cold that comes to me so quietly and creeps into my body and my day is a tentative and ambivalent visitor. Always, it is an unwanted guest that I try not to see and simultaneously direct elsewhere, away from my body and life. It is as though the cold and I stand at a distance inside me and appraise one another. When I finally name the cold, I mobilize my health and resources against it: I take multiple vitamins and minerals, I let a homeopathic remedy dissolve under my tongue, I swallow an extra dose of vitamin C. A while later, I make a ginseng tea. As I peel an orange, I promise to eat more fruits and vegetables. With these rituals, I push the unwanted visitor out of my personal life and back into the streets. If only this cold will go elsewhere, I promise to take better care of myself in the future. If only it will go away, I will change my bad habits and learn the lessons the cold threatens to bring me. Often, I outdistance the cold. Occasionally, my body succumbs; I admit defeat as I become ill.

When I am ill, my relations to myself, my body, and my life shift. The Carol that is ill is less able than the healthy Carol. My energy and optimism are less available to me. My busy life, which gives me many pleasures, becomes a burden. Rather than doing, changing, and growing, I want to stop, rest, and be comforted. I find myself withdrawing from the world; the emotional tone of sensory experiences and interpersonal events has shifted to one that disinterests and even burdens me. Everything is too close and crowds me or is too far away to engage me. I feel unusually caught in myself and my life and, at the same time, strangely detached. In the same way, time slows down and thickens. My movements are slower, take longer to execute, and take me only a short distance from where I began. Minutes lengthen but lose their depth and vitality. The past and the future, which are usually so alive and vibrant with meaningful connections to the present, recede into grayness. My illness brings me starkly into the present, but it is a present within which I feel caught and imprisoned. It is a present that does not contain my healthy self.

Illness reduces me to my body in ways that are uncomfortable and frightening. I am my body, but my body is in trouble. When I am physically ill, my body becomes all that matters about me; it is the me that needs attention and care. To be ill is to be called back to my bodily-being-in-the-world-with-others, precisely because it can no longer be taken for granted. When I return to my body under these circumstances, I am made aware of my thrownness in the world and the fragility of my existence. My ill body tells me that I have limits, that my life will end, and that vulnerability lies just below the surface of competence and power.

My first experiences of becoming ill bring me back to a body that has let me down. Depending upon how aggressive my healthful life has been, I can even feel betrayed by my body. The forward thrust of my life is stopped, suspended, even aborted, and I am dropped out of my "about to be finished" projects. Loss—of the future, health, ableness, and life itself—is my first experience of sickness. The presence of sickness is an experience of my loss of a healthy self. The loss of my healthy self calls me back to my bodily being and to attending to and caring for my bodily self. Illness ruptures the taken for granted union of myself and my bodily being-in-the-world-with-others. It returns me to my body as a dysfunctional instrument, one that needs rest and rejuvenation. If I am able to relate to my sick body with acceptance and kindness, to listen to it and to care for it, I can transform my objectified body into a body subject, one that again embodies my whole being. If, on the other hand, my cold becomes bronchial pneumonia, I must take to my sickbed either at home or in the hospital as a means back to health.

The Patient's Experience
of the Sickbed

When we become ill, our world shrinks to our body, as well as to our sickroom and sickbed. We retreat into our room and crawl into bed, to be held and cradled by softness and warmth. Reduced to our physical being, we seek physical comfort. Having become overburdened by duties, tasks, and stimulation, we are comforted by the confining and protected space. Especially at first, the sickroom and sickbed are havens from a world that is too heavy and demanding. Here, alone in our room and bed, we are comforted by the silence, by the smoothness of the sheets against our skin, by the plumpness of the pillows. We are soothed by the stillness of resting, of motionlessness, of feeling our chest rise and fall as we breath, and of listening to our heart beat and our blood pulse through our ears. The room that is usually rushed in and out of becomes all there is, just as our whole selves become our bodily selves. Senses awake to new aspects of the room and bed; previously hidden sounds, lights, and objects enter awareness. We see colors and shadows shift upon the walls of our sickroom as the day recedes into dusk and night darkens before being lit by the moon.

As receptacles and havens, the sickbed and sickroom form protective walls between us and the larger world. Residing there, the present moment becomes large and compelling. Just as the sickroom becomes our world, so also does the present overpower and pre-empt the past and future. When we are sick and give in to it, we stop living our lives so strongly in the future. Projects lose their vitality, our hands become too weak to hold onto them, and we fall back into the present. Here and now are focal, and future becomes trivial and uninteresting. The past, too, loses its grip upon us, and our minds trail off when we try to trace patterns of influence that brought us to our sickbed. Suspended in the present, everything has a different meaning. Now is all there is; now is where meaning emerges. The life themes that surface when we are sick—pain, love, life, and death—are different from those of our healthy life because their meaning is now and not in some distant future.

Once in our sickbed, we must let go of our old self and let a new self take its place. Stephen Levine (1982) discusses the extreme questioning and reordering of the self that occurs when we lie in our sickbed and experience death coming closer. Although the questions that he raises are deeper ones than those we ask when our illness is minor, they are the same questions that arise when we are ill in any way. Any illness brings our finitude and our death into our living. To some degree, the process of experiencing our old, healthy self dying is part of every illness. When we are sick, we cannot continue as usual. We are pulled around a corner of our life, face-to-face with our vulnerability to death. When we are ill, we cannot help wonder who was living, who is sick, who might be dying, and who might continue living—and for what purpose.

The new self that emerges within the sickbed is more frail and fragile than the old self. As the hardier and healthier self falls away, new awarenesses and pleasures come to us. Although our sick, inactive body is soft, pale, and weak, new strengths of understanding and presence may more than compensate for these losses. The new self is grateful for little pleasures and can rest more comfortably in life's balance of joy and sorrow, hope and loss. Eventually, the new self is more at home with death's place in life than the old one. Life becomes precious and even sensuously present in small moments and realizations. The presence of death can make life come alive. Contrasting the healthy person and the sick person, van den Berg (1972b) sees that the person who lies in the sickbed gains deep understandings of life:

Who misses more of life, the healthy person, when he throws himself into the avalanche of ever more respect, with an ever more wonderful house, an ever more expensive car and ever further reaching holiday trips, and consequently a frantic drive for money; when he throws himself into this avalanche which bears the dazzling name of "career"? Or the sick person who makes his room, his window sill, his window and his view a world full of significant and breathtaking events? Who— now in a completely different sense—is more ill? The illness of the body can be the condition for a soundness of mind which the healthy person misses easily. An existence devoid of sickness lacks the stimulus to live, just as an existence devoid of mental problems degenerates into complete insignificance. Probably there is no better guarantee for a really healthy life than perfect health. But this only means that health and existence without conflict are not synonymous. The really healthy person possesses a vulnerable body and he is aware of this vulnerability. (pp. 73-74)

Sickness returns us to the meaning of life and helps us be present to ourselves and the lessons of small moments and experiences. It stops our rush to find life over there and helps us be present to life that is here and now.

Life is deepened and expanded by physical, as well as psychological, social, and spiritual, pain. When we are physically ill—whether acutely or chronically or in major or minor ways—we face the possibility or the actuality of death and enter the dark side of life. Knowing this darkness orients us to life and heightens life's form and content. Van den Berg (1972b) explains it as follows:

Can it not be said that every intensification of our personal existence is the result of difficulties, sorrow and affliction? No one becomes mature unless he undergoes the crisis of maturation. No one experiences old age as a fulfillment of his life unless he deprives life of many of its desires. Marriage is seldom a real partnership without hardships. A deeper insight into the wonder of our existence, a more human and consequently a more acute way of experiencing the paradoxes and controversies which characterize our existence is always the result of an uneasiness akin to despair, and the challenge of a pressing uncertainty. Death only becomes a friend after a fierce and painful duel. Therefore, it cannot be right to reduce difficulties and sorrow to a minimum artificially. Only where the dark side of life is really present will the light side become light. A life which tries to remain on the light side all the time runs the risk of finding itself in a constant darkness. (pp. 96-97)

The Sensitive and Caring Visitor

People who are attached to the physically ill person's life—mates, relatives, and friends—are all implicated in the patient's sickness. Through the loved one's illness, human vulnerability and finitude enter their lives. If the patient is sick enough to be admitted to a hospital, visitors who walk through the hospital doors enter the realm of sickness and the reality of death. Visitors who wish to comfort patients must attend to their own issues regarding pain and death before crossing the threshold into the hospital room.

Even the most courageous person is frightened by physical illness. The visitor who truly wants to be with the patient must notice and deal with all the feelings that are evoked by illness and death. A mixture of anxiety, fear, sadness, anger, and guilt often surfaces when someone we love is ill. When a loved one's life is threatened, loss enters our hearts. Feelings must be dealt with before we can be with a sick loved one. If we are in touch with our own fears, we can more easily stand within our loved one's changed and often frightening new experiential world.

In his book *Psychology of the Sickbed*, van den Berg (1972b) steers the hospital visitor around some mistakes in sensitivity. Many of his instructions simply remind the visitor to bring normal rules of social interaction into the sickroom. Upon entering the sickroom, van den Berg tells the visitor to take off her or his coat and hat, to set down packages and purses, and to take a seat. Like a visitor entering someone's living room, the visitor should not sit on the patient's bed (in his or her chair) but in a separate chair. Positioning oneself at an angle that enables the patient to talk without neck strain is also helpful. All of these usual, considerate, and relational behaviors tell the patient that the visitor came to be with him or her and to stay for a while.

Like any normal visit between people, the visitor gains important information by attending to what the patient says. By listening to the patient's words, the visitor discovers the patient's concerns, understands how far from the healthy world the patient feels, and assesses the patient's ability to talk about fears and concerns. Van den Berg (1972b) tells visitors to enter the sickroom without prepackaged conversations and to listen to the person's greeting and spontaneous words. He explains:

> In general, it is not advisable to prepare for a visit to a patient. The chances are that the prepared conversation will prevail over the topics the patient really wants to discuss, so that, although he may be taking part in a lively conversation, he is never given a chance to say what he wants to say. One thing should be kept in mind though: the visitor should always realize that the human threshold he crosses is higher than the one at the door of the sickroom. He should also be aware of the fact that the exact height of the threshold will be unknown to him until the words of the patient have made its measurement clear. Abandoning our metaphor, the visitor should try to find the patient in the latter's own world and discuss there the subjects that are significant in his exceptional existence. (pp. 78-79)

We truly visit the patient when we listen and respond to the patient's concerns.

Along with listening to the patient on her or his terms, the visitor should talk honestly and normally. Like any conversation, a visit with an ill person is a dialogue of speaking and listening. A normal visitor talks about oneself, about daily events, about problems and happy moments, and about future plans. By talking of these matters, the visitor invites the patient into his or her world. A visitor who talks about everyday concerns invites the patient into everyday life. Such a visitor brings the healthy world, like a fresh breeze, to the sickroom.

The visitor has a delicate line to walk, one that participates in the world of the healthy, as well as that of the sick, a line that recognizes the patient's different existence without excluding her or him from healthy everyday life. The visitor must be able to enter into the fears, darkness, newly gained wisdom, and joys of the patient's sick world without losing a footing in the taken for granted world of physical health. He or she must remember that the patient is ill without depersonalizing the patient, talk about sickness without excluding the patient from health, and remind without pressuring the patient of his or her place in normal everyday living. While being sensitive to the new meanings, discomforts, and concerns of the physically ill person, the visitor acts as a liaison between the sickroom and the everyday world. The caring and sensitive visitor heartens the patient by taking illness seriously, by noting the real changes it has and will have in the patient's life, and by continuing a respectful acceptance of the whole person of the patient. Being sensitive to the realities of illness, the visitor invites the patient back to his or her essential place in the full human world.

Good Nursing Care

The nurse is also on the edge of two worlds: the world of health and the world of sickness. Unlike the visitor who is a liaison from the everyday world, the nurse is the patient's bedside companion in the unfamiliar world of illness. She or he is a knowledgeable and well-seasoned traveler in this world of pain, disability, and death. As a professional, the nurse inspires the patient's confidence and trust. The nurse literally takes care of the patient's physical needs and efficiently and effectively manages the patient's hospital care. He or she must win the patient's cooperation in the treatment plan and must encourage the patient to hand over responsibilities and worries that disturb rest and healing. The competent nurse manages the emotional, as well as the physical, needs of patients.

The good nurse manages the patient's pain without becoming overburdened and defeated by it. This is a difficult task that must be fine-tuned differently, on different days, with different patients. As a professional helper, the nurse joins the patient without feeling the patient's feelings for him or her. The nurse remains in her or his world but is present with the patient. The continuous demand upon a nurse's understanding, support, and helpfulness can overburden the nurse. Then he or she becomes emotionally exhausted and can use physical caretaking procedures and efficient action as buffers, procedures that distance the patient's problems, feelings, and experiences. To protect oneself, a nurse may develop a formula bedside manner that is false, one that is a little too cheerful, too rushed, too impersonally personal, and even too efficient. This nurse slips beyond the patient's human grasp. Not being present as a person, this efficient nurse explicitly and implicitly trains the patient to keep frightened, needy, and vulnerable parts of the self out of their interactions (Jourard, 1971, pp. 179-181).

The nurse who has retained ties with a healthy emotional self can be empathic with and present to the patient's real emotional self. If a nurse is self-present, she or he can be present to the patient. By acknowledging and talking about emotions evoked by professional duties, nurses can transform raw feeling responses into ones that are more balanced and caring of patients. An emotional self that is listened to, discussed, and treasured can mature and become a strong professional resource.

The nurse who does not use professional distance to shield from the patient's experience must be at home with the fears and feelings that are part of hospital life. Having experienced, worked with, and lived through the difficult feelings and moments of life, this nurse can welcome and help articulate the patient's real concerns and cultivate the patient's disclosure of experiences, feelings, and meanings. If training programs for nurses build upon, rather than eliminate, genuine emotional life, they can graduate nurses who are skilled in caring for the experientially troubled patient, as well as the physically ill one. A nurse trained like this can be technically and interpersonally skilled. To truly care for a patient, the nurse must know each patient as a unique and ever-changing person. He or she must also enter into a patient's unique phenomenal world. To learn about and understand a patient's phenomenal world, a nurse must be able to foster the patient's self-disclosure. Jourard's (1971) research has proven that people disclose to people who are warm, permissive, concerned, and genuinely interested in their experience (p. 193). These qualities help nurses give competent interpersonal care.

A nurse's interpersonal competence depends upon her or his contact with and understanding of personal, emotional selves. A nurse who values and cares for the real self will be able to care for the whole person of the patient. Then the patient will be well taken care of, physically and psychologically. Jourard (1971) describes the patient who is well nursed:

> We can assume he is as comfortable as his condition permits, he knows why he became ill and what is being done for him, he feels his nurses really care what happens to him, he knows that they *know him as a unique person* because they took the trouble to learn about him, and he knows he told them much about himself. He feels free to call

for help when he wants it, and does so. His nurse "tunes in" on him at regular intervals to sample his private, personal, psychological world as it were—not with an empty question, "How do we feel"—and she uses this information as the basis of actions which make him say "ah-h-h!" He wants to get well and to get back into the community, and if his place in the community is one which imposes a lot of sickness-producing stress on him, the nurse has found this out and conveyed the information to a social worker, or the physician, or somebody who might be able to help improve the situation. (pp. 201-202)

The well-nursed patient feels understood, supported, and taken care of by the hospital staff. From the confines of the sickbed, the patient steps back into the future and reenters the fullness of healthy, interpersonal existence. As the patient moves back into healthy living, the body and health can again be taken for granted—but now, with new respect of and gratitude for life.

16

Relational Aspects
of College Teaching

Like physicians and psychotherapists, teachers are involved in asymmetrical relationships with their students. They stand before their classes to teach: to help students pass the course, to communicate knowledge, to stimulate learning, and to inspire creativity and thinking. Teachers in various disciplines—math, biology, psychology, sociology, art, music—are given different tasks by their subject matters. In math and biology, for example, students must be led through numerical formulas and physical body systems. These subject matters leave personal lives behind. In the social sciences and the humanities, however, the student's personal life is often the landscape within which facts and ideas are planted and take root.

The explicit goal of the teacher-student relationship is for the teacher to help the student master subject matter. All participants, then, are focused upon something beyond and, in some ways, separate from their relationship. This transfer of information takes place, however, within a relational context. Not only is the person of the teacher part of this process, but the students in a class also influence learning.

In this chapter, I look at the relationship between teacher and student rather than at a phenomenology of learning. Other phenomenologists, Colaizzi (1971, 1973) and Giorgi (1971, 1975) have developed structural descriptions of learning. These studies focus upon learning as a reorganization of meaning for the learner and emphasize the usefulness of understanding each learner's experience of the task at hand and the situation in which learning occurs. In contrast, my discussions will focus upon the interpersonal context of learning within the college classroom.

My Experiences as a College Teacher

As a university teacher, I have stood before thousands of students in over a hundred classes. Each time I walk into a new classroom, I have a unique but familiar experience. A typical first day of a class looks like this to me.

I walk into Room 2106 and am surprised. The room is different from the year before, now filled with new faces. The students quit talking as I walk toward the lectern, but the silence is unnatural. It began in the middle of sentences left unfinished. I feel uncomfortable in the soundless room because the air is heavy with unspoken expectations. As I reach my destination and turn to face the class, I see that all of the students are watching me. In the instant before I speak, I feel the timelessness of this day and moment. Without having seen each other before, we are here to learn together. What will our journey be? Where will it leave each of us when our relationship ends in a silence not unlike this one, in the intensity of the final examination.

These people meet my gaze and I see them becoming students, just as I feel myself becoming the teacher. I imagine daily lists and problems being set aside in their minds as they wait for me to speak. I realize that I will sound like a teacher for the first time since summer break. Dr. Becker introduces herself, states the name of the course, hands out the syllabus, discusses the readings and the course structure, clarifies the system of grading, and begins her first lecture. The students are silent and attentive.

As I lecture, I feel the impossibility of my task. I am speaking to people I know nothing about and am acting as though they are interested in what I am saying. Besides, my words probably mean something slightly different to each person in the room. My roster shows that students from different majors are enrolled in the class.

In this room are liable to be as many different expectations as students. As I lecture, I look for clues of interests and understandings in facial expressions and body movements. But faces are unnaturally expressionless and bodies are strangely still. When I ask for comments or questions, I am met with awkward silence.

Over the years, I have learned to fill this silence with enthusiastic words. I feel relief that I have my lecture topic to keep me company as I speak to these unspeaking strangers. With gratitude, I look down at my familiar notes filled with interesting ideas before I again glance up to meet the unanswering gazes of these immobile students. At least I have the thinker I am lecturing about to converse with as I develop my thoughts in front of these silent, strange students.

Each year I experience something similar to the foregoing description. Sometimes, a student asks a question during the first lecture. Often, I get students to laugh at a joke I weave into the serious lecture. Either of these events eases the tension in the room. After the first day of classes, I am always reminded of the relational aspects of teaching and learning.

At the college level, teachers are not taught how to teach. In fact, a Ph.D. in an academic discipline is all that is necessary to become a university instructor. Implicit in this criterion is the assumption that ideas and information are the important aspects of teaching and, thus, learning. To teach, one must simply know a lot and speak it to an audience of students. From this point of view, teaching is the passing of information from more informed persons to those less informed.

As a university teacher, however, I have noticed important relational components to teaching and learning. When I began teaching in 1968, I excitedly saved my notes to a well-received lecture. I believed that the organization of ideas and the choice of words had made it interesting and meaningful to students. I was befuddled when the same lecture, given to another class, was dull and unengaging. For years, I kept working on the organization and sequence of ideas, definitions, and examples. I thought that if I finally got it right, it would effectively engage all of the students who rotated through the class year after year. I slowly realized that different things engaged different classes; what had been boring to one group generated questions and discussion in another. Topics that had been main arteries of some class discussions were politely sat through by other groups of students.

After 22 years of university teaching, I understand that I can prepare for, organize, be in charge of, and direct my classes. But I cannot really teach if I am not engaged with my students or if my students are not involved with me. Teaching and learning happen between me and the students and among us as a group. Even in large lecture classes, people are changed by the speaking and listening of the classroom. The activities of the classroom are planned, and yet, they depend upon the spontaneous actions and reactions of the teacher and students. This spontaneity brings life into the established structure and opens it to include real people and living concerns.

For me, teaching is a complex, relational, and creative event. When I teach, I am simultaneously involved in several dynamic relations: with myself, with my everyday world, with my subject matter, and with my students.

First, as a teacher, I have an ongoing, changing relationship to my own thoughts, feelings, experiences, and interests. My relation with myself involves being aware of what interests, excites, and preoccupies me in each moment. Standing before my class, I am a prepared but spontaneous self; I am myself in familiar and also new ways. In touch with my old and new thoughts and feelings, I become an evolving, thinking self. As I speak, I discover how I have changed since the last time I spoke about a topic. Elaborations, connections, and examples come to mind that had not occurred to me as I prepared my lecture notes that morning. Over the years, I have even learned to leave blank spots in my notes, to be filled by spontaneous comments. I know what I am going to say, but I think on my feet. My notes are a foundation that guides me as I am myself in front of my class. When these notes replace me and I begin reading them rather than using them to speak, the lecture becomes stale. In being with myself, I am emotionally and intellectually alive and present. I say things that I did not plan to say but that embellish the lecture I prepared.

Second, I have an ongoing relationship with my everyday world. The salient events of my life, both painful and joyful experiences, focus and shift my lecture topics. As I speak, my last visit with 3-year-old Sarah, my experiences with my 77-year-old father, my latest interpersonal conflict, my observations of a mother and son in the grocery store line find their way into my lecture. In these ways, my everyday world enriches ideas and updates them. These parts of my lifeworld, in turn, touch the diverse experiences of students and bring to mind similar and different events in their lives. Examples from my life help me communicate my thoughts to the students in an applied context, embedded in real events and relationships. They tell about the people in them, show a more real everyday part of me to students, and interlace the lecture with life. In this way, the everyday world is a shared context that supports my lecture and enables the students and me to talk together and to understand one another.

Third, when I lecture, I have a relation with the subject matter. To be convincing and coherent to students, my subject matter must be alive to me. I must believe what I expect students to learn. As the teacher, I am an inside guide for my students. I show them, for example, Buber or Freud, but I also show them Buber or Freud-for-me. When I teach a particular system of thought, I must return to and once again become immersed in it. In doing so, I see what I have already understood and what I can believe in, but I also see anew. Fresh connections present themselves to me, and I see the material from different vantage points. The basic building blocks of the subject remain the same, but their broader implications shift, expand, and deepen. Subtly or explicitly, I discover that the lens of my being has changed each time I return to a subject matter. I cannot simply do what I did before. Each lecture, then, is a different hermeneutical movement between myself and the text, theory, or subject matter. In some ways, the old view and a newer one blend in a unique expression of what has stayed true along with what has changed.

Fourth, my relationship with the class as a whole and the individuals who compose it is a central, developing one. The atmosphere of a class is greatly influenced by students who are talkative and enthusiastic, appreciative of the reading or the lectures, critical of academic knowledge, distrusting of teachers, disinterested in the subject matter, quick to apply topics to everyday life, or scornful of students' questions taking up lecture time. No one knows what will develop when a class convenes. The teacher often sets the tone, but the students are influential as well. Sometimes, one class member serves as a student advocate with the teacher. One outspoken student can also coalesce an entire class against him or her. More frequently, after one student dares to speak, several others follow. As a class develops, student concerns—about grades, about the usefulness of the subject matter, about their everyday lives—become part of the class periods. How students engage in a class influences the class's direction and outcome.

In many ways, the students set the parameters for how much of all my other relationships—to myself, my lifeworld, my subject matter—I share. Even silent students make me be, think, and speak differently. Each of the other relations with myself can, however, enhance the stilted and vacuous initial relationship—really a nonrelationship—between the students and me when we are still strangers. I can fill in this impersonal teacher-student relationship with my enthusiasm for the subject matter, my own experience, or my beliefs. When I do this, I become personally present in front of the class and, thus, set a tone and direction for the relationship, one that invites emotional presence and personal involvement. If I as the teacher am personally present and invite the students to value their life experiences, the chance that they will become more actively present within the class structure increases.

The subject matters that I teach, such as life span development, intimate relationships, phenomenology, lesbian and gay life-styles, and women and their bodies, are permeated with values and worldviews. They are about life and relationships. These relational components of my subject matters highlight the relational context of teaching for me. Even though I am very focused upon relationships, however, I sometimes get caught up in the course content and exam scores. This year, Darlene reminded me that learning can be about emotional issues.

Darlene, an attractive, well-dressed black woman in her early 30s, came to see me after the first exam in a course on life span development. She had received a D on the test and wanted to know how she could improve her grade. We went over her wrong answers; some of them were far afield from the right answers. When I looked at her highlighted textbook, I saw that highlighting was sparse and at times did not include the topics on the test. These discoveries encouraged me because this information would help her do better on the next test. The pattern of wrong answers seemed the same on the lecture material, so I asked to see her class notes. Darlene's notes on my first lecture were even more thorough than my memory of it; she had neatly written down everything I had said. I was amazed, said with genuine appreciation, "These are great notes, Darlene!" and continued to leaf through her spiral notebook. When I looked up, Darlene had tears streaming down her face. She gulped for air and said how hard she tried to learn. Her tears helped me stop focusing upon the subject matter and pay attention to Darlene, a hardworking, defeated student.

Oddly enough, my expressed appreciation of Darlene's class notes seemed to be the most helpful part of our meeting. By complimenting her, I acknowledged her effort and ability and joined her in believing that the test score was an unrepresentative one. After seeing Darlene's notes and witnessing her tears of defeat, I felt personally committed to helping her do better on the next exam. We scheduled another appointment to go over the course material for the next exam.

In fact, Darlene missed our appointment and we never did see each other outside of class. But each time I saw her in class, I said hello to her and expressed my interest in her doing well. As I recorded grades at the end of the term, I paused at Darlene's last exam score. It was a B; she had jumped two grades and raised her final grade to a C. I sat back and smiled over her personal triumph. Although I do not know what caused this change in Darlene's performance or how she experienced our interactions, my contact with Darlene underscored the emotional and relational components of teaching for me. I did not explain one idea or study technique to Darlene, I only sympathized with and expressed belief in her.

Shifts in the Relational Context
of the Classroom

I have often wondered what students experienced at different points in a college class. As the term progresses, my perceptions tell me that students become more comfortable with themselves, with each other, and with me. In large lecture classes, in fact, I have to work hard to get the students' attention and then to complete my lectures. As the class continues, spontaneous discussion of the lecture topic becomes a normal event. Even walking into the classroom midway through the term shows me that the class is different. Here is a brief description, during its fifth week, of my experience of the class on life span development that met in Room 2106.

Today when I enter Room 2106, my experience is different from the first day of class. As I walk toward the lectern, I greet and speak informally with students. Most students are sitting in their usual chairs; many are talking energetically to one another. I glance at my notes and face the class, ready to lecture. The students seem unaware of me. I raise my voice and say that I would like to begin. Students finish their conversations, turn toward me, and prepare paper and pens for note taking. Their attention is more natural, their silence is less strained, and their bodies move more spontaneously than on the first day.

As I lecture, some students nod, frown, ask questions, make comments, and even speak directly to one another about the lecture topic. Other students are preoccupied with matters removed from the lecture: some read, others whisper to one another. This undifferentiated group of students has become separated into small subgroups—the quiet ones, the questioners, the ones concerned about grades, the radical thinkers, the entertaining ones, the confused ones. My presentations are now peppered with students' questions and comments, and I twine previous discussions into current topics. As the class and I respond to one another, our interactions force me to balance many concerns: covering the lecture material, communicating effectively to diverse students, holding students' interest, highlighting the required reading, tying the course content to daily concerns, and clarifying, expanding, or simplifying what I did the year before.

Within several weeks, most classes form a loosely cohesive unit that has a predictable but dynamic rhythm and energy. Individual students act in expected ways: some describe personal experiences, some ask questions about the facts being presented, some are silent. Each class develops unspoken norms of behavior: some groups focus upon tests, others discuss the meaningfulness of course topics, still others develop friendship groups. In every class, however, are moments when something unexpected and gripping happens, when someone speaks with unusual conviction or openness. Last quarter, Mark, a student in my adolescence class, brought the discussions to a new level of honesty. This is what happened.

Enrolled in the class on adolescent development during fall quarter are 33 students. Besides the multiple-choice midterm and final, students receive 10 points of their grade for doing a class presentation. They can do almost anything: They can bring an adolescent to class, discuss their own teenage years, report on adolescents they know, show a video clip, play music, give a small lecture, or talk informally about personal experience. Only two students signed up for the first day of presentations. It is always frightening to be the first presenter because students do not know each other very well and, no matter what they do, the presentation is a personal statement about themselves.

Mark, a tall, stocky, good-looking, and articulate white man in his early 30s, is the first student to present. He looks around, says that he is nervous, and announces that he will talk about being an obese adolescent. A special stillness settles over the room as Mark tells of being called fatso, tubby, tub-of-lard. He remembers how worthless and humiliated he felt and how he stayed home from school during his sophomore and junior years of high school to avoid being ridiculed. Mark also mentions skills that he gained from this period of his life: He learned to entertain people with humor, to anticipate and avoid anxiety-provoking situations, and to relate to adults. But even now, as a mature and emotionally secure person, Mark sees himself as extremely obese. In spite of his attainments, he feels socially and physically incompetent.

hen Mark finishes, he looks exposed and unsure of himself. He has risked being vulnerable with us and does not know how we will respond. I speak first because I want Mark to feel safe. I thank him for talking about such painful experiences. The students follow my lead. Some also talk about being obese adolescents. Many of their experiences reinforce what Mark has said. Others describe less painfully isolating experiences of being fat. We all forget time, and talk past our 10-minute limit. Mark has risked bringing himself into the class, and all of us are changed by the experience. As I leave class, I feel that Mark's presentation took us beyond the readings and lectures into the experiential world of feeling and struggling adolescents.

If a teacher and students provide a safe enough relational context, class members bring their personal experiences and important life concerns into class discussions. These moments of the teacher and students being real people together develop dialectically. Often, the teacher must show that she or he values personal remarks and believes that they help accomplish the course purposes. The teacher alone cannot, however, create an atmosphere that welcomes personal involvement. It must be created among class members.

As the relational context becomes familiar and reliable, students relax into their niches in the class. They loosen up when they know that their concerns—getting good grades, absorbing interesting information, experiencing a lively class period, balancing the class with other pressures in their lives—will be taken care of and that they have found a place for this class in their busy lives.

One year, I asked students in my course on life span development to write down their experiences of the class. Their responses showed diverse concerns and experiences. By the time the class was half over, students had figured out what helped or hindered learning for them. Some even told me how to improve my presentations. The following are representative of their descriptions during the fifth week of class:

> For myself, the class is interesting. I like the content of the lectures. However, I get bogged down with the amount of reading required. I think that discussion is good, to help understand the material better, but I would like it to be kept to the material covered in class. Otherwise it becomes a source of anxiety. I feel anxious about the midterm exam, because I don't know what we'll be expected to know.

❖   ❖   ❖

> Overall, this class has been a little bit over my head (I'm talking about the lectures only; the book is great). Sometimes I have a hard time grasping what concept is being taught, and I have an even harder time putting it into my notes. I like the class discussions we get into, and I would rather just read the information instead of being lectured to about it.

❖   ❖   ❖

The book that is required reading is not as stimulating as the lectures. As much as I have planned to catch up with the reading assignments, I haven't been able to do so. I'm mostly depending on the lecture.

❖　❖　❖

There are differing forces at work in this class—the films presented their material clearly and from a central point of view. The discussions tended to be too divergent, which is good (you get differing views), but also bad (in that I feel pulled in different directions).

❖　❖　❖

I feel that the class has become more conducive to learning since the first day. There is more discussion taking place and we all seem to feel comfortable with each other. You, as the instructor, convey a true interest in the opinions of the students.

❖　❖　❖

I have found it a little difficult to follow the lecture in an organized manner. But the class has been a good experience for me. I enjoy the material we discuss, especially as it pertains to our lives. The feedback from other classmates is very valuable to me. I feel that I learn as much from the class discussions as from the lectures.

❖　❖　❖

My experience of the lecture material is confusion. If you would remind my brain whose theory we're talking about and when they lived in relation to the others, it would help. Also, did these people get their ideas from people in the same country and era? I need a broader picture.

❖　❖　❖

I'm more comfortable than before, but I still have a problem taking notes. If you could write the important things on the blackboard more, it might be very helpful to me (and probably to some others, too). I quit bringing a tape recorder to class, because you started talking slower. I really appreciate it. But, sometimes, you talk as fast as before, and I can't take notes.

Different students experienced this same class in a variety of ways. What helped one student learn proved problematic for another. All students had a sense of themselves and the various aspects of the course and were actively pursuing what interested and helped them learn.

When a class is about to end, students are even more actively involved than previously. At the end of a college class, changes in the students are more pronounced than they were midway through the course. Here are some of the changes that I noticed in the previously discussed class that met in Room 2106.

On the day before the final, a wave of sound composed of many voices hits me when I open the door to Room 2106. I pass by many animated conversations as I walk to the lectern. The room is full of students; everyone is here today. My efforts to gain the attention of the class go unnoticed until I jokingly say that I will not be able to review for the exam if they do not stop talking. Amid laughter and further talking, students turn toward me. They immediately raise questions about the final exam. They are especially alert as I review the exam structure and content.

During this last lecture, numerous questions are asked that clarify and qualify my remarks. Even students who have never talked before speak up. Everyone is attentive, vocal, and lively. Students bubble over with knowledge, critiques, opinions, jokes, and asides; many are knowledgeable about my topic and freely add to my lecture.

Student descriptions from the previously cited research project in the course on life span development attest to their active evaluative stance toward the class as it ends. They access what the class had added to their lives, what they have liked and disliked about it, and what I could do to improve the course. Some of their comments follow:

> I have finally finished all of the reading, but I do not comprehend all that I have read. I enjoyed the movies, they put Piaget's theory into a real live action place. How all of this helps me in later life, I'm not sure. Interesting in a way, but is it really necessary?

❖   ❖   ❖

> I have become increasingly interested in the class. The topics discussed are interesting because they can be applied to our own lives. It's fun to

listen to some of the experiences that other students have had. Working in a convalescent hospital, I am familiar with many of the topics related to adulthood and elderly people. This last part of the class has made me stop and think about what I have to look forward to.

❖   ❖   ❖

I have found that this class has given me a better knowledge of the processes that human beings go through from birth to death. This knowledge has begun to make me more aware of the people around me and the problems they face throughout their lives. Your humor has been enjoyable and appreciated.

In my last two descriptions, I relayed a negative attitude towards the class. I expressed feelings of bewilderment, confusion, and boredom towards the lectures and readings. Now that I have read the entire book and looked over the class as a whole, I have found that everything fits together. Human development is a complex subject, but I feel that this class has helped me to understand people better and ultimately to learn about myself as a person.

❖   ❖   ❖

I would have liked to delve more deeply into Jung's theory and Kubler-Ross's works. I felt that too much time and emphasis was placed on child development at the expense of adult development. I feel that we should have broken up into small groups for discussion, and I would have enjoyed an optional reading list.

During a class, but especially as it nears its end, teachers and students can become co-authorities; they can build knowledge together. On one of the last days of class in a course on women and their bodies, a quiet but powerful development of the lecture topic occurred among the students and me. I was lecturing on two illnesses covered in our required reading, arthritis and diabetes, and surveying the facts and definitions that students would need for the final exam. In the middle of my remarks, Jan raised a question about rheumatoid arthritis that I was not sure I could answer. I responded with what I knew and asked students to help me out. Karen, a woman in her 40s, identified herself as someone who was living with rheumatoid arthritis. She listed the problems that had brought her to the doctor and the symptoms her doctor used to diagnose the condition. She told us how medication had enabled her to live symptomless for several years. A younger woman, Sally, asked Karen about dietary cures for arthritis. Karen could not answer the question, but I responded with what I knew. A third student, Johanna, confirmed and expanded what I said. When this spontaneous building of the lecture/discussion ended, I summarized our reading's suggestions for managing arthritis: healthy diet, exercise, rest, and lifting habits. Other class members added information from their lives, and we moved on to discuss diabetes.

Something similar happened with this topic. I outlined the prevalence of diabetes in different ethnic groups and cited four danger signs of diabetes: tiredness, thirst, frequent urination, and slow-healing cuts. Jessie added sudden weight loss to my list and told of her experiences with a friend who recently discovered that she was diabetic. I defined insulin dependent and noninsulin dependent types of the disease and read an experiential account of a 53-year-old black grandmother's diagnosis and treatment. Jessie spoke up to say how important it is for friends and loved ones to notice the cognitive and behavioral changes that accompany low blood glucose. Other students chimed in with questions to Jessie and to me. Before we knew it, our class period was over.

As a class evolves, the relationship between teacher and students, and among students, can become increasingly dialectical. Over the years, I have identified a number of factors that facilitate a shift in the one-way, hierarchical relation between teachers and students to a reciprocal one that builds knowledge through dialogue.

Relational Aspects
of the College Classroom

In a certain sense, teachers and students enter classrooms without knowing what they are doing. By agreeing to spend an entire college term with one another, they begin a predictable journey that has a definite purpose and goal. The required readings, the lecture schedule, and the exams provide the structure for their contact, as well as their reason for meeting. The beliefs, values, characters, and lives of the students and the teacher lie dormant, however, beneath these foundational elements of the class, and on another level, teachers and students begin co-created unpredictable journeys together. These deeper journeys are formed by the confluence of people who compose a class. If the class goes well, more than the explicit goal of the class, the transfer of knowledge from teacher to student, will be accomplished.

A successful class contains some degree of dialogue between the teacher and students. For students, class periods become alive and meaningful when fellow students enter into lectures by raising issues, giving examples, or asking questions. Then classes become living events; the class happens among people, and both sides of the teacher-student relationship are essential in forming its content and structure. In such classes, the teacher's notes do not always contain the important things learned by students. Spontaneous discussions prove to be the most interesting and informative, as ideas move back and forth between teacher and student, as well as among students. Class periods like this are verbal dances in which a pattern of thought is woven among class members. In this verbal dance, even students who only listen are important in the movement of ideas. During these rare moments, all are present. Students rarely take notes, but much is learned. Although such moments as these only happen occasionally and are not on the final exam, they are some of the most compelling reasons teachers teach and students attend classes. Having built knowledge and personal understanding of each other together, the teacher and the students leave class touched by one another, carrying pieces of class members' lives and thoughts with them.

An unnerving part of being a teacher is that I have agreed to teach people whom I have never met and of whom I know little. In limited ways, I have agreed to extend myself to them and to let them into my life. My fate is, thus, not completely in my hands, and I am vulnerable to the unknown others I am about to face. In his writings on education, Buber (1985) states that a teacher's inability to control the composition of a class is one of the most important aspects of teaching; the teacher finds the students already in the classroom and is unable to select and arrange them. According to Buber, the wise educator accepts this "indiscriminate confusion" (p. 121) of the classroom as a microcosm of the universe. All of the issues of life can be found in the diversity of a class. For Buber (1985), a first class contains the grace of beginning life afresh, and doing this with others, within the context of community (pp. 109-130). This grace of newness promises potentials—for added meaning, hope, enjoyment, self-understanding, and understanding others. Learning with others ties knowledge to the wholeness of human life, to being-in-the-world-with-others.

Buber believes that teachers can cultivate greatness of character by facing, time after time, the unknown challenge of a new class. According to Buber (1985), each new class is a living situation that demands nothing less than the teacher's complete presence. He explains:

> In spite of all similarities every living situation has, like a new-born child, a new face, that has never been before and will never come again. It demands of you a reaction which cannot be prepared beforehand. It demands nothing of what is past. It demands presence, responsibility; it demands you. I call a great character one who by his actions and attitudes satisfies the claim of situations out of deep readiness to respond with his whole life, and in such a way that the sum of his actions and attitudes expresses at the same time the unity of his being in its willingness to accept responsibility. As his being is unity, the unity of accepted responsibility, his active life, too, coheres into unity. (p. 143)

If a teacher brings her or his presence and active living and thinking to students, students usually respond with matching vitality. Then, dialogue that ignites life and being occurs, and an integration of learning and living is achieved.

In Buber's (1985) words, each educator selects a world to present to students and is, thus, an embodiment of a world that matters to him or her. A teacher brings this personally crafted world to students, one that is imbued with personal life and meaning. It is this personal wholeness that differentiates a classroom from a text; the teacher embodies and stands for the subject matter as it is integrated into the world. The teacher who stands thus serves as a human bridge among self, students, subject matter, everyday world, and life in general. When the teacher teaches a subject matter, she or he also teaches about self and life. Standing before the class, the teacher offers his or her concreteness as a manifestation of the subject matter, as a symbol of learning about life and the integration of different worlds that coalesce within the classroom. The educator draws the world into herself or himself and presents it to students (Buber, 1985, p. 129).

True education unites the contents of the classroom with the everyday world. It touches the personal lives of the students by engaging with themes that are meaningful in life. Further, it strengthens the interpersonal network of dialogue and community that surrounds and supports individual lives. When teachers and students silently sever their relationships during the final exam, they turn away from one another to continue their diverse journeys separately. All, however, carry the experiences they have shared and the people they have encountered with them as they continue to live their lives and to be transformed by life experiences.

Cultivating Teacher-Student Dialogue

The teacher who wants to strengthen relational components of the classroom can do several things to prepare the foundation for a dialectical experience.

First, a teacher who truly wishes students to participate in the class must take charge of the class and fulfill his or her explicit responsibilities as the teacher. This involves setting forth a schedule of lecture topics and assigned readings and having a clear and predictable grading system. In these ways, the teacher shows students how she or he will handle power and authority. Once the power relationship has been clarified, students can orient themselves vis-à-vis the class structure in order to accomplish personal goals.

Second, the teacher can invite students to bring life experiences and understandings into dialogue with readings and lectures. By affirming the life understandings students bring to a class, the teacher welcomes them as whole people and not just students. Students have been and continue to be active participants in lives that are larger and more dynamic than the class itself. By recognizing the importance of knowledge gained through living, the teacher validates students' experiential expertise in the class's subject matter.

Third, the teacher who wishes to find whole people in students must be a whole person in front of them. Being a whole person involves showing oneself to students: by talking about beliefs and concerns, by sharing personal experiences, and by interlacing the course content with everyday life. When a teacher is honest and spontaneous, students are given more than the teacher's thinking; they are given access to someone who will be present with them, extend essential understandings to them, and let them into his or her existence. Spontaneous remarks endear a teacher to students because these comments make the human instructor visible to students. By being herself or himself, the teacher invites students to do likewise.

Fourth, the teacher stimulates students to become active participants in the class by responding to them and including their contributions in lectures and exams. This inclusion gives students' ideas equal status with those of the instructor and encourages students to listen to each other. Then knowledge can be built among people and something more than what has been planned by the teacher can happen. When this occurs, the task oriented, hierarchical relationship between the teacher and students can evolve into a dialectical one that, in special moments, transforms the very beings of teachers and students.

Afterword

The foregoing discussions of human nature, life span development, intimate relationships, and helping relationships have touched upon, dwelled within, and opened up fundamental dimensions of living and relating. Above all, phenomenological descriptions present human life from the inside, from the viewpoint of dynamic, intentional, experiencing, and meaning-giving people. By attending to everyday situations and events, phenomenologists plumb the depths of life, reap large and small understandings from it, and harvest new awarenesses of universal and unique life themes. Phenomenology renews our interest in knowing ourselves and others. It inspires us to learn about ourselves and others as co-created, dynamic beings. As technology shrinks the world and people of different ethnic groups, races, classes, sexual orientations, and life-styles coexist, knowing how to build a functional community from this diversity becomes vital. The phenomenological perspective is a valuable approach to a heterogenous world because it enables us to know people within their lived meanings, desires, values, and purposes.

I have tried to show the phenomenological viewpoint as it has been most alive, meaningful, and useful to me in my work as a teacher and a psychotherapist. These are the treasures that phenomenological theory, research, and praxis have offered to me, those that have enriched my personal and professional living. I hope that the descriptions and insights presented in *Living and Relating* have invited readers "back to the things themselves," back to lived experience in the everyday world. Reentering the everyday world through the perspective of phenomenology, I hope that readers have seen the complexities, essential qualities, transformative movements, and mysteries of human existence with renewed interest and respect.

Like any book, this one has developed some topics and not others. Those that I have concentrated on are the ones about which I know the most, those that have touched my life and added meaning to my existence. *Living and Relating* is not a thorough overview of the phenomenological orientation within the social sciences. In writing it, I have drawn upon my areas of expertise, as well as my interests in a variety of relationships. Even within these areas, however, I was selective and did not reference all that has been written on each topic. I tried, instead, to provide evocative glimpses into each topic area, ones that stimulate readers to search out other phenomenological works.

Living and Relating leaves much to be done, and many scholars, researchers, and practitioners are in the process of doing it. Numerous graduate programs, journals, conferences, and professional societies are available to readers who wish to pursue the study of phenomenology. What follows is an overview of the main resources available to people interested in learning more about phenomenology.

Amadeo Giorgi (1986) lists universities or institutes in ten countries around the world that are international centers for the study and practice of phenomenology: Brazil, Canada, Denmark, England, Holland, Japan, Republic of South Africa, Sweden, United States, and Venezuela. Scholars in a number of organizations in these countries are experts in diverse disciplines: communications, geography, nursing, pedagogy, psychology, and sociology. Conventions of the Association of Humanistic Psychologists, as well as Divisions 32 (Humanistic Psychology) and 24 (Theoretical and Philosophical Psychology) of the American Psychological Association, provide programs on phenomenological theory, research, and psychotherapy each year. On a larger scale, the International Human Science Research Conference, now in its 11th year, began at the University of Michigan in 1982 and has been hosted in subsequent years at the following universities in North America and Europe: Duquesne University, West Georgia College, University of Alberta, Saybrook Institute and California State University, University of Ottawa, Seattle University, University of Aarhus, University of Laval, and University of Gothenburg (Aanstoos, 1990). At this lively conference, academicians, researchers, psychotherapists, and artists present on far-reaching topics under the wide umbrella of human science research.

In North America alone are 11 journals devoted primarily or exclusively to humanistic, phenomenological, and existential concerns: *Journal of Phenomenological Psychology, Phenomenology + Pedagogy, The Humanistic Psychologist, Theoretical and Philosophical Psychology, Review of Existential Psychiatry and Psychology, Methods, Journal of Humanistic Psychology, Journal of Qualitative Studies in Education, Human Studies, Holistic Education Review,* and *Humanity and Society.* In addition to these publications, the *Duquesne Studies in Phenomenological Psychology,* volumes 1 through 4, are a valuable chronology of phenomenological writings from 1971 through 1983. The references cited in *Living and Relating* also offer avenues to further study of the phenomenological perspective.

At this point we face an increasingly delightful array of approaches, methods, and applications within phenomenology. Some resources are reconceptualizations that nourish the mind. Some provide penetrating insights into specific aspects of human life. Others touch the heart by illuminating deep, existential themes of life and death. Still others tickle the soul and push us into the wonder of existence. Each has its place and its contribution within the changing, developing, and maturing applications of the phenomenological viewpoint to living and relating.

More than a century old, existential-phenomenology is a loosely interconnected family of scholars and practitioners. Like a human family, it contains different generations and personalities; people with particular interests and aptitudes. Its members come together in university or conference settings and from varied geographical areas and backgrounds to build a community that sustains and supports each of them. They search out one another to talk, to listen, to share food, to rest, to dream, to plan the future, to honor elders, and to guide future generations. Like a human family, members have conflicting ideas and ways of proceeding, disagree over values, and form special loyalties and attachments. Now, in the 1990s, the phenomenological viewpoint in the social sciences has diversified in its identity; many members have matured, have found their professional stride, and have separated and individuated. Like any healthy family, its task is to retain the wisdom of the elders without its reification and rigidification, and to make room for the new life that younger generations bring. Old members guide it along proven paths; new members reform its structure and content and strike out to explore new horizons of possibility. Like any resilient family, the people within a phenomenological orientation must search out what they want to know about and do, what they can contribute, and what work nourishes their minds, hearts, and souls. And occasionally, they must come together to catch up with one another and to build a sense of community that sustains their heart paths and rekindles the dreams sparked by this alternative approach to life.

References

Aanstoos, C. (1990). A brief history of the human science research conference. *Journal of Humanistic Psychology, 30*(3), 137-145.

Alapack, R. J. (1984). Adolescent first love. In C. Aanstoos (Ed.), *Exploring the lived world: Readings in phenomenological psychology,* West Georgia College Studies in the Social Sciences, *23,* 101-117. Carrollton: West Georgia College.

Alapack, R. J., & Alapack, M. (1984). The hinge of the door to authentic adulthood: A Kierkegaardian inspired synthesis of the meaning of leaving home. *Journal of Phenomenological Psychology, 15*(1), 45-69.

Bachelard, G. (1964). *The poetics of space* (M. Jolas, Trans.). Boston: Beacon. (Original work published 1958)

Bachelard, G. (1969). *The poetics of reverie* (D. Russell, Trans.). Boston: Beacon. (Original work published 1960)

Baird, M. (1983). *Fathers' experiences in launching their first child.* Unpublished doctoral dissertation, California School of Professional Psychology, Berkeley.

Baker, R. (1982). *Growing up.* New York: New American Library.

Bandura, A. (1986). *Social foundations of thought and action: A social cognitive theory.* Englewood Cliffs, NJ: Prentice-Hall.

Barritt, L., Beekman, T., Bleeker, H., & Mulderij, K. (1983). The world through children's eyes: Hide and seek & peekaboo. *Phenomenology + Pedagogy, 1*(2), 140-161.

Becker, C. S. (1973). *A phenomenological explication of friendship: As exemplified by most important college women friends.* Unpublished doctoral dissertation, Duquesne University, Pittsburgh.

Becker, C. S. (1987). Friendship between women: A phenomenological study of best friends. *Journal of Phenomenological Psychology, 18*(1), 59-72.

Becker, C. S. (1988). *Unbroken ties: Lesbian ex-lovers.* Boston: Alyson.

Becker, C. S. (1991). A phenomenology of friendship families. *The Humanisit Psychologist, 19,*(2), 170-184.

Bentz, V. M. (1989). *Becoming mature.* New York: Walter de Gruyter.

275

Binswanger, L. (1963). *Being-in-the-world* (J. Needleman, Trans.). New York: Basic Books.

Blos, P. (1962). *On adolescence*. New York: Free Press.

Boelen, B. (1978). *Personal maturity: The existential dimension*. New York: Seabury.

Boss, M. (1963). *Psychoanalysis and daseinsanalysis* (L. B. Lefebre, Trans.). New York: Basic Books. (Original work published 1957)

Briod, M. (1989). A phenomenological approach to child development. In R. S. Valle & S. Halling. (Eds.), *Existential-phenomenological perspectives in psychology* (pp. 115-126). New York: Plenum.

Buber, M. (1985). *Between man and man* (R. G. Smith, Trans. with an introduction by M. S. Friedman). New York: Macmillan.

Colaizzi, P. F. (1971). Analysis of the learner's perception of learning material at various phases of a learning process. In A. Giorgi, W. F. Fischer, & R. von Eckartsberg (Eds.), *Duquesne studies in phenomenological psychology: Vol. I* (pp. 101-111). Pittsburgh: Duquesne University Press.

Colaizzi, P. F. (1973). *Reflection and research in psychology: A phenomenological study of learning*. Dubuque, IA: Kendall/Hunt.

Craig, E. (Ed.). (1988). Psychotherapy for freedom: The daseinanalytic way in psychology and psychoanalysis. *The Humanistic Psychologist, 16*(1).

Cushman, P. (1990). Why the self is empty: Toward a historically situated psychology. *American Psychologist, 45*(5), 599-611.

de Saint Exupery, A. (1943). *The little prince* (K. Woods, Trans.). New York: Harcourt Brace & World.

Devine, H. (1984). The workout: The phenomenology of training. *Phenomenology + Pedagogy, 2*(2), 163-177.

Dienske, I. (1984). Self-understanding in the lives of women. *Phenomenology + Pedagogy, 1*(3), 365-371.

Dillard, A. (1987). *An American childhood*. New York: Harper & Row.

Erikson, E. (1963). *Childhood and society*. New York: Norton.

Fischer, C. T. (1971). Toward the structure of privacy: Implications for psychological assessment. In A. Giorgi, W. F. Fischer, & R. von Eckartsberg (Eds.), *Duquesne studies in phenomenological psychology: Vol. I* (pp. 149-163). Pittsburgh: Duquesne University Press.

Fischer, C. T., & Alapack, R. J. (1987). A phenomenological approach to adolescence. In V. B. Van Hasselt & M. Herson (Eds.), *Handbook of adolescent psychology* (pp. 91-107). New York: Pergamon.

Fischer, C. T., & Wertz, F. (1979). Empirical phenomenological analyses of being criminally victimized. In A. Giorgi, R. Knowles, & D. L. Smith (Eds.), *Duquesne studies in phenomenological psychology: Vol. III* (pp. 135-158). Pittsburgh: Duquesne University Press.

Freud, S. (1935). *A general introduction to psychoanalysis* (J. Riviere, Trans.). New York: Washington Square. (Original work published 1924)

Freud, S. (1949). *An outline of psychoanalysis*. New York: Norton.

Freud, S. (1957). Mourning and melancholia. In *The Standard Edition of the Complete Psychological Works of Sigmund Freud, 14*. New York: Hogarth.

Friedman, M. S. (Ed.). (1991). *The worlds of existentialism: A critical reader* (2nd ed. with new preface). Atlantic Highlands, NJ: Humanities Press International.

Gendlin, E. T. (1981). *Focusing*. New York: Bantam.

Gilligan, C. (1982). *In a different voice*. Cambridge, MA: Harvard University Press.

Giorgi, A. (1970). *Psychology as a human science*. New York: Harper & Row.

Giorgi, A. (1971). A phenomenological approach to the problem of meaning and serial learning. In A. Giorgi, W. F. Fischer, & R. von Eckartsberg (Eds.), *Duquesne studies in phenomenological psychology: Vol. I* (pp. 88-100). Pittsburgh: Duquesne University Press.

Giorgi, A. (1975). An application of phenomenological method in psychology. In A. Giorgi, C. Fischer, & E. Murray (Eds.), *Duquesne studies in phenomenological psychology: Vol. II* (pp. 82-103). Pittsburgh: Duquesne University Press.

Giorgi, A. (1986). Status of qualitative research in the human sciences: A limited interdisciplinary and international perspective. *Methods, 1*(1), 29-62.

Heidegger, M. (1962). *Being and time* (J. Macquarrie & E. Robinson, Trans.). London: SCM. (Original work published 1904)

Hesse, H. (1968). *Narcissus and Goldmund* (U. Molinaro, Trans.). New York: Bantam.

Hornstein, G. A., & Wapner, S. (1985). Modes of experiencing and adapting to retirement. *International Journal of Aging and Human Development, 21*(4), 291-315.

Husserl, E. (1962). *Ideas* (W. Gibson, Trans.). London: Collier. (Original work published 1913)

Husserl, E. (1977). *Phenomenological psychology* (J. Scanlon, Trans.). The Hague: Nijhoff. (Original work published 1925)

Jager, B. (1979). Dionysos and the world of passion. In A. Giorgi, R. Knowles, & D. L. Smith (Eds.), *Duquesne studies in phenomenological psychology: Vol. IV* (pp. 209-226). Pittsburgh: Duquesne University Press.

Jourard, S. M. (1971). *The transparent self.* New York: Van Nostrand Reinhold.

Jung, C. G. (1960). *The structure and dynamics of the psyche* (R. F. C. Hull, Trans.). New York: Pantheon.

Kierkegaard, S. (1954). *Fear and trembling* (W. Lowrie, Trans.). Garden City, NY: Doubleday.

Kimmel, D. C. (1980). *Adulthood and aging.* New York: John Wiley.

Knee, P. (1990, June). *Merleau-Ponty's critique of Sartre on intersubjectivity.* Paper presented at the Annual Meeting of the International Human Science Research Conference, University of Laval, Quebec, Canada.

Knowles, R. T. (1986). *Human development and human possibility.* Lanham, MD: University Press of America.

Kohut, H. (1977). *The restoration of the self.* New York: International Universities Press.

Kohut, H. (A. Goldberg & P. Stepansky, Eds.). (1984). *How does analysis cure?* Chicago: University of Chicago Press.

Kubler-Ross, E. (1969). *On death and dying.* New York: Macmillan.

Kvale, S. (1983). The qualitative research interview: A phenomenological and a hermeneutical mode of understanding. *Journal of Phenomenological Psychology, 14*(2), 171-196.

Laing, R. D. (1959). *The divided self.* New York: Penguin.

Lapointe, F. (1974). The phenomenology of desire and love in Sartre and Merleau-Ponty. *Journal of Phenomenological Psychology, 4*(2), 445-459.

Levin, D. M. (1985). *The body's recollection of being.* London: Routledge & Kegan Paul.

Levine, S. (1982). *Who dies?* Garden City, NY: Doubleday.

Levinson, D. (1979). *The seasons of a man's life.* New York: Knopf.

Levy, S. M. (1981). The experience of undergoing a heart attack: The construction of a new reality. *Journal of Phenomenology, 12*(2), 153-171.

Macdonald, B., & Rich, C. (1983). *Look me in the eye.* San Francisco: Spinsters/Aunt Lute.

May, R., Angel, R., & Ellenberger, H. (Eds.). (1958). *Existence: A new dimension in psychiatry and psychology.* New York: Simon & Schuster.

Mealy, J. B. (1972). *An empirical phenomenology investigation of swearing.* Unpublished doctoral dissertation, Duquesne University, Pittsburgh, PA.

Merleau-Ponty, M. (1962). *Phenomenology of perception* (C. Smith, Trans.). London: Routledge & Kegan Paul.

Merleau-Ponty, M. (1964). *Signs* (R. C. McCleary, Trans.). Evanston, IL: Northwestern University Press. (Original work published 1960)

Merleau-Ponty, M. (1973a). *Consciousness and the acquisition of language* (H. J. Silverman, Trans.). Evanston, IL: Northwestern University Press. (Original work published 1964)

Merleau-Ponty, M. (1973b). *The prose of the world* (J. O'Neill, Trans.). Evanston, IL: Northwestern University Press. (Original work published 1969)

Michalko, R. (1984). The metaphor of adolescence. *Phenomenology + Pedagogy, 1*(3), 296-311.

Miller, A. (1981). *The drama of the gifted child* (R. Ward, Trans.). New York: Basic Books. (Original work published 1979)

Miller, A. (1983). *For your own good* (H. & H. Hannum, Trans.). New York: Farrar, Straus, & Giroux. (Original work published 1980)

Miller, M. P. (1978). *A phenomenological investigation of anticipatory grief for the survivor-to-be.* Unpublished master's thesis, California School of Professional Psychology, Berkeley, CA.

Miller, M. P. (1981). *A phenomenological investigation of the creative process of women poets.* Unpublished doctoral dissertation, California School of Professional Psychology, Berkeley, CA.

Moustakas, C. (1961). *Loneliness.* Englewood Cliffs, NJ: Prentice-Hall.

Offer, D., Ostrov, E., & Howard, K. I. (1981). *The adolescent.* New York: Basic Books.

Piaget, J. (1952). *The origins of intelligence in children* (M. Cook, Trans.). New York: Norton.

Polakow, V. (1986). On meaning-making and stories: Young children's experiences with texts. *Phenomenology + Pedagogy, 4*(3), 37-47.

Romanyshyn, R. D. (1982). *Psychological life: From science to metaphor.* Austin: University of Texas Press.

Romanyshyn, R. D. (1988). Psychotherapy as a creative process. In E. M. Stern (Ed.), *Psychotherapy and the creative patient* (pp. 35-46). New York: Haworth.

Romanyshyn, R. D. (1989). *Technology as symptom and dream.* New York: Routledge, Chapman & Hall.

Romanyshyn, R. D. (1990). Life-world as depth of soul: Phenomenology and psychoanalysis. In J. E. Faulconer & R. N. Williams (Eds.), *Reconsidering psychology: Perspectives in continental philosophy* (pp. 234-251). Pittsburgh: Duquesne University Press.

Romanyshyn, R. D. (1991). Complex knowing: Toward a psychological hermeneutics. *The Humanistic Psychologist, 19*(1), 10-29.

Rubin, L. (1979). *Women of a certain age.* New York: Harper & Row.

Santrock, J. W. (1989). *Life-span development.* Dubuque, IA: William C. Brown.

Santrock, J. W. (1990). *Adolescence.* Dubuque, IA: William C. Brown.

Sartre, J. P. (1956). *Being and nothingness* (H. E. Barnes, Trans.). New York: Washington Square.

Selman, R. L., & Selman, A. P. (1979, April). Children's ideas about friendship: A new theory. *Psychology Today,* pp. 70-80.

Shneidman, E. S. (1973). *Deaths of man.* New York: Quadrangle/New York Times.

Skinner, B. F. (1938). *The behavior of organisms: An experimental analysis.* New York: Appleton-Century-Crofts.

Sullivan, H. S. (1953). *The interpersonal theory of psychiatry.* New York: Norton.

Titelman, P. (1981). A phenomenological comparison between envy and jealousy. *Journal of Phenomenological Psychology, 12*(2), 189-203.

Valle, R. S., & Halling, S. (Eds.). (1989). *Existential-phenomenological perspectives in psychology.* New York: Plenum.

van den Berg, J. H. (1961). *The changing nature of man.* New York: Norton.

van den Berg, J. H. (1971a). Phenomenology and metabletics. *Humanitas, 7*(3), 279-290.

van den Berg, J. H. (1971b). What is psychotherapy. *Humanitas, 7*(3), 321-370.

van den Berg, J. H. (1972a). *A different existence.* Pittsburgh: Duquesne University Press.

van den Berg, J. H. (1972b). *Psychology of the sickbed.* Pittsburgh: Duquesne University Press.

von Eckartsberg, R. (1971). On experiential methodology. In A. Giorgi, W. F. Fischer, & R. von Eckartsberg (Eds.), *Duquesne studies in phenomenological psychology: Vol. I* (pp. 66-79). Pittsburgh: Duquesne University Press.

von Eckartsberg, R. (1986). *Life-world experience: Existential-phenomenological research approaches in psychology.* Lanham, MD: University Press of America.

Welty, E. (1984). *One writer's beginnings.* New York: Warner.

Wertz, F. J. (1984). Procedures in phenomenological research and the question of validity. In Aanstoos, C. M. (Ed.). *Exploring the lived world: Readings in phenomenological psychology, 23,* 29-48. Carrollton: West Georgia College.

Winnicott, D. W. (1965). *The maturational processes and the facilitating environment.* New York: International Universities Press.

Yalom, I. D. (1980). *Existential psychotherapy.* New York: Basic Books.

Index

About the Author

Carol S. Becker received her Ph.D. in Clinical Psychology from Duquesne University in Pittsburgh, Pennsylvania in 1973. She is currently a Professor of Human Development at California State University, Hayward, California, as well as a Licensed Psychologist with psychotherapy practices in San Francisco and Berkeley, California. Dr. Becker's first book, *Unbroken ties: Lesbian ex-lovers*, was published in 1988. She has published articles on phenomenological research, friendships, and friendship families in the *Journal of Phenomenological Psychology, Methods,* and *The Humanistic Psychologist.* She has held Excutive Committee offices in Divisions 24 (Theoretical and Philosophical Psychology) and 44 (Society for the Psychological Study of Lesbian and Gay Issues) of the American Psychological Association and has been Convention Program Chair for the Hospitality Suite of Division 32 (Humanistic Psychology). Dr. Becker has been a consulting editor for the *Journal of Phenomenological Psychology, Theoretical and Philosophical Psychology,* and *The Humanistic Psychologist.* She has given numerous talks on various aspects of intimate relations to local and national groups. Her current research concerns family relationships among kin and friends.